When Fat Men Flew

By

Dan Kingsley

When Fat Men Flew

by

E. Daniel Kingsley

Former Corporal, United States Marine Corps

CW4 United States Army, Retired

Silver Quill Publishing

Spanish Fork, UT

When Fat Men Flew

By E. Daniel Kingsley

© 2023

Published by Silver Quill Publishing

Spanish Fork, UT

Manufactured in the United States of America

Interior design and finishing by E. Daniel Kingsley

Cover Design by Michael P Kingsley

Editing by Drollene P. Brown

ISBN: 978-1-7335223-2-8

Library of Congress No. N/A

Price: $22.99

Library of Congress Cataloging-in-Publication Data: N/A

Kingsley, E. Daniel, 1949 -

When Fat Men Flew by Dan Kingsley

Autobiography

1. Kingsley, E. Daniel, 1949- 2. Marine Corps Enlisted Service. 3. Army Aviation Warrant Officer Career. 4. Army Aviation. 5. Military life impact on family life. 6. Latter Day Saints Military Service. 7. Military Life and Humor.

Dedication

This book is dedicated to Warrant Officer One (WO1) Daniel Hallows. 1n 1967 we were high school pals. I got word of his combat death in Vietnam in June 1970, and it took a moment to sink in. I sat down in a lonely stairwell and did something I still cannot explain. Marines don't cry, but whatever I did, it was leaky; it was gut wrenching; and it was not very dignified.

He was my precious friend, my brother, my confidant. I know I am not worthy to speak his name, but I hold his example as noble and the stuff heroes are made of.

Nineteen seventy may seem like a long time ago to you, but it is yesterday to me. Those relationships do not age or change over the years. Danny is still alive in my heart, still my buddy. His sacrifice brought honor to my flag, my uniform, my nation. I believe he paid for all that I cherish. I followed him into the ranks of the Warrant Officer Corps, but I was allowed to find my potential without the sacrifice he made. If I ever find anything he left undone, I will give almost anything to make it good. On the other side of the veil… if he should ever need ground support or an armed escort, maybe I can fly his wing.

Dan Kingsley
CW4, US Army, Retired

Contents

Introduction

You paid for this book. If you do not want to know some background, just skip to the beginning of Chapter 1.

The Title

This is my story. It is my own opinion, without permission of or coordination with the United States Marine Corps or the US Army. It is not *Gone with the Wind*. It is a peacetime soldier's story.

This is not intended to be a historical document, but it is true. This story is fact and as well rendered as I can make it. The facts may be slightly out of order; they may not be quite on the right date, or they may represent too much coincidence for you to swallow undiluted. I don't care. *But you cannot imagine how I felt about some of this stuff.*

Before you start reading the following chapters, note these things.

My children do not remember when I was a stallion or for that matter very much about my military career. Today I am the King of Grandfathers, and my adoring grandchildren think I am a chubby hero. But when one of them hears I was a Marine and then an Army Cobra pilot, their inevitable responses are:

First, "What is a Cobra?"

Second, "You?"

Third, "Grandpa, are you teasin' me … again?"

And thus the title of this book is one to which they can relate: *When Fat Men Flew*.

The Real Heroes

In the event you are not an old soldier, and for the purposes of this book, there is a required definition of "combat soldier." This term requires that a soldier must have been, at some time, within earshot of hostile gunfire or explosions or must have experienced something indicating hostile intent. That is all. Let's be clear about this. *I am not qualified to claim this honor.*

Soldiers are pretty quiet about it, but "combat veteran" is a title truly considered an honor, claimed only by one who has paid the price. The act of fraud and cowardice committed by someone lying to claim combat experience cannot be overstated, and I want no part of it.

I am what is scorned and known throughout the military as a REMF. This is an ugly term I hate. It is pronounced *rimf,* like the word *rim* with an *f* at the end it. It is an abbreviation, as PIC means Pilot in Command, or CIC means Commander in Chief, or CIB stands for Combat Infantry Badge.

But it means nothing so noble or respected.

REMF stands for ... wait for it ... "Rear Echelon Mother _____ ."

In order to get the real feel for the mood of this scornful label, you have to sort of snort and spit, then wipe off your chin

INTRODUCTION

on your shirt sleeve. It means someone who has never seen
real combat. But it is more scornful if the faker claims the real
sacrifice for the purpose of recognition or favors granted to this
brotherhood.

I hate it, but it is true. It is ironic, actually. I never intended
to avoid combat or to hide from my responsibility. Serving six
years in the Marine Corps and 17 years as an Army gunship
pilot tells you I should have seen some sort of conflict. The
worst fighting I ever saw was a couple of idiot platoon leaders
in a scrap. Oh yeah, once I even pointed a loaded weapon at a
man ... only once. He was bigger'n me, and drunk as a hoot
owl. I was serious about not getting my butt kicked, and he
sobered up as soon as he saw me pull back the slide on my .45.

I never shot at any opponent or took incoming fire of any
kind. While I am truly grateful for my safety, I have found
special solace in the fact that *this status is not uncommon.*

Now, in the real world when the battle is raging and the
Commies are coming over the hill, every cook, baker and
candlestick maker will be issued a rifle and will sight it in on the
perimeter. The real truth—and thank God for it—is that not all
of us see combat. This book is the story of an average soldier
surrounded by heroes. I think my story has merit, but the heroes
here are real easy to pick out. And I am not one of them.

Finally, a Word to the Young Soldiers of the Coming Generations

First, don't give me any guff about the term "man" or "woman" in this book meaning anything more than it does. Old fashioned as I am, a fighting man, male or female, is the soldier I am discussing—Soldier, Sailor, Airman, Marine. I might slip a Coastie in here for good measure. I ask women who read this to know I mean no disrespect when I use the male noun and pronoun almost exclusively. It doesn't matter to me so long as she or he is part of the team. That is what I am talking about.

This book is about my career. It is not a story of battle or war or death and bloodshed. There is a lot of great stuff here, but no glory. It is the real story of a real Marine turned Soldier in a peacetime career. There is risk, pride, humor, challenge and patriotism. Career advancement always meant preparing for promotion. And preparing for war. It would come, I was sure.

I hope you will recommend this book to a realistic young serviceman ... or someone who is a soldier in embryo ... perhaps someone who wants to enlist or take a commission ... maybe wants to be a basic Jarhead or Squid or Slogger ... maybe a Green Beret or Special Forces ... a Ranger ... maybe an Airman of some sort ... Seal ... Submariner ... Pilot ... Infantryman ... Armor Crewman ... Artilleryman. Every calling has its adherents. If you are not military, these may not

INTRODUCTION

seem significant to you, but to me, they are like the glorious Great Seal of the King. I am a specialist, as every soldier is.

If you are not looking to be a soldier, then be proud of your soldier, and tell him so. He is proud now. One day he will have to provide leadership and courage that may cost him his life. When he is alone making those tough decisions, your faith and trust and adoration are the counterweight to terror, privation, thirst, heat, cold and exhaustion. These burdens, in fact, are no more than what he puts up with until he can go home to his family, where the *really* important things in life are going to happen ... just as soon as he gets there. And he loves you for being that loving counterweight.

This book is for the young serviceman who shares my values but who has no mentor. Sometimes a military career needs a boost, a direction, a leg up to face the administrative crap that will bury that career as a nameless number in a sea of numbers. A simple word from a loving mentor, well-spoken at the right moment in a career, may turn a dying, discouraged ember into a soaring rocket. Do not doubt it. You owe your serviceman whatever you can dredge up to lift him through his trials. I had no mentor. Your serviceman will laugh at my mistakes. Maybe he will learn from them

Remember here, every American soldier has one advantage shared only by a few of the free nations of the world, and it is sniffed out by every starry-eyed young American who wants to test the military waters. This advantage, this critical difference, I believe, is the *virtue of high ideals*. It may not seem so obvious today, but most American children are taught this virtue when we honor the flag, say the pledge, take an oath we consider sacred, or honor a hero or veteran. Or when we vote. When we go to church. When we honor our dead in a military funeral. When we honor our parents. And when they see us doing other worthy things, we set the example.

We may not do all this as we used to. I believe the liberal culture has demeaned and denigrated these values. But we still need bold and fearless youth who will stand up to be counted as the cutting edge of our nation, who are willing to fight defend to the principles we love. Who submit to hardship and stress and danger willingly for the cause they hope is right. These examples of righteous and faithful patriotism, are the principles of high ideals of which I speak.

I pray our nation can maintain those high ideals—duty, honor, country—and let those virtues strengthen and uplift our fellow servicemen. Only then, when they are in a moment that demands their deepest effort to survive and endure, will they have a firm foundation on which to base their beliefs and bear their trials.

INTRODUCTION

WHEN FAT MEN FLEW

INTRODUCTION

PART I
The Marine Corps

WHEN FAT MEN FLEW

1

In the Beginning

The Recruiter

Most of my high school years were spent at KOFA High (named after the King of Arizona copper mines in North Yuma County, Arizona). When I was a freshman I wrote an essay describing why I wanted to be a US Marine. In my research I had found a famous picture of a dead Marine on Iwo Jima hunched over his rifle, a prominent hole in his helmet. The picture of that brave Marine only strengthened my resolve to become a Marine. That genuine desire stayed with me until I was in college.

There were other fine examples to follow. I knew Gil Tijerina (forgive me, Gil, for misspelling your last name), a great kid selected for West Point from KOFA High School, and I envied him. But I did not have what it took to make that sort of commitment.

My family and I moved back to Holland, New York, in 1966, when I was seventeen. I managed to graduate from Holland High School in 1967 and found a way to get into Arizona Western College, back in Yuma. I became a route salesman for Stewart's Sandwich and Bar Supplies. I was making pretty good money, when on the Saturday before Easter in 1968, I flipped my truck and survived with a large bruise. But I lost my source of income. I had pretty much eliminated all my financial options to stay in college when I called a Marine Corps recruiter to visit me out at my college dorm, Kino Hall.

He was handsome. He was not John Wayne, but he was fit; he was "gung-ho," and he fed my desire to be a hero of sorts. Besides, after a year of hard-earned school and the grind of everyday living, all that working and studying had lost its allure. In my crackers-and-cheese budget world, a Marine uniform had lots of appeal.

I felt I was well prepared for his pitch, but I did not know how good it would be. I had known a couple of Marines, and I knew the Marine Corps reputation. Vietnam was not popular in 1968, but it was not as unpopular as it would become, and

IN THE BEGINNING

I was fiercely independent. I could make my own decision. This is the *Marine Corps* we are talking about, after all. And the sergeant impressed me with more than his uniform. He was clean-cut, smart, a real professional, and he exuded confidence. He was confident in himself and in his Marine Corps.

Well, I wanted it to be *my* Marine Corps. From a distance he could see I wanted that *esprit* ... that work ... that job, which was as much a "calling" as it was work. A career. A military profession. Some real adventure where you could be proud, and if you were really good, you could survive. I did not understand it, but he did.

He showed up at Kino Hall and got a lot of stares. My college mates were very surprised to see a recruiter there, since we all knew Vietnam was *bad*. And we were all good and faithful anti-establishment folk. My friends could hardly believe I had summoned a recruiter.

He was not intimidated, and I thought he might strut a bit. But he was a pro. He acquired his target (I refuse to be called a sucker), focused on me with a laser eye and did not beat around the bush. In a few moments he learned I was serious. So he laid it all out for me. In fact, he was so sure of himself he went directly to the enlistment options without even so much as a "howdy-do." After all, this was the Marine Corps. We were two *men* talking about undeniable, glorious Marine Corps stuff, and there was no reason to discuss anything but commitment.

If I enlisted for *six* years, he began, I could probably pick my own job (MOS, the Marine Corps jargon for Military Occupational Specialty). Of course, that would depend upon my test results. But he pointed out the obvious. I was a bright boy, in college, physically perfect and ready for the challenge of boot camp. He did not bother to comment on my growing arrogance or my prideful confidence.

Hell, I growled to myself, he did not even know I was a superb shot, too. *Great! Let me at 'em!*

"Now," he added almost as an afterthought, "if you enlist for *four* years, you will very likely get a great MOS because of the term length."

He reminded me again that I had a special advantage over other recruits, being fresh out of college and experienced in a testing environment and all that stuff. I should be able to test well and still cut a great deal. I wondered aloud why I would want to do that four-year thing; he placed his hands behind his head, and leaned back in his chair.

"Didn't I mention to you that a career Marine ..."

(*Did you hear that? Me! A career Marine!*)

IN THE BEGINNING

"…a career Marine gets a re-enlistment bonus when he re-ups? Why, a four-year enlistment should let you earn pretty much all the rank you can get in one hitch, and you would get that bonus that much *sooner*. Why, they are offering up to $10,000 these days for special MOSs to reenlist!"

Whoo Hoo! I thought, barely containing my delight. So, *okay! Great! Let me at 'em!*

"Now, you also have another option." He interrupted my thought mid-sentence. I did not hide my impatience too well, but I listened as he drawled on and on.

"If you enlist for *three* years, you will likely get a great MOS because they need guys who are willing to stay more than two years. And if you are qualified for some sort of rocket-science job, they will give you an opportunity to extend your enlistment to meet your commitment requirements."

I nearly choked out the words. "For cryin' out loud, why would I want to do that?"

"Money, pure and simple. If you are a career Marine, you might as well make as much money as you can. You can re-enlist that much *sooner*. Not only that, but they may even bump you up a pay grade earlier than normal and give you a *higher* bonus … just because they want to keep a good career Marine around."

Dang, he was good. "A good career Marine" was the catnip phrase that paralyzed me.

So, okay! I get it! I thought as I tried to ponder this parade of endless options. Six years, four years, three years. *Great! Get outta my way and let me—*

He looked at me again, and I knew he was going to spring something else on me. I bit my lip and said nothing. He continued.

"Just hear me out. You *could* enlist for *two* years. You would get no other schools. You would almost certainly get a combat arms MOS (that job jargon again), but you would not get a choice. (In that case, most likely, I would become an Infantry Marine, MOS 0311.) You would probably go through ITR (Infantry Training Regiment) at Camp Pendleton, California, and go directly to Vietnam. And you can count on it … you can re-up that much sooner!"

I sat up and looked directly at him. Was he ever going to let me enlist or what? But even as I considered this with sarcasm, something terrible occurred to me.

Other MOSs? Those other opportunities that would come to me because of my great merit or intelligence or whatever he was talking about, well that might just be recruiter-speak for … well … wimpy, or certainly some less-than-worthy Marine Corps job—one that might normally be done by some lesser entity, like the Army or Navy or maybe even (perish the thought) the Coast Guard.

Was there such a thing? I mean, was there some special Marine Corps job that was less than a fully Marine Corps-certified manly-man job? I wanted to be a *real* Marine, not some sort of imposter.

"Am I going to have a gun?" I blurted it out. He was sort of stunned.

"What?" He looked at me closely. I was a sure-fire enlistee, and my timing chain had slipped a cog. He wanted me back in the bag.

"Well, I thought all Marines were infantry. If I get another MOS, will I still be a real *Marine?*"

He leaned over and looked at me. Hard. He was a combat veteran, and I wilted. His forehead furrowed, and his eyes narrowed as he stared at me face to face.

"You listen to me. *We* ..." he paused to let me absorb his meaning that I would be part of the elite few ... "*We,*" he repeated, "are *Marines*. No matter what we do, we are all Marines, and we are all *infantry.*"

He watched as my naive mind tried to put this all into perspective. He leaned back in his chair, put his feet up on the table and laced his fingers behind his head again. It was his pose for every deft strike of irrefutable logic.

"Look. You get yourself into a jam in any bar in the country, and yell '*Marine!*' Every Marine from 18 to 80 will come to your aid." He paused for the full effect. Then he smiled and winked.

"Just you yell '*Coast Guard*' and see what you get."

We both laughed.

And I signed up for three years.

As it turned out, when my three-year hitch was up, I wanted to kiss that recruiter's butt and give him 30 minutes to draw a crowd for not tricking me into a longer enlistment. Contrary to all the experience I saw around me in the Corps, my recruiter's every word about means and opportunity came to pass just as he said. I did not make great rank and did not reenlist for big money. But I was offered promotion to sergeant, a bonus of $15,000, and an opportunity to go to Officers Candidate School. In the end, I did an honorable tour, and I found a path to a better career.

That day he also gave me a *bona fide* little US Marine Corps identity card stating I was a Marine on reserve status and due all the respect, privileges and honor of my station. It was a harmless hook, designed to remind the owner that very soon, he would have his moment basking in the Marine Corps glory.

A few days later, after a quick physical and the signing of all those papers, he gave me orders requiring me to show up on 28 September 1968 at the Yuma Greyhound Station to catch a bus to Los Angeles to go through the mustering in process.

You know, I showed that card, my badge of honor, to everyone who would look. And I kept that little card for 20 years.

WHEN FAT MEN FLEW

2

The World of Boot Camp

Induction Center

My first day on active duty was spent taking a Greyhound bus from Yuma, Arizona, to Los Angeles, California, and the rest of the day in the processing station there. We stayed in a flea-bag hotel with common bathrooms and a terrible restaurant accessed with a single meal card worth whatever their cheapest meal cost. At age 19, I was the old man. And I was the most educated, with one genuine year of college behind me. There were all kinds of kids for all the services; some were scared; some were worried; and some were spending the night with friends, with women of the night or with family. I was alone. My last meal as a free man was a trip to the Orange Julius stand. I have chased my culinary talents since that day trying to create an orange drink that tasted as good.

The in-process was pretty interesting for a country boy. Seemed if you showed up, you were automatically treated like an idiot. They told us everything we had to do, and they acted as though we simply could not do it without supervision. Of course, some of their instructions were bizarre. When they got us all naked and standing in a circle they told us to "… bend over and spread your cheeks." They sure as heck were not doing an oral exam, and a doctor walked around the circle behind us and got a rear view, close up.

I was stunned to learn that sometimes the Marine Corps drafted folks in those days. A kid was wailing about how he should never have accepted the draft into the Army, that he should have joined the Marines, and we were all real sympathetic. When an old gunny came around looking for draftees to take into the Corps, the kid got kicked over into the Marine Corps line, and you never heard such squawking.

We had a big ol' kid who was scoffing at all us little guys who were crying about the shots, which were given with air guns. There were, however, a few needles, and when he saw his first needle, he passed out. One kid sort of jerked when he was getting his shots, and it ripped his arm open. The whole day was like that.

THE WORLD OF BOOT CAMP

Arrival at Boot Camp

We Marine recruits got on the bus next morning and rolled into MCRD (Marine Corps Recruit Depot), San Diego, that night. The ugliest, best Marine I ever knew met us there and ran us off the bus. SGT Ralph Neville.

We got there around 10 P.M., and we were chased, yelled at, showered and put to bed before 2 A.M. They ran us upstairs and downstairs repeatedly to shower, box up our civvies, start into the madhouse routine of boot camp and get our first partial issue of stuff. We were naked or barely dressed, still wet, and cranking at full speed to throw our civvies in a box for mailing home. We grabbed our initial issue of boxers, T-shirts and moth-ball smelling utilities. In the morning, we discovered we were in Platoon 1091, and we had three DIs (drill instructors). I am not sure I have all the spellings correct, but they were SGT Ralph Neville, and SSG Patterson, I think his name was. I am not sure because he separated from the USMC during our training. We later got a corporal who somehow was made a DI (probably some sort of reenlistment deal), but he was an idiot and was eventually "relieved for cause" (i.e., he was removed from drill instructor duty and sent back to his MOS.) He was the only dishonest DI I ever knew.

My record of boot camp experience is a hodge-podge of moments that stand out because of one odd thing or another.

Gomer Pyle

We were all billeted in Quonset huts. A Quonset hut is a tin building that looks like a coffee can cut from top to bottom by a blade through the middle, laid on the open face with a door at each end. Each hut housed about 11 double bunks, if I remember, meaning 22 men, give or take the occasional medical transfer into or out of the platoon. That made three fire teams, or one squad, and we all got to know each other really well in that tiny space.

If you have watched the old comedy TV series *Gomer Pyle,* you have seen replicas of the Quonset huts and uniforms I was trained in. In fact that series' opening shot (of marching Marines with the DI jumping around yelling at Gomer Pyle) was filmed on our grinder (parade field) less than a year before I started boot camp. Heaven knows, we marched a million harassed miles on that grinder.

I remember other things that stood out. (No pun intended, but leading to the next topic.)

Short Arm Inspection

On one of the first nights we spent in boot camp, at about 2100 hours (9 P.M.), we were all in our Quonset getting ready for showers. We were ordered into our skivvies and onto our foot lockers for our first "short arm inspection." There we were, all standing on our foot lockers, staring at each other. But we all obeyed, in confusion.

You have to try to imagine this. I do not have to tell you, but there was simply no dignity in this ritual … 22 men in their boxer shorts, standing at the position of attention, facing inboard on footlockers, all with their diminutive manhood (the aforementioned "short arm") hanging in the wind. Add to that the intimidation of the spit-shined drill instructor, carefully inspecting each one and offering gentle words of encouragement like: "Get the damn thing out where I can see it," or "Skin it back, stupid." There were other offerings of wisdom, but you get the idea.

Anyway, you did *not* want to see him bore in for a deathly stare, point at you and yell, "*Get Out!*" That indicated, in drill instructor speak, that yer equipment was not being properly … well … maintained, and that you were at risk of a brutal cleansing.

There were three points to this exercise. The first was the immediate identification of any obvious cases of disease. The second was the irrevocable realization that hygienic dignity was a readily perishable and needless luxury. The third, we had already been told if we did not clean ourselves well with our two-minute showers, we would be treated to the wire brush treatment, and we were terrified this would be the night.

In point of fact, all timidity in keeping the combat troops clean was removed by this exercise, and even though we had guys who did not shower well—and even got into trouble over it—we did not have a dirty dinger in the entire platoon. Ever.

The Finer Points of Hand To Hand Combat

Marines were taught to fight in several ways.

First, we were taught the fundamentals of *block, parry and punch* in unarmed, hand to hand combat. We were not experts, but it made us active participants in event of real battle. Physical contact in this manner became, if not common place, certainly a part of the expected "close with and destroy the enemy" mentality. We were also inspired to understand that the first strike was generally the one that would carry the day. I never had to do it, but I suspect it made the execution of battle less intimidating. These valuable lessons made my willingness to engage in physical fighting throughout my life a much more carefully considered event.

THE WORLD OF BOOT CAMP

Do not suppose that "carefully considered" is a term I take lightly. It means, basically, that if I did not have a reason to strike first, my ego could generally endure the embarrassment of departure.

Second, we were taught the basics of using the bayonet in hand fighting. The use of the bayonet was taught using rubber hoses about 10" in length. The intent here was to get the feel of maneuvering next to an enemy combatant and stabbing or slicing him without actual injury.

Third, we used pugilist sticks to learn the art of executing the infamous Marine Corps bayonet attack.

I am going to pause here to discuss the Marine Corps bayonet attack from the perspective of a Marine private. Remember, if you will, the mental brick that boot camp had placed in my spirit. I was undefeatable. I was indestructible. I was Superman with a USMC on my T-shirt. I feared but clung to the Marine Corps tool of battle signaled by, "Fix bayonets!" There I was, scared, excited, a new private in the Marine Corps, trying to get my head around this most important concept.

A bayonet attack is normally executed by a defiant group of Marines, each holding a rifle with a sharp pointy thing (bayonet) attached to the muzzle. You can imagine that preceding execution of that attack, the battle is already at a fever pitch, everybody is hungry, scared, in need of a hot shower and mad as hell. Generally the enemy is gaining the advantage, or these men would not be hungry, scared, in need of a hot shower and mad as hell. By the time this tactic is applied, the ammunition is very low or the enemy is real close-in, probably close enough to smell, and making life … well … very difficult.

There comes a moment in the battle when the choice is—to keep it simple—attack or die. It just cannot go on like this. Something must be done to turn the battle. As many Marines as are still standing are ordered to attack, ammunition notwithstanding. They may not have much ammo, but they still have their weapons, and that sharp pointy thing on the end of that M-14 makes a real handy spear.

On the order to attack, the Marines leap into the open and charge the enemy. They yell. They look as big and mean as they can. Even if they are being fired upon, each Marine attempts to skewer the nearest enemy soldier, thereby creating motivation for his immediate and irrevocable departure and provide inspiration for his fellows to follow. Every Marine knows if you can just get them started panicking, the fight will be over. According to boot camp doctrine, the fearsome bayonet attack is unique to the Marine Corps and, in many cases, the cause for victory in the face of incredible odds.

THE WORLD OF BOOT CAMP

Now, a pugilist stick may look like a poor substitute for a rifle and bayonet, but it provides the terrifying physical contact that teaches a Marine to take a licking and keep on ticking. The stick consists of a four-foot-long broom stick with large Q-tip-like ends. It was certainly nothing like the sleek M-14 rifle we loved so. But it was an effective training tool.

The DI would march us down to the practice area, where we gathered around to watch the combatants and await our turn in the fight. We learned a lot from watching. We practiced fighting against each other in several formats. We fought one-on-one and two-on-one, sometimes with sticks and sometimes with bayonets (the aforementioned rubber hoses, 10" in length). In one-on-one combat, you can correctly imagine two Marines in pads battering each other until one is injured or a winner is declared. There were no rules beyond wearing your helmet and pads and wailing away on your opponent. The DI was the authority. He called all the shots, and whatever he said, that was the rule.

Two-on-one combat was slightly more complicated. The principle guidance in trying to deal with an attack by more than one enemy is this: kill one at a time, and use one to tangle up the other. First, you must keep one of your antagonists between you and your other enemy until you have disposed of him by your skillful and fearsome bayonet assault. Then you take on the next poor sucker and dispose of him.

C'mon. We are Marines, after all. You must understand that we all assumed it would be the logical outcome. After all, two deposed suckers for every Marine seemed only right and proper.

Learning to accomplish this with a pugilist stick was a clumsy affair. I was not very impressed with those pillow-ends. They were just not as soft as billed … and if I recall correctly, I took an ignoble beating in my turn. I did not realize it but there was real danger in this training.

In our platoon, I saw a kid take a terrible blow to the "nether parts," and he squealed and trembled for half an hour until an ambulance picked him up. The DIs had a specific philosophy on injury during most boot camp training. "Man up" and limp off the battlefield with some kind of dignity … for the Corps. No matter what the injury. But as I watched that poor kid quivering and squealing on the ground, I was certain.

That Marine would never, ever have children.

When it came my turn to do this with a hand-held bayonet (rubber hose), I did pretty well. A bayonet is smaller, quicker, and more manageable than a 10-pound rifle (or a four-foot-long stick with pads on the end). I got credit for killing one guy and disabling another. To my everlasting shame.

I shoulda kilt 'em both.

Combat Medals in the Marine Corps, Explained

The first and foremost thought and instruction in Marine Corps boot camp is attack. Attack and kill the enemy. Be aggressive. Be vigilant. Bravery was never mentioned, primarily I suppose, because bravery was only incidental to the Marine Corps attack.

No one ever discussed bravery, and no one discussed medals. We all knew Marines simply didn't get as many medals as other services, and the culture dismissed that consequence as beneath us. We were Marines, after all, and our standards were higher. We felt that medals in other services were often not as worthy as the ones earned in the Marine Corps. We were sure of it. We were arrogant about it. Hell, if you earned a medal in the Marine Corps, you were Superman. Even Marine officers were given medals more easily than enlisted men. So medals granted to an enlisted Marine were very respected. We truly felt it was beneath us to covet a medal or to be thinking of personal glory in battle from a place so far removed from reality as boot camp.

But once in a while, someone had to pierce our training (propaganda?) and insert some plain good sense. These young Marines had to have some perspective that included reality. We clung to that stuff about being the baddest, the most lethal weapon on the battlefield and living the fearless image that was the envy of all nations. Well, deep down inside we all knew we would gain some new perspective with the first bullet fired downrange. The outside world called this part of our career experience *reality*.

To cultivate this spirit of aggression, boot camp taught us a tremendous amount of combat tradition. Chesty Puller, Commander at the Chosen Reservoir in the Korean War, was a heroic household name to each of us. Legend had it that his son, a Marine lieutenant, lost his leg in Vietnam … and how cool was that? SGT Dan Daily, *twice winner of the Medal of Honor* (first in the Boxer Rebellion in China and then in Korea, if memory serves), is known to every Marine to this day as the go-to example of impossible odds and leadership.

On a local level, this sort of image building continued. Most notably, one of our Drill Instructors, SGT Ralph Neville, that homely old rascal, was reputed to the most irresistible hunk of catnip the women of San Diego had ever known, the best shot on the West Coast, and there was a rumor he could throw a knife accurately at 50 yards. But I learned to love our DIs because they seemed to have a sense of balance between the Marine Corps brainwashing and the aforementioned reality. I loved the entire Marine attitude … but I always tried to place my survival skills just beyond the reach of Marine propaganda.

THE WORLD OF BOOT CAMP

This, the very personal training of troops by a drill instructor, occurred almost as though by osmosis, one tiny bit at a time. Our DI did not ever just stroll around the area and strut. He prowled; he tracked his victim; he stalked for issues to teach to the Marines during class or any gathering. He was always sharing personal wisdom or life lessons or experiences. We were his platoon. He loved us in his peculiar, gruff, no-nonsense way. When he spoke, sometimes we were just plain scared, but no matter what, we all listened very attentively.

The routine for the all-important personal training went like this. The walkway in front of the Quonset was called the street. We fell out as ordered, lined up our buckets and sat on them in the street. We field stripped our rifles into pieces for cleaning. We rubbed and polished and rammed; we hosed down our weapons with WD-40 and gun oil and then wiped them dry. Then we did it again and again. We did it in our sleep. We did it blindfolded. And the most important lessons were taught during these times.

SSGT Barrera approached the platoon one afternoon as we were field stripping our weapons. We were all watching him carefully. If you let a DI surprise you, it was not good. Suddenly and without a word, he reached down and snatched up a rifle. The owner flinched for the butt chewing or the lesson to be taught at his expense for some heretofore unknown violation of some obscure Marine Corps law. But Barrera held it up and announced loudly, "*This* is your safety!"

Now we were on alert. What was he doing?

He pointed at the safety, a little flag-like item in front of the trigger guard. When you flipped it on or off, that little flag actually passed through the trigger guard.

"This here safety is there primarily to ensure prevention of accidental discharge. You do not want to shoot your buddy or shoot your foot off by accident. That is all it does. It is not magic."

What the hell was he doing? He looked around with his barn-owl stare, ensuring we were all riveted to his instruction. We were still confused.

"The weapon will not fire if the safety is *on*. It is *on* if it is *inside* the trigger guard, with your *finger*. Remember. You do *not* want to shoot your foot or your buddy by accident. *He* is a Marine"—he pointed at one of the men—"We do not shoot Marines. The safety is *on* because it *interferes with easy access* to the trigger."

So much for *not* firing. He changed his track now to firing the weapon.

"Turn it *off* to shoot the weapon. Point your rifle and gently pull the trigger. The trigger is the item you will use to *kill* your enemy. Not your buddy."

His steely eyes surveyed his minions again.

"The weapon will fire if the safety is *off*. It is *off* in the forward position, clear of the trigger guard. You will remember it is *off* because there is *lots* of room in the trigger guard for your finger to find the trigger."

On and on he yammered. Louder and louder. The lesson had to be soon.

He poked his finger obnoxiously through the trigger guard.

"After you aim your rifle, the trigger is the item you will use to *kill* your enemy. To fire the weapon and kill your enemy, you must push the safety forward to turn it *off*, then aim, then pull the trigger."

He pushed the safety forward and pulled the trigger, letting us all hear the comforting click of the faithful M-14 as it fulfilled its part of the lesson.

"Turn the safety *off* when you want to shoot the weapon. *Off* when you want to shoot the weapon."

Holy smokes. He had spoken often to us before as though we were idiots. Maybe someone had swallowed a stupid pill today, and we needed this special harassment.

But Barrera was not done. He had a purpose. He had a personal lesson. He next pulled a newspaper clipping out of his pocket and unfolded it. He held it up. He pointed at a picture.

"This is a damn good Marine. He was asleep in his hooch when his post was overrun by the NVA (North Vietnamese Army). He heard sappers come through the wire. He jumped out of bed like any good Marine, and he began to fight. He picked up his rifle …"

Barrera picked up a bayonet and clicked it into place on the muzzle of that M-14 and raised it high for all to see, then continued his rant.

"… and he bayoneted the first soldier … just as we have taught you."

SSG Barrera stopped again for effect and thrust the weapon into an imaginary enemy. His cold, stony stare almost sucked the warmth out of the air. We did not blink. We thought he was now going to sing the praises of Marine training. Heck, we *knew* he was going to brag about our training. But we were in for a surprise.

"He then butt stroked and killed the second gook (enemy soldier), breaking his M-14 in two pieces …"

He gave back the rifle and pointed at the broken M-14 in the picture, right next to two dead soldiers. He looked around at us and paused.

"… Then he ran outside and killed another one in hand-to-hand combat. Just the way we have taught you."

He stared at us again, but this time there was scorn. He shook his head.

"They wanted to give him a medal."

So, that was it. Why, hell, who needs medals? We are all Marines. Why are we having this discussion?

Barrera finally arrived. The lesson. We were all sure we understood. We were wrong.

He pointed at something in the newspaper clipping. It showed the dead enemy soldiers and a broken M-14, complete with inserted magazine, on the floor of a room.

"But you will notice that the dumb son of a bitch forgot to release the safety."

He pointed carefully at the picture and at the safety that was obviously in the *on* position. He gathered us all around so he could show the picture to every recruit.

"It is mighty damn hard to kill three men unless you elect to *shoot* a couple of them. *Don't forget it.* If one of my Marines ever does this … (we were all so damn proud … we were *his* Marines) … I am gonna come over there and kick your butt myself."

So now we knew the bottom line.

In the Marine Corps, you can never earn a medal for hand-to-hand combat until you are out of ammo. And SSG Barrera is gonna kick your butt if you screw it up.

In a final note: Long after our graduation, I was told that one-third of Platoon 1091 was overrun at Khe Sanh, Vietnam, in 1969. Khe Sanh was not a single engagement fought in a couple of days. It was huge, fought over for months, and the scuttlebutt I got was strictly gossip. It was the way word was passed in the Corps.

One of those kids, a black kid named White (how else would I remember a name so long ago) lost an arm repelling an attack and won the Silver Star. That was the last time I heard of any of those who shipped out right away.

It is unimaginable now, but when we heard of this brave man and the honor he had earned, we were awed. Not by the merit of this person in our midst. Not in gratitude that he was back home, safe. This was, after all, the Silver Star, the third-highest medal given for bravery, bestowed on an *enlisted* Marine at that. We all sat around dumbstruck. We did not even engage on the idea that this brave Marine had lost his arm in combat and survived. After all, that was what Marines did.

Our united thought was, *Holy shit. What could he have done to win the Silver Star?*

Boot Camp Oddball Stuff

Marine Corps Number

In the old days, all Marines were issued a Marine Corps number. In fact, I think the USMC started using social security numbers after January 1969. I still remember my Marine Corps number and have a very rare trophy—a dog tag with my original Marine Corps number on it.

In fact, in my fortunate career, there are two odd things other men seem to quietly envy. They are not useful or especially worthy. But I put them where they can be seen and appreciated.

1. Young Marines envy having a Marine Corps number. It sort of lends more ownership to the Marine *Esprit.* It reeks of "Old Corps."

2. And Army Aviators envy having a Broken Wing. More on that later.

Old Corps Boots

Remember, *my* Marine Corps had spit-shined boots, not some of the ultra-comfortable, hi-tech suede boots issued today. In the *old days*, I mean the *really old days*—before me—issue boots were *brown suede*. I am not kidding. Marines were required to shave them, dye them and polish them. (I am not kidding about that, either.)

In my day, Marine recruits were all supposed to be issued regular black leather boots. Not the kind with the smooth overlaid toe (they were called "jump boots," or Corcorans), but a simple black leather boot with leather soles that could hold a respectable polish and shine on the toe.

Some of the Marines in our platoon, instead, received the last brown suede boots in supply. Not all of us got them, of course. They were the last ones left, in odd (that is, small) sizes. But the Marines who got them had to soak them in hot water, shave them (it took a day and a whole pack of razor blades), dye them with Kiwi black boot dye, and then polish them to a mirror shine. It was a pain in the neck, but it was possible (actually, it was required). You could tell which ones of the lucky Marines got a pair of the "old Corps" boots because no matter how well they were shaved, the bend-creases in the boots always showed a tiny bit of unshaved suede in them. It was a lot of trouble, but we were

Marines. Like every challenging moment, it turned out to be just another badge of honor.

The Beloved M-14

We were each issued a rifle, and we field-stripped that thing a zillion times. It was an M-14, a wonderful, powerful, dependable weapon that we each knew and loved. It was supposed to have been developed to reduce the size of the M-1, provide the automatic firepower of the BAR (Browning Automatic Rifle), and still be the faithful platform of the famous Marine Corps bayonet. We loved that thing, and we memorized our rifle number. I remembered my boot camp rifle number until I was 50 years old. I am not sure now, but I think it was 1219317. If you look it up on the internet, that number is valid for the timeframe of my Marine career.

The M-14 was especially handy because it was smaller and more powerful than the old M-1, and it fired a NATO 7.62 mm round. If you followed an M-60 machine gun around the battlefield, it would periodically throw away a belt of ammo, which also used that NATO 7.62 mm round. If ammo was scarce, you simply pealed the rounds out of the M-60 belt, and you had fresh, clean ammo for your magazines.

Remember here, the M-16 was brand new, and not even issued to the Marine Corps yet. Compared to the new M-16, the M-14 had a longer bayonet and was more effective in bayonet assault due to its physical durability. We sort of scoffed at the plastic, lightweight M-16. The early models jammed easily, and they broke fairly easily. The M-16 used the NATO 5.56 mm round, smaller and less powerful than the M-14 round. And beyond 200 yards, the rounds of the M-16 tumbled and were less accurate.

Nowadays, the usual assault technique is close-in and uses high rates of fire. The M-16 is considered perfect for this sort of combat. Its reputation as a dependable weapon has been enhanced by experience, and it does not need to shoot beyond 300 yards very often. However, the M-14 is still the Special Forces medium-range sniper rifle of choice, and it is periodically called out of retirement for specific units or missions. A bi-pod and a small scope make it easily transportable, deadly accurate and feared around the battlefield.

If they ever recall old, fat, ex-Marines, I will carry the M-14.

The Boot Camp Schedule

Our days started at 0500 or earlier. We fell outside in our shorts and T-shirts or sweats and went for a run. It was San Diego, after all, and it wasn't *that* cold.

BOOT CAMP ODDBALL STUFF

Immediately after our run we hit the showers, dressed, went to chow. The shower lasted two minutes and the chow lasted until the last recruit sat down; then all got up and left. We ran everywhere; we had a purpose for every task. We each had a footlocker, a bucket, two pairs of boots and the standard-issue utilities (dungarees to all you non-hackers) and basic equipment. When we were not being trained in class, we lined up in the street, sat on our buckets and performed a myriad of tasks. We polished boots, cleaned our weapons and equipment, starched our covers (caps). We got and read our mail. We wrote our letters there, read our manuals, all of it. *I got more butt time on that bucket than anywhere else in my Marine career.* It was an old-fashioned zinc bucket with a thick bottom rim, and I think I still have a scar where I sat on it.

The Black Eye

Should it occur that a Marine, in his training, got a black eye or some such mark of external motivation—and mind you, it could be from his platoon or his platoon sergeant—we would say he tripped over his footlocker. If it was especially obvious, it was said he *fell off his wall locker*. I am not talking about hazing or random brutality here. If a recruit refused to comply with the rules, or if he embarrassed or dishonored the platoon in a serious way, he would be properly motivated by the laying on of hands. It might not be a religious experience, but it could be life-changing.

No thought was ever given to the fact that *we had* no *wall lockers*.

The Smoking Lamp

In 1967, the Surgeon General had just come out with a paragraph statement on every pack of cigarettes warning that the habit was dangerous. Cigarettes were still being issued in C Rations, in four-cigarette packs. We used them or bartered chow for them. But on a regular boot camp day, before we could smoke, we were told, "The smoking lamp is lit." We fell out into the street with our buckets, got out our cigarettes and a match, placed the bucket over our head. Then we called out in unison, "The smoking lamp is lit, *Sir*! *Danger*! The Surgeon General says that smoking is dangerous to your health. Aye aye, *Sir*!"

Then we would light the cigarette and smoke it under the bucket. Now, no one exactly said this, but with such a stern warning about smoking, a lot of us did what the Marine Corps might expect. We all quit ... wait for it ... *reading.*

Religion

I thought I was doing pretty well in boot camp, but my family was fairly dysfunctional, so boot was just a different kind of stressful fun to me. Anyway, my first Sunday there, I went to church. I went to the Protestant service. It was in the movie theatre, and it was really strange. It was filled with silence. A moment of peace apart from the noise of boot camp. Except for the sniffling. All of a sudden I was crying. No sound, just crying. Most of us were. The enormity of our situation and the focus of our preparation for war, I suppose, made the spiritual moment nearly overwhelming.

Milestones of Boot Camp

I had a thousand one-on-one personal experiences with my DIs. I am convinced that such moments, right or wrong, whether course or refined, represent the weave that makes the fabric of Marine Corps *Esprit*.

The Swimming Hole

As we progressed through training, there was a rumor that SSGT Barrera cultivated with precision. He would get real mad from time to time about this or that ... and he swore in his wrath that if we did not get our act together, he would take us to the swimming hole. We lived in constant fear that he would one day get peeved and take us to his "swimming hole." We did not know just what that meant, only that it was horrible and filled with torment, and it haunted us.

SSGT Barrera was a straight-up Marine. Chiseled, a proud Mexican, not sort of pudgy like Neville. If you could call Neville pudgy, it was only because you compared him to the rest of us hungry wolves. Barrera was just as heroic to us as Neville. In the "old corps" the DI would accompany his recruits to war. This must have bothered Barrera considerably. Twice he apologized in a gruff sort of way that he would not be going over with us.

Once he suddenly stopped our march and set us down. He was not polished … he was sharp-tongued; he had an accent I think he kept up for his image, and he was Marine Corps through and through. He attempted to tell us what the flag meant to him. His flag. Our flag. His words failed him, but his heart could not be hidden. I do not remember a single word, but I recall perfectly the burning I felt in my soul for the sacred charge of my flag. I still feel that.

One day he was trying to teach a couple of fat kids to march. They were scared; they were not athletes, and he started slapping them around. He swore. He made reference to their complete lack of merit in this life and in the Marine Corps in particular. He threatened to send them to the "Fat Platoon," where it was rumored you would never eat and you would seldom sleep. They simply were not getting it, and he locked onto the fact that they were fat and inept. He started yelling … and swearing … at them and at us … and we could see it coming.

Barrera flipped. He fell us in, turned us around on the grinder and marched us behind the Quonsets to an area where the wash racks had been removed. We knew he could not beat us all up, so we were confused. But we figured it out pretty quick. It was calf-deep in sand. He became more angry and frustrated as our marching became uncoordinated. He swore some more … he yelled some more … he continued to slap those kids around, getting madder and madder at each mistake. At each mistake … at each *suspected* mistake.

He halted the platoon at the position of attention in the sandy field, and he started working us in close-order drill … calling cadence faster and barking change-steps faster and faster. The dust hung in great clouds. The dirt was everywhere. He fell us into pushups, sit-ups, swimming and crawling exercises.

"Splash! Faster! … I want to see waves! … Count! Louder!"

We were called to attention … it wasn't fast enough. We started over with close order drill. Then he dropped us directly to crawling. Then to attention.

We were ordered to crawl. We were ordered to get on our backs and paddle. Onto our faces and swim. On and on we went. We were not just filthy … we had dirt and sand in our noses, our skivvies … our boots … our eyes and ears … there was no respite. Our sweat turned it to mud. Mud that covered us. Soaked into our underwear, our socks. And still it went on.

The afternoon passed away. We missed a class. We missed chow. We missed mail call. The sun went down, and we missed shower call. We did not hear reveille in the commotion … still we swam; 2200 hours came and went; we knew he could be court-martialed for this. Hitting a recruit. Missing scheduled events. Missing chow. Missing lights out. Showers. Still he went on.

Then somewhere, the Marine Corps Hymn. One voice … then two … then a dozen. Louder. Clear, without apology, no whimpering. It was pride that we all felt, not anger or humiliation.

Barrera was suddenly quiet. He stood up straight and looked us over. He called us to attention. We stumbled into formation and stopped singing.

Barrera had tears running down his face. We marched back loud and proud. He called cadence and we responded. We woke the sleeping platoons; he marched us back for our gear and fell us out for a late shower. We marched back to the Quonset and fell out for mail. He dug out every snack he could find in the DI office; we munched, and then we got ten minutes with lights on to read mail. We had been to the "swimming hole." We racked out and never heard another word about it. From that moment, he never gave us such a load of crap again. From that day, we were *his* platoon. Neville and Barrera pretty much owned us after that.

Knife Throwing

SGT Neville was always one for macho shock value. We had a sister platoon, Platoon 1090 with Platoon SGT Gunny Silverman. Silverman and Neville were always jabbing each other about their platoons.

One day we were all out on the wash racks. Somehow Silverman had found out about Neville's prowess with a knife. After sufficient torment, Gunny Silverman bet Neville $20 he couldn't throw a knife into a Quonset hut door … and in front of our entire platoon. Neville made a 60-foot throw with a bayonet.

You will note here that he was our hero. There was no discussion of his ability, the miracle of the throw, the open mouth that Silverman flashed for only a second after the throw. There was no mention of the terrible balance of an M-14 bayonet. Or the fact it is was not sharp, for we were not allowed to sharpen them. This was SGT Neville, after all. He was our DI. Just ask any damn body. He was *ours* every bit as much as we were *his*, and nothing he did amazed us. He musta had a big red "S" on his chest, and it didn't stand for stupid.

The Quonsets were gray, and their doors were painted battleship gray. That bayonet had stuck in the plywood door. We quietly covered the hole with a bit of gray tape that made it nearly invisible.

You know damn well I was determined to become that good with a knife after that.

Rifle Range

In our fifth week (I think it was), we went to the rifle range with Neville. Somehow it never occurred to us that his being there alone with us might indicate his lower standing to the two staff sergeants who were also our DIs.

In those days we fired our weapons from the 200-, 300- and 500-yard line. It seems to me we fired 50 rounds to qualify—10 at the 200-yard line. kneeling; 10 at the 200-yard line, freehand (standing); 10 at the 300-yard line, kneeling; 10 at the 300-yard line, prone (lying down); and 10 at the 500-yard line, prone. If you fired a high score, you were Expert. If it was just a good score, you were Sharpshooter. If you passed, you were Marksman. The Expert and Sharpshooter badges were beautiful. The marksman badge was supposed to be shaped like a target, but it looked like a toilet seat. And that's what we called it.

Don't doubt it, many men wore that marksmanship badge gladly. It symbolized success at the bottom rung. It meant there was no set-back for failure to pass on the range; there was no outward shame for simply passing, even for this. Anything but failure. But many men went back to the range later to do better.

The procedure was this: The Marine would take his firing position at the line and was given five rounds (bullets) in a clip. He could load the magazine by hand and then place the magazine in the weapon, or he could insert the magazine, place the clip in the back of the chamber over the magazine and press the rounds into the magazine. When the range was declared live … he would fire five-round increments at a target with a life size black silhouette on it.

The targets were on stands in the "pit," and Marines in the pit would handle the targets and report the scores. Over the silhouette was printed a large set of circles, the inside one being the "bull's eye." After firing, the pit would lower the target, patch it, then raise it again.

Using a black or white disk on a long stick, the target handler would hold a disk up over the target for all to see. The disk was shown relative to the location of the strike, and each strike was presented in the order of the strikes from center to edge. If a Marine hit the bull's eye twice, two white disks would be shown relative to the proximity of the strike in the bull. If the silhouette was struck twice outside the bull, two black disks would be raised over the target relative to the strike.

But if you should (heaven forbid) miss the target completely, you got a Maggie's Drawers.

Now, the subtlety of some Marine Corps ego traditions cannot be measured with a nanometer ... but the Maggie's Drawers was a large red flag attached to a long stick. Did I say it was large, and red ... and obnoxious as hell? Well, SOP (Standard Operating Procedure) required the flag to be waved ***once*** slowly from right to left in front of the target ... *once* for each miss. Maggie's Drawers meant that Private Helen Keller, that dumb SOB, had missed the target completely, and it usually meant a kick and loud abuse from the shooting instructor, not to mention special attention from the DI who was standing on the line ready to motivate his platoon.

MILESTONES OF BOOT CAMP

So, as we were plugging away, a kid down the line from me was having problems. He managed two Maggie's Drawers. That was out of his *first* clip of five rounds. He was catching heck from his instructor, and his DI was waiting to climb onto his poor ego.

That DI was Neville. And he was not losing his cool … not yet. His cold stare was enough, and he knew it. Anyway, the kid was obviously nervous when he fired another five, slowly, carefully, and with all the finesse of a great artist.

What followed was classic Marine Corps. The kid raised his head from his spot weld (the way his cheek lay on his rifle butt) to see the spotting over the target, when the first Maggie's Drawers was waved. He knew then that four more were coming. He sagged as they were presented. Slowly, each one being called out, "*Miss*" by the spotter. The personal attention heaped on the aforementioned Private Helen Keller by the shooting instructor was the stuff legends are made of.

But it was not to be so simple. There was a Marine back there in the pit with a criminal mind and evil in his heart … and *he* was the flaming ass waving the Maggie. So, when the fifth Maggie's Drawers was waved appropriately, that turkey paused before pulling it down and waved it back and forth at least four more times.

First there was stunned silence all along the line. Above the laughter you suddenly could hear the shooting instructor yelling at that kid a mile away, and the spotter was on the phone to the pit reminding the pit crew NCOIC (Non-Commissioned Officer In Charge) of the relative lack of merit in his career, his ancestors and his upcoming days off … and in all else he may have held precious in the Marine Corps. Poor old Helen Keller was whining about the lousy rifle. It had to get better.

Neville was pure class. He said nothing. He stepped past the line instructor and up to the kid, took his rifle and stood freehand at 500 yards … and fired. For a moment, everyone there was still stunned. The range was still hot, but it had happened quickly, and no one had cleared him specifically to fire and *no one* ever fired 500 yards freehand.

Well, it was a DI, and it was a legal shot. The spotting officer called for a check on the target, and when it came up, it was a bull. The spotting officer thought it was wrong and called for a recheck. It came back up again as a bull's eye. Neville did not even blink, just gave the kid back his rifle and spat scornfully, "Try keeping your eye open."

Now, Neville was in the true tradition of the Marine Corps DI—course, rude and intimidating. He didn't speak with a lisp, but he did not enunciate his words very well, and they sometimes slurred. I am certain it did not lend much to his career, since in the Marine Corps perfect looks and manners are too often the measure of the man. Neville was just a work-dog Marine. Now, we loved that bum, but after this, he was the god of our platoon.

My personal experience at the rifle range was mixed. I was a country boy with a lot of freehand shooting, and for three days I fired Expert. On the fourth day I had a terrible day, and I fired Marksman. On the scoring day, I had another "iffy" day, and I fired Sharpshooter.

I felt as though I had let the whole platoon down. I actually cried in the back of the bus as we returned to the barracks. I was feeling pretty low when Neville walked past me as we got off.

"Wait until they are shooting back," was all he said.

Boot Camp Progression

As we went through boot camp, our progress was marked in some way by the uniform we wore. We were issued utilities (fatigues in Army language), covers (caps) and boots. Initially, we were not allowed to spit-shine our boots, wear starched utilities or starch our covers. We were not allowed to roll up our sleeves, blouse our boots or unbutton our top blouse button. If I remember correctly (forgive me if I am off either in order or length of time), we did eight weeks or so of boot and six weeks or so of ITR (Infantry Training Regiment), not including some weeks of guard duty and KP (kitchen patrol duty) assigned along the way.

The order of progress was, as well as I can remember it:

Week 1— Mothballs and Floppy Hats. We smelled like mothballs in our new, unpressed, unwashed utilities, buttoned to the neck; new, unwashed and unblocked caps with the perfect, unfaded chicken and fishhook (globe and anchor) on the front of the cap.

Week 2—Sleeves. We were allowed to roll up our sleeves.

Week 3—Boots. We got to wear spit-shined boots.

Week 4—"Starchies". We broke starch (wore starched utilities).

Week 5—Rifle Range. During the week of rifle range training, we were allowed to blouse our boots.

During training we were allowed to go to the PX for soap and shaving gear once, but after the Range, we made a real PX run and one of the guys managed to come back with a contraband radio. We had not heard a radio for more than a month, and the first song I heard on it was "Crimson and Clover." I have always loved that song since.

Week 6—Top Button. We had finished the rifle range, and we were allowed to unbutton our top button

Week 7—Starched Covers. We were allowed to starch our covers and wear them.

Week 8—Senior Platoon. We were the senior platoon, and we swaggered around acting as though we knew it all. We all started to crease and shape our covers as though we were really devils.

MOS Day

One afternoon before graduation, just after mail call, we all gathered in one Quonset hut for an important meeting. We were, at long last, being assigned our MOS (military occupational specialty). By this time, we all understood the truth as well as our eight weeks in the Marine Corps could let us. Infantry was not any glory day; it was the work-dog Marine, honored but tough. And scary. Unlike most of the other Marines in my platoon who got a combat MOS, my story worked out with all the fluff just as my recruiter said, and I got a special MOS—2847, Ground Radio Repair. Me. Given a specialty MOS. And I was still a respected Marine.

All but a very few of us received combat arms MOSs. I knew guys who were in for four years, very bright and educated men, who were assigned infantry, armor and artillery MOSs. I did not know a soul with a six-year active duty hitch, but I knew a bunch of guys with two-year commitments, and they were all assigned 0311, Infantry.

Why? Why didn't I go off to war as I expected? No one knows. Today when I am caught up among vets being honored for their combat service, as they are periodically, I am keenly aware of my own fraud in the presence of this elite group.

When we graduated, I knew only one person in San Diego, Sue Sweitzer. She alone attended my graduation. She was very cute and a bit older than I. We had met when we served Methodist Missions at the same time, and we always had been good friends. When I spent my school year at MCRD (Marine Corps Recruitment Depot), I became active in her Methodist Church.

When the graduation ceremony was complete, I had a free afternoon to walk around the area, to the PX and such. Seems I bought a burger and fries and dined gloriously with my friends. I called home and told Mom how proud I was to be a Marine. She tried to be happy that I had not been disappointed.

3

Infantry Training Regiment (ITR)

Following graduation I went directly to ITR at Camp Onofre, in Camp Pendleton, California. I was to be trained in a specialist MOS, and so my stay there was only about six weeks, not the 10+ weeks the combat arms guys stayed. In addition to endless fire-watch (night security) and mess duty, my training covered familiarization with most infantry weapons, marching, some tactics, marching, reenlistment propaganda and marching. This was in-between some forced marches and long march exercises.

During my first two weeks, when I was assigned extra duty but not yet in training, I got so deathly ill I was afraid I might live, and I was afraid to go to the hospital because they would set me back to another class, causing me to miss Christmas leave. So I tried to just suck it up. It got so bad that when I couldn't control my bowels, my corporal gave me a night off. Hong Cong Flu—worst thing I ever had.

Also, I was terribly cold. We were issued two blankets and had the option of everyone doing two hours of fire watch while the gas stove burned at night, or just getting a full four or so hours sleep in the cold … so we slept cold. I wore all my clothes, including field jacket and liner with two pairs of wool socks, and still I was frozen. But I lived. And I never was set back.

We got Thanksgiving off. I spent hours waiting to get into a pay-telephone booth for a call home and another to my sweetheart.

Frankie and Little Joe

One evening when I was walking guard, I saw an old friend of mine, Frankie Estupinian (forgive my spelling, ol' pal). This is typical of the meetings you have with folks from home. Just in passing you create in a moment a lifetime memory. I was homesick, and so was he. He was actually the older brother of a friend, Gilbert. Frankie and I didn't really know each other very well. But we were old comrades when we met that night. He was carrying an M-60 (the standard

7.62 mm machine gun of the day), a dependable and worthy companion to the M-14, the 7.62 mm rifle. He was going somewhere, either for a class or to clean it, I suppose. I surmised he was an 0311 (pronounced "oh three eleven," the Marine Corps Military Occupational Specialty of "grunt," an infantry man), with a machine-gun specialty. He mentioned another mutual friend, Little Joe Sanchez, a short leftie in the tradition of Little Joe Cartwright, our cowboy hero from the TV series *Bonanza*. Joe was also in the Corps; seems as though he was also an infantryman, but he was not there just then.

I never saw Frankie or Joe again, and I heard they had been killed in Vietnam. I searched and tried to look them up on casualty lists but never found them, so I hope the scuttlebutt was wrong this time.

I managed to survive until Christmas and went home on leave to South Wales, New York, to see my honey. Still the love of my life, and I absolutely intended to marry her, and … what else can I say?

WHEN FAT MEN FLEW

4

Young Love

Pardon me while we take a minor stray thought to its conclusion here. This is out of order but logical in its context.

Christine

Her name was Christine, an angel's name to be sure. Short, petite, sweet as she could be, she was such a beauty the sight of her would take my breath away. She was smart. But "pretty" simply did not cover this girl. She was more than just pretty. She was perfect. Or nearly perfect. And she was crazy about me. Her brother, Jay, was my best friend; her Mom loved me; her sister loved me. Even her Dad loved me. But she had only one small, eensy teensy little flaw … a minor issue as far as I was concerned, or at least it seemed a minor issue when compared to the merits in such a wonderful girl.

It was just this: Every time I was more than a grenade blast-radius away from her, *she fell in love with someone else.*

Damn, I hated that. But I was sure I could forgive almost anything, so long as she loved only me … and I was absolutely sure … well, pretty sure … well, fairly certain, sort of … well, that she was *in love* … or *in like* … or *in something* with *me* … her true love, I was certain.

Our adventure went like this. Whenever I went away, we were in love. Deeply, irrevocably, wonderfully consumed with each other. And after a couple of months or so she would sort of fade away to an infrequent letter and an emotionally distant, occasional phone call. And I could almost hear the fizzle as the spark went out. I would moon for several months, then come home on leave and suddenly she was nuts about me again.

On a side note … just remember that this is *my* sob story. I claim the right of poetic merit in this story. The actual merit (to her) of a private in the Marine Corps with his rather less-than-intellectual approach to all things, his constant absence and his refusal to acknowledge the difficulty a long-distance relationship placed on her … none of that is up for consideration here.

YOUNG LOVE

Anyway, we survived this cycle at least three separate times. Once it was when I went away to boot camp, and twice when I returned on leave at different times during my tour.

Now, let's say that I was pretty stupid. (This is 50 years of hindsight, painful hindsight, speaking now.) I spent about two years trying not to have a nervous breakdown over this girl. I was always away, and the Marine Corps knew no other way of business. I was still writing, still calling, still planning marriage and all those sweet things a young man and woman do to build a life.

Then one day I got a letter from her little sister. She was a cute little sister. I had noticed her before, but not too seriously. She had been in touch with me all along, she being my really dependable "long distance pen pal," as it were. But I did not really put little sister on my radar until the day I got that special letter. You know the deal. She was one of the few people-from-home writing. Among the other things of home, she was covering all the things that had to be done before the wedding, and the people involved, *blah blah blah*, when … *shades of a bolt from the blue* … it occurred to me that I was *not* going to be included in or involved with this wedding.

Boy, I was sort of in shock, still playing the "grenade blast radius blues" in the back of my mind. I got mad! I pulled up my britches and decided I would show her a thing or two. Just see if I ever ask *her* to marry me again. I was wounded. I put in a request for Vietnam (never went) and stepped out on the wild side awhile. I got pretty stupid. Stupid enough so that even I could see it (ditto the aforementioned 50 years of painful hindsight), and finally I had to grow up. When it was over and I was out of the Marine Corps, I took stock.

Christine turned out lucky … married a sweet guy, had a few kids, and became a nurse. He became a teacher, was always at home, and their family is still pretty well connected to all that tradition.

Little Sister

Not so for that sweet little sister. Her name was Gail, and she married an Army bum. He dragged her all over the world and had six kids; they now live all over the country … with 24 grandchildren and, if there is any justice, more on the way. Her life was not always easy or fun, but it was always exciting.

I am the one who made out like a fat rat. Turns out that marrying that little sister was one of the best decisions I ever made. It was never easy for her, but she turned out to be the angel I could not see, and our six children are the best in the world, for which the credit goes primarily to her. But I am the *king* of Grandpas!

YOUNG LOVE

Well, I am no longer married to this wonderful woman, but my esteem for her and for all the family she raised with me knows no bounds. Whatever our differences, I know my debt to her, and I hope one day I might find a way to repay her for the happiness she gave me.

WHEN FAT MEN FLEW

5

Basic Electronics Course (BEC)

Okay, back to the Marine Corps. I went home on my first Marine Corps leave for Christmas of 1968 and returned to MCRD for Basic Electronics School (BEC). I struggled through school but got a meritorious promotion to PFC (E-2) and then to Lance Corporal(E-3). I was no rocket scientist, but I did okay. For a while.

The Marine Corps Mission

Seems as though I returned to MCRD around 5 January 1969.

I still remember signing into the company for BEC followed by the Ground Radio Repair school. I was standing in a rain-soaked uniform when an old warrant officer, a CW2, if I remember, supposedly the last USMC Warrant on active duty, ordered me to a Quonset with my sea bag. It was lonely and impersonal, but I was finally serving and was *not* a recruit.

The next day we were marched down to the theater for our in-briefing. We marched on the same grinder where we had marched during boot camp, and to the same theater where we had graduated from boot camp. I was especially proud because I was now a full-fledged Marine, albeit a private, in a real Marine uniform. None of that slinking through the shadows because you're a (cough … spit) *recruit*. And it was the best-looking darn uniform in history.

We all marched into the theater and were seated. The theater smelled of popcorn, and the seats were cushy. I was liking my start in the Marines just fine.

Suddenly, out on the stage marched a crisp, sharp looking major, Commander of Basic Electronics School. His pleasant demeanor departed with his first words. An old sergeant yelled *"Ten, hut!"*

BASIC ELECTRONICS COURSE (BEC)

We popped to attention quicker than you could say, "Bob's Yer Uncle." The major looked around at us and yelled, "At ease!" And we popped back down. You could hear a pin drop. He clasped his hands behind him. Then he walked the length of the stage and back to the center, searching our august body with all-seeing eyes.

When he spoke, it was as though a foghorn from Hades was piercing your soul. He did not draw a big breath or rear back or perform any of the theatrics you might expect. But wow … the sound. It resonated with your heartbeat. It was a deep, booming voice, dripping with *Esprit*. It made you want to sharpen a bayonet or pull a pin from a grenade with your teeth or something.

"*Who* can tell me why you are here?" I knew a loaded question when I heard it, and I did not want this guy hopping onto my prize uniform, filled to the top with his newest Marine, at least not until I had completely unpacked my sea bag. Neither did anyone else.

"Oh, c'mon! C'mon! C'*mon*! Talk to me! You! Marine!" He had his victim. He wasn't letting go. He pointed at one of our timid fellows who suddenly grew a pair. He leapt out of his chair with a conviction he did not really feel. With quivering legs, in a soprano voice, he belted it out.

"*To fix radios!*" Then remembering his place, the private cleared his trembling throat and added, "*Sir!*"

"*What*?" The major was incredulous.

"To fix radios, *Sir!*" The private choked it out rather more feebly.

"*Bullshit! Sit down!*" The major nearly spit as he slapped him down and moved on for effect. It is funny, but it was only a proclamation for motivational effect, not a belittling or shaming of this young Marine. We all knew it. We were all still Marines. The major, *he* was a Marine. And that private, *he* was also still a Marine.

"You are Marines! All of you! You Marines are here to *close with and destroy the f'in' enemy. Never forget it!* The world knows *the most dangerous weapon in the world is a Marine and his rifle*! That is your purpose, your *only* purpose. You remember the Marine Corps is as awful and as terrible in battle as anything that history can record. The enemy, when he is in a fight with Marines … why the only thing he can think about is, "*How the hell can we get* out *of here!*"

We all started to laugh, to howl, then applause broke out. We got on our feet and cheered! His talk engendered pride and deep commitment to the Corps. And we all felt it. Heck, when he was done, we would have happily followed him into hell!

BASIC ELECTRONICS COURSE (BEC)

Pride was the single, universal virtue that we lived for. The Marine Corps demanded this single source of total satisfaction, the symbol of devotion and sacrifice for our beloved Corps. Pride. It was what we had in common. It was what we all did. And we did it proudly.

We all marched back down the grinder to our Quonsets and got settled in. While I was in BES later that year, I took a day off and went back to visit my old DI, Sgt Neville. He was in the same Quonset area and doing the same training, happy to see me.

He was proud to introduce me to his platoon, all on their buckets in the street, working on personal gear, and made it a point to remind them that one day, *they* could come back to visit. He winked at me, and I followed him into his hooch. I watched as he reached into a 3x5 card box full of tiny lesson plans for his day. Each card had a small topic to remind him of something to train … er … yell about. "First word out of mouth … *Sir!*" was one. "DI—Dumb Idiot?" was another. "Don't call me sir. I work for a living!" was another.

He stepped out into the street, found a private to yell at in front of the platoon and drove home this critical point by virtue of yelling and intimidation. This particular card indicated fault with the private's uniform. He berated the private about the condition of his spit shine, and with one mind, the entire platoon immediately bent over their boots to touch them up before our DI could catch them, too.

Neville turned on his heel and marched back into his hooch for another card.

No one said he was a rocket scientist. Just a damn fine Marine.

Marathon 1969

In the summer of 1969 I was still attending Basic Electronic School, USMC, at the very same MCRD in San Diego. I was a typical, confused young Marine, trying to get through a year-long electronics school and enjoy my time off in such a pretty town. As a Marine, I was expecting to go to Vietnam. All Marines who were real men, according to the Marine Corps Commandant, were going to Vietnam.

So I was taking in the whole world as fast as I could go. I loved the downtown coffeehouse areas, the beaches and the neighborly atmosphere of San Diego. I was fairly sharp; most of the kids in this school were, but I was looking for some distraction. I was wandering around on my off time looking for a sweet girl, a church that mattered and a genuine purpose when I stumbled onto the San Diego March of Dimes.

BASIC ELECTRONICS COURSE (BEC)

The rules were fairly loose. They wanted money. Any legal way you could get some was okay ... which pretty much meant you had to beg or coerce your contributors to choke up some money. In other words there was not a lot of accountability for the nickels and dimes we little folk could bring in. The drive was cause for big events, and they came up with a lot of community involvement for events, one after the other, for the summer.

One was the marathon. They were going to sponsor a 26-mile marathon along that wonderful stretch of waterways, beaches and coffee houses I loved so much. There was a five- and 10-mile section, but the object was for folks to run it and find sponsors to pay something for every mile completed. I decided to walk it and collect what I could. It turned out to be pretty exciting for me.

I was really energized when I went into a Chevy (Pontiac maybe?) dealership and asked for the manager. He was young and handsome, a confident stud, bronze from the San Diego sun, and he was lord of all he surveyed. He came up, shook my hand with a big grin and greeted me like a fellow member of royalty, practically begging me to let him contribute! When we were done, he committed to $3.00 per mile, and it seemed as though there would be a bonus for a speedy run. Suddenly I was a player, someone who was going to bring in over a hundred bucks ... *wow!*

Now, you may have to look with a blind eye to see it now, but I was a stallion then. I was tall and straight and trim and fleet of foot. Nothing was better than me, and this puny 26 miles ... why hell, this was just another long walk in the park. A very long walk in the park, perhaps, but a *park*, nonetheless. There would be free water and stuff along the way. There was bound to be bikini clad girls along the route who might be impressed by such a man ... and the real men in my world would pay homage to such a feat ... *blah blah blah.*

I showed up with six or seven sponsors, and I had bought a new pair of sneakers just for good measure. I wore a tank top and a pair of shorts. I had a fashionable "farmer's tan," which meant I had brown forearms and hairy legs the color of a young snow fox.

I was so damn handsome I could hardly believe it was *me.* In a moment of supreme, immodest and irrevocably ignorant self-confidence, I decided I was in better than average shape and would run it if I could. It was a cold-turkey run, without any preparation or training.

It is safe to say I did not give this idea any serious thought and even less preparation. I took one look at a few of the spindly guys who showed up (who actually prepared for the run), and I simply could not understand how a puny man that skinny could be serious here.

BASIC ELECTRONICS COURSE (BEC)

Well, reality started tapping me on the shoulder around two miles out.

I noticed my shoes were sort of tight, and I tried to adjust them. I finally realized my tenny-runners were simply too small, and I needed some help. Like any sensible Marine, I whipped out my pocket knife and cut out the toes. I started running again, and in no time, I stopped to carve on the edges of those soles. In fact, I started to hack more out of the toes every so often, just to smooth down the rough edges and keep the hot spots under control. It seemed to work. At least the blisters didn't start to bleed until around 20 miles.

My normal work attire was the issue utilities, and my exposed knuckles and forearms never burned. On this day, I used some sort of mystical tanning oil, which I purchased early on the run based on its claims to attract female attention. I do not remember ever hearing about sun screen until much later in my adulthood, and on that day, the need for it was not apparent until I was on the run. I did not even notice the sunburn until later in the morning. By that time, my ears, nose and neck were suffering.

I fairly glowed from my liberal but fruitless application of this stuff. Instead of the Hawaiian god on the label, I looked like that idiot on the cover of *Mad Magazine*.

I did wear a good pair of shorts. But not having decided to run the route until my arrival at the starting line, I had not prepared for or even considered the wisdom of a good athletic supporter. Though I did not even consider the battering 26 miles of jogging might impose on my diminutive manhood, it *did* distract me from the chafing. In fact, the barely noticeable chafing during the run became very painful ... awful, terrible and very personal, beginning the very first moment I stepped into the evening shower. For good measure, this lesson was driven into me by four exhausting and sleepless nights, lasting through the next four days of duty.

Well, I made the run in less than six hours, if memory serves. That may be too generous. I actually finished, running or whatever it was I was doing. I had bleeding feet. I suffered the above-mentioned severe and very personal injury, and I was burned to a crisp. My new tenny-runners were trash. I was starving; there had been no food along the way. There was not a single female impressed with my effort, and I had to walk bow-legged for a week.

Oh no ... you don't get off that easy. There is more. Unknown to me, there was a PT (physical fitness) test Monday morning. In those days, regulation forbade careless injury by sunburn. Missing duty for sunburn rated an Article 15 (company-grade punishment) for failure to perform. I passed that PT test, limp and all. And, for duty, I continued to break fresh starch, meaning that each day's uniform (standard utilities, or dungarees, as the Army would say) were freshly and very heavily starched to hold creases and look very sharp. They woulda looked better without me in them.

Anyway, the final tragic moment was yet to come. It took me a few days to get up the motivation to make my rounds and collect the donations from my sponsors, but most of them paid up immediately.

The Chevy dealer was closed the first time I went there. And the second time. It seemed odd because there was no reason for it to be shut down. The third time I went, the place looked like a morgue. All the staff were wearing black, and there was no person to greet me in the usual car dealership fashion.

I went up to the secretary and asked for the manager; she burst into tears and ran off. Soon some official-looking salesman came up and asked what I wanted. I went through my story, ending with my victorious 26-mile run, and he choked back the tears.

Seems that his manager had purchased a new boat and had gone out that weekend with his family. I cannot remember how many of them died in that accident, but he did.

No one offered to pay up. I hadn't the heart to ask. And the March of Dimes forgave me and even thanked me for the $30 I did collect. I learned three very important lessons that stand me in good stead even today.

First, the right shoes, at any price, are a bargain.

Second, you cannot go wrong with industrial-strength sunscreen.

Third, never underestimate the value of a good athletic supporter. A little anti-bacterial crème can also be helpful

Knife Throwing, Refined

I had a buddy named Crease, a tall, backwoods guy from the deep south. He and I were both quietly smitten with the art of knife throwing. In those days, there were several movies of great renown that touted the merits of knife throwing skill. Jim Bowie, a hero of Alamo fame, comes to mind. Anyway, having witnessed the knife throwing prowess of my Superman DI, SGT Ralph Neville, I was very impressed when Crease bought a top-of-the line boot knife, a Gerber.

Gerber was famous for the "soldier of fortune" appeal, and it was a fine piece of stainless-steel cutlery, very handy in a field situation. It was the long one, and it held a very fine edge well. And it slipped perfectly into your boot, if you were sure to carefully protect your tender ankle from that wonderful blade. I don't think you could jump in it (from an airplane, I mean), but you could run with it and carry it in the field without any problem.

Crease and I would sneak back into an old handball court behind the barracks and throw the Gerber at the back wall. Every once in a while we actually stuck it, and we seemed to be getting better each day. But, wouldn't you know it, I reared back and let fly with that thing, and it hit the wall oddly. I broke that damn thing right off at the handle. We were both stunned, since it was made of expensive, high-quality steel that ran from the point through the hilt. I felt bad … no, I felt terrible about it. He is probably still mad.

Anyway, I was undaunted. I decided to buy a set of throwing knives and become proficient in this skill. After all, I wanted all the skills involved in the fine art of Marine Corps legend-building.

These knives could endure any stupid throw. They were chrome, one single piece without a separate handle. The knife was not fancy, just one piece of metal, shaped like a knife. The handle was on the end opposite to the blade, and it sort of looked like a normal handle, and it was covered in plastic. The knives were a lot cheaper than the Gerber, they felt balanced, and they threw fairly well. I admit now I was not sure precisely what "fairly well" meant. But they flew straight, and they never broke on me.

I invited Crease to go out back with me, but he still was pretty mad. Anyway, compared with that beautiful piece of combat cutlery, these were like the Yugo compared to the Pontiac GTO. He declined my generous offer.

The throwing knives were illegal and expressly forbidden. Marines simply were not allowed to arm themselves and damage the handball court in pursuit of combat proficiency. I had slinked into a pawn shop to buy them and thought I was pretty clever. I was not one to break rules, but *this* was different. They made me feel as if I were adding to my Marine skill-set. I was a secret killer, and my self-image was, for the moment, enhanced.

The knives were not refined pieces of equipment, but they worked until they were both stolen. I had hidden them outside the barracks in a palm tree, and obviously some moron had better use for them than I did. I simply could not afford to invest in any more foolishness, so I gave up all my knife-throwing aspirations.

Quit laughing. I may not have been Dan Daily (a twice winner of the Medal of Honor, to whom all Marines pay homage), but neither was I Gomer Pyle.

GT Smart

I hung out with a great kid, Gordon T. Smart ... just like the infamous comedy TV character. But GT (as we called him) had a peculiar identifying feature. He had five fingers and zero thumbs on each hand. And he had a little Sunbeam, a wonderful little sports car we could actually afford to keep on the road. I found that guy recently. He is retired now in Oregon. (Can I really be that old?)

It is a small world. GT became an aviation electronics repairman and returned to my home town of Yuma, Arizona, to be stationed at MCAS (Marine Corps Air Station), Yuma. Then he married a girl from my high school (KOFA high, in Yuma). How weird is that?

The Prom

I had been a Methodist and served a Methodist mission before joining the Marines. While I was in San Diego, I was active in a little old Methodist Church down near 42nd and El Cajon. It is not there anymore, but I went every week and knew all the young people there.

There was an odd family there. The mom and one daughter were enormous. Dad was a Sailor, and as a Navy family, they were sensitive to the demands of the service. They were very sweet, and they made a lonely Marine feel right at home with good company and a nice home-cooked meal from time to time.

Well, I wasn't dating much—remember, I was mooning about my true love back home—and I discovered that the sweet daughter had no prom date. Her social life was fairly limited, and I was determined that if nothing else good happened, I was going to ask her to the prom. She accepted. I came in uniform, and I brought a corsage that you would have thought was to die for. I can tell you I have never been as appreciated or loved the way that family loved me after that. And Joyce was forever a dear friend. I wish I knew where they are now.

Balboa Park

I had several places, beaches and such, that I often visited in my off time. One of these was Balboa Park, and if memory serves it is quite close to the San Diego Zoo and the Naval Hospital there. I would go over there and spend hours wandering about, taking in the beautiful park. I could take a bus ride over there for cheap, and half a book later, I was a new man.

Thirty years later, I went back to that wonderful park. It looked the same, as well as I could tell from three decades of dusty memory. It was clean, trimmed and perfectly groomed. I was lost in my fog of memories for 20 minutes before I realized I was the *only man* on this side of the park *without another man* holding my hand.

Sorry if I challenge your sensibilities. I am not gay. I was offended to realize that because I am straight, I must now stay in my own part of the park. It seems that the old San Diego, the one I used to think was so liberal but in fact was fairly conservative, has taken a leap into the illusive pursuit of "progress." I hope it works for them. I still love that town, but the lure of progress has taken something that cannot be replaced. I was not there long enough to see what else has changed, but I am certain there is more.

Graduation

I do not remember much about my graduation from Basic Electronics School. I got to wander around post, eat pogey bait and have a coke with friend Sue. But it was topped off by another flight back home to my sweetie. And she would soon be in love with me again.

The Marine Corps handed me another set of orders to 29 Palms, California, to prepare for shipment to Vietnam.

WHEN FAT MEN FLEW

6

29 Palms

The Banning Bullet

I arrived in Palm Springs via commercial flight. In those days, Marines often were sent via bus to CONUS (CONtinental US) duty stations. I found a booth in the airport where I could inquire about transportation. There was a bus I had to catch to 29 Palms ... nicknamed "the Banning Bullet."

It was an old blue bus, owned by the man who won the contract to carry Marines back and forth to Palm Springs and a few other places. It must have been fashioned after a Vietnamese bus because it took hours longer than necessary to get there and it was never on time. Some of this was due to the maintenance skills of the operation, and some of it was because it carried everything from cargo to chickens and goats to every barn, farmhouse, outhouse, dog house, hen house and roadside stand along the way. There were no chickens or goats on my initial trip, but there was a dog.

This was my first real Marine line unit, and it was a bit of a disappointment. I arrived after my Thanksgiving leave. I was sensitive to the freedom of the married men to go home, so I volunteered to stand mess duty over the holidays and weekends. But I hated KP.

The NCOIC of the mess was an old staff sergeant who was so crooked they will have to screw him into the ground when he dies. Hungry Marines came to his mess hall to be fed swill and minimal portions, while he carried food out the back door to sell or do something else with it. He even bragged about how many men he could feed with a 10-pound roast. Everyone there was unhappy, and one day I was pulled into an office by an investigator to answer questions. After I had asked about my own status there, I gave him straight answers. I was too naive, too new and too junior to be accused of much, and I was not trusted enough to know all the details. But I knew enough. That sergeant was arrested before I was released from KP.

During that time there was a disc jockey on the radio named Wolfman Jack, and we all loved that crazy guy. There was only one record player in our barracks and only one record, which was by Credence Clearwater. "Proud Mary" played all day and night, every day and night, and I hated that song. Still do. I had my heart set on buying a Norton Motorcycle, a big sponsor of the Wolfman Jack radio show, but I just never got it done.

I made friends with two married Marines who lived in town, and I tried to take care of them. They were always broke; I was always hungry for some sort of distraction. I would buy steaks or chicken, then go and visit for a barbeque. One had kids; the other's wife was pregnant. I would often lend money … and I think I lent them around $500 … which I never saw again. Remember, I was making about $135/month. The amount I lent them was a lot of money to me.

I also met a wonderful woman, Marian Wise. Ah, Marian Wise … she was a middle-aged woman with some teenage kids, and she was the costume maker for the Joshua Tree Theater Guild. She found out I could sing, and she asked me along. Before you know it, Ken Althaus, another buddy, and I were playing in the musical *Kiss Me Kate*.

It was a blast. I loved that bunch, and especially the Wises. I met two wonderful girls there, but I do not remember their names. I don't suppose I ever made an impression on either of them, but they were all part of it. I even sang a tenor solo, "Too Darn Hot." It was just too high for me, but I belted it out, and they did not kill me for my performance, so it was all good.

Ken was my best friend then, and he got into trouble. He ended up in the brig and was going to be AWOL if he did not return to duty immediately, possibly charged with missing a movement. In a moment of supreme selflessness, I went to the credit union and took out a loan to pay off his $500 fine. You cannot imagine the questions I had to answer for that loan ... and I paid it off in a year. Ken stayed out of trouble after that. was true to his word ... until it came to paying me back. As you can guess, I never saw any of that money again, either.

Anyway, Marian Wise was a trusted friend. My Grandfather Marsh had given me an elk-horn knife, made in Germany, and I left it with her for safe keeping. I could not send it overseas; as far as I know, she still has it.

Dishonorable Discharge

Now, I was a fairly new lance corporal, and I suppose I was rather naive. The US Military career is designed to be one progressive event after another, and promotion is naturally a part of that. Most of the men (vets) who had returned from Vietnam who were still under the rank of corporal were, generally, duds. Not all, but as a general rule, these were the dregs of the Corps, and there was always trouble afoot. Especially drugs. Alcohol was simply accepted as the natural reflection of the frustration there, but drugs were also all around. I began to try to report some of that stuff, and I was immediately outcast and threatened. My bunk and laundry bag were urinated on, and I started spending my nights with the Wises in town.

Anyway, one day one of our career privates was dragged away by the MPs, and no one saw him for a week. Unexpectedly we were all called out into formation, and he was hauled out in front of us as a PFC (Private E-2) in full greens.

We were called to attention, and a statement was read about his courts martial, his reduction to the rank of Private E-1, and his dishonorable discharge. An officer then stepped forward and unceremoniously began to cut off all his Marine Corps emblems. The officer cut off the private's stripes and every USMC button on his uniform … and removed the globe and anchor from his cap.

Whatever our faults, we were all still Marines, and we were in this together. We were all ashamed. I am sure the display was designed to add shame to our motivation for better behavior, but it was not received that way. It seemed to be a symbol of the shame we should have felt for the casual abandonment of our devotion to the Corps. I was still idealistic, and I felt it deeply. I cannot explain it very well. We did not talk about it, but I never forgot it.

The private was escorted by guards to a jeep and tried to wave an uncaring and cheery goodbye as he was driven away. It was just as empty as the ceremony. He was taken to the gate and set out. He walked away, and we never saw him again.

29 Palms NCO

Walking around in the town of 29 Palms, I was going by a bar when I saw an old Datsun pickup with a sticker from the Silver Spur Rodeo in Yuma, Arizona. Yuma was my hometown, and I still had friends there. Anyone from home was okay with me.

I went in and asked who owned it. An old staff sergeant stepped up and shook my hand. We became fast friends. He was from Yuma, and he went back there most every weekend. His family was settled in there, and he was finishing his career as a bachelor at 29 Palms. He was an odd guy who did not mince words. Once, in heavy traffic, we were driving along, and he got real frustrated. He pulled out an old thumb-buster .44, and two rounds of that into the air cleared the road ahead just fine. He owned a Toyota pickup and had never changed the oil, due to various odd circumstances. He was running it just to see how long he could make it, and with more than 100,000 miles, it still did not burn much.

Although I do not remember his name, I recall what a good guy he was, and that because of him I got back to my beloved Yuma a couple of times a month when the duty roster let me. He taught me a lot. One day I smarted off about how unhappy he should be to retire staff sergeant rather than Gunny. He looked at me and I shut up.

"I love being a Marine, and it has been a good career." He said it reverently.

"There is no way you can pay a man to be a Marine. His mission is not the same as that of someone in the Army or any other service. You simply cannot give the toughest job in the world to a man and ask, 'How much is it worth?'

"What job, you ask? Just put 80 pounds on a man, give him a rifle with a bandoleer and a sharp pointy thing on it; give him several grenades and bring him in to shore under artillery fire in a giant bath tub filled with vomiting men; have him jump into neck-deep water and swim ashore, cross an open beach under fire, all the while watching his friends getting killed and maimed, and jam that thing into a living person all the way to the flash suppressor.

Now, *that* is a job description. And only *pride* can *make* a man do it. Did I say *make*? Yep. If you think he will let his buddies down, if you think he won't die before failing them, well, you have never been a Marine."

About this time, I had a clear understanding of my recruiter, though he said it a bit differently when I enlisted.

"Just you yell 'Coast Guard!' and see what you get."

The Smoker

I remember my first real lesson in image. Rather, it was the limits of image as opposed to character. The battalion was having a smoker, a boxing match, and there were prizes, cheap beer and food, and it was going to be a great time.

The biggest match on base was supposed to be with this giant, murderous, arrogant Marine who ran around, trained loudly, sparred with all comers and was going to display his manhood for the world to envy. I do not remember his name.

He finally got a challenger, a former Golden Gloves champ of a significantly lower weight, a nice guy who we did not want hurt for the sake of show. He said little. He simply went about his business.

On the day of the smoker, all the lighter weights fought first, and it was a good day. As the heavyweight match was presented, the loudmouth had several folks in his corner. The little guy had a man to hold a towel, and who knows, maybe to throw it into the ring. The crowd cheered for the big guy as he bowed, preened and soaked up the glory something like the way old Max Baer did in all his fights. The little guy simply warmed up and said nothing.

In the first round, the loudmouth came out all business. He started confidently, but he quit talking. The little guy went in low and worked the body, often, hard, always two shots at a time. The shots he took were to the head, mostly deflected and impotent. The crowd started to quiet down. In fact, the entire concessions section was silent except between rounds.

In the second round, the loudmouth began to drop his hands, and the little guy continued to work the middle of his opponent. Every strike seemed to shake the big man's entire soul. At the bell, he staggered back to his corner for refreshment and encouragement. His crew waved a towel over him, poured water, propped him up for his victorious comeback in the third round. But the crowd was silent.

At the beginning of the third round, he took one to the liver, and a second or two later, he stopped, sagged and fell to the mat in a ball. The place went wild.

That was the second best fight I ever saw. The best fight happened years earlier, and it was ended by pure arrogance. One man was beating the other to a pulp, and after hitting him with a staggering liver shot, stood over him as the poor guy was catching his breath, barely on his feet. Instead of finishing him, he taunted his victim and stood directly against him as his victim was sort of hunched over in pain and with the shame of being the loser. Suddenly the injured boxer stood upright and ripped that guy's head off with a surprise uppercut. It knocked him cold. The victor could hardly stand while the referee raised his hand in victory, and his corner helped him back to the stool.

The fight was so surprising that the narrator interviewed the loser, who was bitterly ashamed of his foolishness. But in his humility, I think he learned a valuable lesson.

Three Stooges in the Impact Area

I had one giant stroke of luck when I was there. I was in the back of a jeep riding around the back trails at 29 Palms with two other Marines, and we went through an impact area. An impact area is on an artillery range, where targets are used. Often dud ammunition was left in the ground without being set off or destroyed.

As we were driving along, one of the guys yelled to stop, and he jumped out. There, beside the trail was an old bomb, nose first in the dirt, fins up, and he was determined to take it home. He ran over there, got hold of it just about the time the driver and I came to life. We shrieked, yelled and hopped up and down. The guy with the bomb released his prize, and we began a pointed discussion on the merits of his ancestors and how quickly he wanted to see them again. We all should have been killed, and only stupid luck saved us.

I believe God had a higher purpose to my surviving that moment, but that kid did not have a clue. He got back in the jeep, and we all lived to fight another day.

21st Birthday

I turned 21 in 1970, and I proved once and for all I had no capability for serious drinking. I also demonstrated that I had very little good sense. I went to Tijuana, got drunk, stayed up 48 hours and accomplished nothing, not even a good time. I did not get arrested, and I returned before my pass expired. (In those days, you had to draw a liberty chit to go off base.) I suppose I was a pretty boring Marine. I didn't whore around and I couldn't drink; my most evil ambition, which never happened, was to buy a Norton motorcycle.

Well, I had gone home for Thanksgiving leave in 1969. My angel was in love with me again and was busy at work one evening when I learned that her little sister, who had a crush on me, did not have a date to the local dance. I volunteered, and of course, I showed up in uniform. There, instead of that little almost 16-year-old girl, there was a gorgeous little woman waiting for me. Impatiently.

Now, her family was very special to me, and they were all sort of taken aback when they saw Gail waiting at the door. When they saw me with my mouth open, Dad stepped up and gave me that proper stare; I closed my mouth and was the perfect gentleman. I did not know then that she would become the love of my life. And I took full note of her disappointment when I gave her a peck at the door as I said my good night.

But her victory was complete when my honey, her big sister, came home. Gail refused to tell her sister what we did or where we went. It was not very exciting, but the evil was in her silence.

7

Hawaii

When I got orders to Hawaii, I was flabbergasted. I had
to read them twice and confirm it was no error. I was a pretty
idealistic kid at 29 Palms, and I was really disappointed in the
average mentality of the average Marine … party, drink, smoke
dope, party some more. In those days there was a terrible
decay in the USMC morale. My going to Hawaii, though I
was ashamed to be a *"firewatch* Marine," probably saved my
life. Actually, I believe my lieutenant, a lifer master sergeant
turned 2LT, got those orders fixed, probably due to my own
immaturity. Anyway, I lived a long time under the illusion that
I had been robbed. So you see, I was stupid as well.

Note: The *firewatch* ribbon (The National Defense Service Ribbon, or NDSR) was presented to all members of the military in those days for serving during war time without doing much. To me, it seemed to represent who served but never went anywhere or did anything *real* Marines did ... like go to Vietnam and get killed. Why hell, even the Guard and Reserves (who may have served 90 days or so) got one.

I flew into Hawaii around March 1970.

Don't Touch the Graves

I was flying in uniform and sitting next to a kid who looked Hawaiian and did not say much. Turns out he had been in the Air Force Academy and resigned. He did not seem too happy, but I pressed on. I sort of sneaked up on him with my big question. I wanted to be friendly with the natives, and I was looking for some fairly straightforward way to do that.

He looked at me with distant eyes.

"*Don't* touch the graves," he whispered.

Holy smokes. I don't think I said another word. I never saw him again.

So I got there with this spooky advice, and I met a kid to be stationed with me for the next 19 months. McIntosh. Don't remember his first name now. We were sent out to the

Naval Ammunition Depot, Lualualei, a collection of ammo bunkers between Nanakuli on the coast and Kolekole Pass, beyond which was Schofield Barracks.

Kolekole Pass and the Headless Princess

Lualualei was laid out in odd fashion. As I recall a road ran along the leeward side of the island, north and south. The town of Nanakuli was on the water, and a road went from there directly through the Marine Barracks, up Kolekole Road, through Kolekole Pass and down to Schofield Barracks, an Army post.

Kolekole road ran along the magazine (mag) area, climbing to the pass, and you could look over the mag area nearly anywhere along that road. About mid-way up the pass was an observation tower, and a guard was always in it. In the blackest and deepest and wildest part of the mag area, there was another observation tower. No Marine ever manned it during my tenure.

There was a legend of a Marine stationed out there in that lonely tower. One night he screamed for help over the hot line to the guard shack at the main gate. A patrol truck lit out there immediately, but before help arrived, the Marine emptied his magazine and ran the seven miles cross country to the main gate. It was not a simple run; he was cut to pieces by thorns and briers in the wild underbrush. The tower had been closed since that time.

Whatever the real issue in this legend, I was in the guard shack one night as patrol driver when Corporal Crenitz got a call. The console had lights for the various locations, and this was from the old guard tower in the mag area. We looked at each other as he picked it up and someone on the other end screamed. He slammed down the phone, and we raced out there (armed, I can tell you) and found nothing. When Crenitz got into the tower, he ripped out the phone and brought it back to the guard shack. That just added another layer to the legend in the Kolekole pass lore.

At the top of the pass we had another guard shack right beside the exit to Schofield Barracks. The building housed the watch each 24 hours and was equipped with bathroom, sleeping quarters and kitchen. Behind that building was a sacrificial site where beheading rituals had been held … including the catch basin for the head and a drain for the blood. I am sorry I never took pictures of it, but we were not allowed to tamper with anything there, only look at it. This was all high adventure for a *Haole*. (Haole is an often-scornful Hawaiian term for a meddling or foolish off-islander, or white guy.)

Kolekole Pass was associated with a headless princess; I do not remember her name or all the story that went with her.

HAWAII

She was reputed to walk the pass often. We were periodically given reports of her wandering the pass by folks who were respectable, believable people. It happened often. We also had folks arrive at the top of the pass insisting a ghost had been riding with them up the pass. And we simply accepted it as part of the local lore.

I never saw her. But as a new guard, I was on duty at a back gate along the Naval Radio Station there, a separate part of Lualualei. Two women pulled into the gate area screaming. They were terrified and incoherent. I drew my pistol and ran into the road outside the gate, and I saw nothing. I returned to the car with my gun in hand and yelled for them to shut up. They were obviously Hawaiian, and they were not military, so I was concerned about their presence in my gate area. I called my Corporal of the Guard, and he sent out the Sergeant of the Relief. In the meantime, the ladies told me they had been driving along and had hit someone … that is, they couldn't have missed but they felt no impact when they ran over him.

The sergeant arrived, and I bit my lip explaining the story. He did not even react. He asked how much they had to drink (hadn't even occurred to me to ask) and convinced them to leave. That was the limit of my personal experience with the ghosts of Lualualei.

Promotion to Corporal

I was in an odd spot for the Marine Corps. Granted, I was
not the brightest bulb in the box, but I worked hard and was eager
to do my duty. Seeing Hawaii, or at least the island of Oahu, was
just another perk. Anyway, I was actually assigned MOS #2847,
Ground Radio Repairman, in which I had trained; it was a critical
MOS. But I was working in the MOS 8151, basically a facility
guard, which I was told was another critical MOS. That means that
during the Vietnam War, I was holding a "critical MOS, "which
means an important MOS with a shortage of qualified men in
it; I was serving in another supposedly "critical MOS." I could
not be released from the MOS in which I was working no matter
what the excuse (i.e., to go either to a qualified, proper MOS or to
Vietnam *because* my MOS was critical). I could not be promoted
because I was working *outside* my trained MOS.

So for 27 months, I remained a lance corporal, E-3. Now
there is excitement for you. I was finally given a "meritorious
promotion" to Corporal, E-4, four months before I was separated
from active duty. I thought it was because I was a heck of a man.
But it turns out that in order to get me to re-enlist, they had to
promote me and then tempt me to another promotion on condition
of my reenlistment.

The real privilege of the promotion turned out to be two
things. First, I was able to stand Corporal of the Guard for

a while and assume some leadership. Second, I was moved into a three-man room, a real treat. After living with 70 men, it was very nice to have a bit of privacy.

There was another element of karma here… note that in this proud promotion picture (I am on the far left here), there is *a garbage truck in the background*. At that time, it seemed like that was symbolic of the rest of my Marine Corps career.

I was finally promoted (they thought I would reenlist for the privilege), and I was proud. But the Marine Corps never really went out of its way to reward my career ambition.

I spent about 19 months in Hawaii all told, and when it was over, I was pretty much disappointed with the Marine Corps. It was thankless, and my initial idealism faded with the constant grind of duty with no change in pace. I had a pain-in-the neck staff sergeant who was always in my knickers about something. The section worked regular shifts for the first few months, then changed to some sort of swing shifts, where our scheduled rotation moved up four hours every day. That meant we were on standby for four hours, on duty for four hours, and off 12 hours. We did that for about a year. It was exhausting, and we were stupid about it.

Under this schedule, the enlisted men tried to save some rest, and once in a while they simply stayed up 24 hours to get some time out in town away from the flag.

The Buddy System

I had a buddy there, not a really close friend, but a newly married guy, L/Cpl Hildebrand, who was a stallion. He knew all about snorkeling, and I was dying to go out and try my hand in the water. I convinced him to take me out. Remember, I was a non-floating good swimmer, and I knew how to fit a mask ... that was it. I was also pale as a ghost.

We went out there with his wife. The water was perfect. The winds were picking up, but I didn't give it a thought. I was with Hildebrand. He was a stud, and I was confident I would get some of that stuff rubbed off on *me*. Hildebrand swam out about a quarter mile, past the breakers, and turned left to parallel the beach about half a mile. He did it like nothing. I was a stallion in my own right, and I could swim. But I was not prepared for this. Strong swimmer or not, I had come without a thought of preparation. I was, first of all, completely without tanning lotion, and my back side was quickly broiling … red as a lobster.

I was no idiot. I had been thoroughly briefed on the merits of the buddy system and the stupidity of solo flight. *He was my buddy*. I depended on it. But to him, I was just along for the ride, nothing more. Even though I knew the wisdom in sticking together, I finally realized he had no such wisdom in that bone head of his.

He was *not* going back, and I *was* going to drown if I did not broil first. So when I said we should go in, he said, "Bye!" He did not look back.

I did the "man up" thing and swam away.

Anyway, there I was, about a quarter mile from the beach, about half a mile downstream from my entry point. The surf was building, but I had no clue. I started swimming directly into the shore and discovered to my great dismay that the breaking waves I could see were breaking over coral. I decided to try walking across it to the shore.

That was soon a no-go. I cut my feet on the way in. I turned around and fell getting back out to the water, cutting my knee. I struggled, but luckily I did not lose my fins, and I finally got clear of the coral. I shoved off out into the ocean for my swim home. I headed for my initial entry point, but I couldn't see the shore now for the breaking waves. The wind was blowing fairly hard, and I was becoming concerned until I finally reached a place I correctly presumed was a beach. I swam in. I was thankful it *was* a beach.

By that time, I wasn't firing on all cylinders. It was really funny. I felt weird, and when I reached the shore, I could not stand at first. I lay there a few minutes and finally, shakily, stood up and walked to a water faucet on a little breaker wall. I had been out there more than three hours, and I was parched from the salt water I had breathed and swallowed. I was blistered from the sunburn and was badly dehydrated.

I never went out with Hildebrand again, but I maintained my Marine Corps attitude. I was too ashamed to tell him how close I had come to not getting back at all.

Education

I took some college courses and some USMC NCO courses while there, and it was a painful effort. Initially I had no car and had to get a military ride to Schofield Barracks for each class. That did not make SSG Roberts happy, but I still went.

Today promotions depend somewhat on the initiative a Marine or a soldier uses to get more education. He or she is recognized for the effort and may even earn points for it.

In those times, it was just another burden to the command.

Enlisted Club

I hired on as a bartender at the local enlisted club, and I worked for Miss Angel, who was sort of the assistant club manager. She was a local Hawaiian lady who was loved by all of us, and she was a legend. While I worked there, I met a wonderful girl, her daughter. About that time I was dumped by the love of my life (is there any other kind of love?), and I wigged out over Miss Angel's daughter. In those days, I was a drinker (a poor one, who could not hold his booze). I was off duty and got very drunk and really sappy over her in front of her mom. Miss Angel and I were good friends, since I worked for her, and we were very honest with each other. She mentioned her daughter was getting a divorce from some Marine pilot, and to my great and all too rare credit, I bowed out. It simply wasn't in me to date a married woman. She took up with a friend of mine, and that pretty much ended my serious romantic escapades until I left Hawaii.

Of course, I was writing my future wife as a pal at that time, and she helped me cling to the tether of reality. So even when I was getting kind of nuts, I had my eye on the important stuff.

Rescuing a Patrol Driver

The barracks we lived in was an open bay. There were about 70 men in it, and there was a rifle rack in the middle of the squad bay that held all our M-14s. There were two twin bunks in each section, separated by wall lockers. We all had a wall locker and a foot locker. It was a public place in all matters of the heart and the world. When I made Corporal and was allowed a brief period living in a three-man room, it meant less noise after lights-out. The communal head and shower was shared by everyone, but our limited privacy was really appreciated.

One night word was passed that one of our patrol drivers was being held in the mag area. In other words, the driver was being held at gunpoint or by force of some kind in the magazine area we were guarding.

Every Marine knew what that meant. Who knows how it started? But out came a big hammer, and the lock on the rifle rack disappeared. The rifle rack was emptied. Out came every secret, hidden and unauthorized round of ammunition. Every Marine not on duty was armed, dressed (in everything from shorts and sandals to swimsuits and grungy sweats) and headed up the hill in every conveyance from POVs (Privately Owned Vehicles) to government vehicles, which we broke into and "borrowed."

There were no lights. The entire mag area was blacker 'n the inside of a cow at that hour, so it was fairly spooky even on a normal night. We had an idea where he was, and as a giant, fast-moving snake, we zoomed up Kolekole Pass to his location.

Suddenly, there they were. The MP patrol driver was standing beside a civilian vehicle and saw us coming. Clearly not expecting us, he started looking about apprehensively. In the darkness, the lights flashing and the glare of a dozen headlights from assorted vehicles was sort of creepy. He was parked behind the vehicle in which was a barely dressed and embarrassed Army couple. An Army specialist and his wife, apparently, had been overwhelmed by family and were in desperate need of privacy to lend some dignity to their family duties. The miracle was that our driver caught them at all, since the mag area was huge. Anyway, our patrol driver was standing next to the driver with a flashlight in hand, pretending to inspect their drivers licenses and not stare at the beautiful girl when all 50 or so of us pulled up.

We had some NCOs with us, but none of it was authorized, and though we would have complied with orders, no one was actually in charge. We all knew our actions were …

questionable to say the least. But when Gunny Coy drove up, our goose was cooked.

He must have come from something official, because he was all dressed in his working Trops (Tropical Worsted, a good-looking, dry-cleaned, semi-formal dress uniform), looking hatefully around as though he were a hawk ready to spring on a mouse. He pulled up, got out and stood straight up. Almost casually, he closed his door.

He looked around severely. *No one* wanted that withering look aimed at *him*. It was so quiet the truck flashers bonked away like thunderclaps. The patrol truck engine was still running, but nothing else. Speaking for myself, my heartbeat was almost too loud for me to hear what Gunny said next.

He cleared his throat and croaked, "I don't ever want to hear about this again."

If you had dropped a nickel, we would have been off that hill before it hit the ground. When we got back, someone gathered up the illegal ammo and put it in a box, which turned out to be an amnesty box. It was placed anonymously on the Gunny's desk. The lock was quietly replaced and the spare keys distributed without comment. The secret "key" (small sledge hammer) was hidden again for another emergency.

Let's put this into perspective. You have to remember what *Semper Fidelis* or *Semper Fi* really means to Marines. Always faithful. Always. It may sound trite, but I can assure you that Coy did more than simply let it slide. It was a measure of our unspoken devotion to the Corps. All of us were prepared to do whatever was necessary that night, without question, without hesitation, with no inspection of legal mumbo jumbo. No one ever spoke of it; no one ever mentioned that drive to watch your buddy. It was never brought up for discussion or definition.

Not often does such a learning moment occur by mistake. Morale in the unit, which pretty much sucked until that moment, shot up. The gunny had been given a gift, and he made good use of it. He had the captain hold a barbeque for the men. Extra days off were scheduled for every worthy Marine. Coy bought beer for the barracks to go with the barbeque. There were even a few promotions. The only time in my career I ever considered re-enlistment in the Marine Corps was that time.

Anyway, I was scheduled to PCS (permanent change of station, in this case, separation from active duty) in Sept '71, and I was called into the office and told I would be promoted in June. In July, Captain CD Collins Jr. brought me into his office for the re-enlistment talk. It was convincing. He was a charismatic leader, and I liked him. He told me I could re-enlist for sergeant and go back to my old MOS or get a new one. He discussed the possibility of OCS with me, but I did not have enough college. I could not be roped into six more years as an enlisted man, so I refused. But I thanked him. Later, when I applied to Army flight school, he wrote a letter of recommendation. The letter does not show him to be the intellectual I once thought him to be, but it was from the heart. And I always appreciated it.

Radar NCO

I was relatively sharp in my work there, mature or not, and I was appointed Radar NCO ... a real cosmic job for a lowly gonna-be-promoted lance corporal. I was responsible for the maintenance of the radar set, management of the tickets and paperwork involved, chasing information when necessary, and recommending sites for deployment.

There was a period when our radar was down, and I rigged a set of mirrors to measure the speed of motorists. It took a bit of math to figure out the speed of a car before it got away, and so we were not as effective as I had hoped. But it was an impressive exercise of initiative.

Now, as I nearly completed my tour there, a squid (the Marine slang designation for a sailor) claimed that one of my patrol drivers struck him on a bicycle. I mean hit him with the patrol truck while he was on the bicycle! I had proved to my own satisfaction that the driver in question was not guilty of this, and aside from my being steamed, all was well.

My last night on station was spent drinking and celebrating. I went over to the Naval Radio Station Enlisted Club with a pal. And there was that slimy little vermin, the little weasel who had caused my driver to be suspended pending investigation. It was he who had cast doubt on our professionalism, who *dared* to accuse a Marine of something evil, *blah blah blah*. There he was within arm's reach, and he had only a few of his buddies with him. Much to the shock of my pal, I marched my butt over to the squid, spun up enough to be really stupid with him.

You have to understand I was a real peaceable guy. This was beyond stupid. And beyond illegal to beat up a squid who showed no ill intent in a club filled with witnesses only too glad to review my stupidity with a jury. My pal got hold of me by the stacking swivel and reminded me of all I had to lose and how little there was to gain in this foolishness. I was leaving the following day. Anyway, that guy showed no interest in any further grief, and I went back to the barracks and went to bed.

The next day I got on a plane and flew home.

Separation and Civilian Life Between

I had gone on leave around February 1971, and I asked Gail to marry me while we were at a showing of *Love Story*. I had bought her a ring at the PX in Lualualei, but I did not give it to her until I returned in September.

In September 1971 I was sent orders to Treasure Island to out-process from active duty. I was there it seems like two weeks and then flew to Phoenix to visit a friend, then to Buffalo. I arrived home to the welcoming arms of Gail and Mom Fancher. Gail had been contemplating the advances of a young man she met in Georgia, and we were glad those decisions were behind us.

We married 1 July 1972, and Dad Fancher made a great deal out of her being only 17. But she had graduated from high school, and it was a great celebration. We lived in and around Holland, New York, for a few years.

The steel mill laid me off, and I sold insurance for a while. My sales boss at Prudential was a major in the Air Force Reserves in Niagara Falls, and he persuaded me to join up. I was to be enlisted as an E-5, and then promoted to E-6 when I completed loadmaster school. Then I would have a career as an enlisted reservist on active duty at Niagara Falls.

On my way back from the flight surgeon for a flight physical, I stopped in at an Army Recruiter. I think his name was Grazinski. The rest is history.

PART II
The Army

WHEN FAT MEN FLEW

8

The Long Road to a Career

I was in a suit and tie. I was fit, and I looked pretty good. I went right up to him and told him I was an ex-Marine Corporal. I told him I had known a good man killed in the warrant officer flight program, and I wanted to fly. He laughed. He said scornfully that I would never pass the tests, and that he might get me in as a corporal.

I was pretty arrogant. I tried to snort and spit and wipe my nose on my shirt. This was the *Army* after all, and they had nothing on me. I could always go back to the Air Force. I told him I had been a corporal where *real* men were corporals, and it was flight school or nothing. It did not please him.

Now in those days, if you enlisted within six years of your Marine Corps initial entry date, you could go into any other branch for which you were qualified without going into their boot camp. This was because Marine boot camp is generally regarded as the most challenging in the US military. I was within six months of that date, so I felt I had him over a barrel, since he definitely wanted to sign up a fit NCO. But he could not see anything but my arrogance. He again stated flatly that I would never pass the test, that no one he had ever tried to sign up to flight school ever passed. Maybe, he said, he could wring out an enlistment as a sergeant. In other words, "Shut up, stupid."

I learned later he would not get recruiter credit for my flight school billet; the officer recruiter, his boss, would get it. As it turned out, Grazinski just needed another distraction to see the light.

As I was becoming more displeased and he was more and more unimpressed, a shabby, barefoot, dirty, unshaven man in a T-shirt and Levis came in. He looked around and said casually, "Man. I gotta get back in the Army." He approached SGT Grazinski.

Grazinski took me by the elbow and nodded his head at another recruiter. "See him. I am busy just now."

I took that test and passed. Grazinski notified me a week later, but he dragged his feet until just before my anniversary date, and I had to threaten him with a personal visit to his recruiting officer. He had to get off his dead butt, give up his credit for enlisting a qualified NCO, and get me a flight school billet, pronto.

Nonetheless, he was the consummate professional administrative NCO. You cannot defeat those guys. And he almost got me, probably because he felt cheated for my credit going to his superior. He enlisted me as a private, not as a Specialist E-5. The document said I would be temporarily promoted to Specialist 5 for the school, and it got by me. It was not a real rank. If I had failed flight school, I would have been a private again.

WHEN FAT MEN FLEW

9

The World of Flight School

I went to Fort Rucker, Alabama, for flight school in April 1974. It made everyone there very unhappy, especially the supply sergeant. I did not have to go back through Army boot camp, but I arrived at Rucker without any uniforms or even any familiarity with Army administrative procedure. I was an odd duck where odd ducks go to flounder and die.

I arrived in civilian attire (coat and tie and close haircut) and was set upon immediately by hollering, unkind TAC (tactical) officers. I actually was harassed a couple of days by several TAC officers who really felt they were doing me in, but it was a joke compared to life in the Marines. The Snowbirds (pre-flight school candidates awaiting a starting class) who were to be in the next starting class with me were all vets. They rallied 'round, and one lent me a belt, another lent boots, another, trousers, until I had a sloppy but regulation uniform. I was a worker, so the class quickly accepted me as we did our daily ash and trash runs and other petty post details. We hauled chairs for the Officers' Club; we set up tables for countless parties and presentations and performed such duties as mowing lawns and doing office work. We did this until the dreaded day we began preflight training.

As snowbirds, we single and geographic bachelors hung around the barracks in the evenings. It was a two-story, white WWII barracks, and we polished and buffed it daily. When I had left for flight school, my wife decided to wait until my graduation in nine months to join me. She made it six weeks and moved to Daleville, just outside Fort Rucker. I couldn't see her often, but it helped my attitude considerably.

Remember now, I thought I had enlisted as a Sp/5 (sort of specialty sergeant), but in fact I had enlisted as an E-2, or private. The Sp/5 status kicked in when I started preflight training; the extra pay was given to help cover the cost of new uniforms and other sorts of professional maintenance. I was lucky because all my uniforms were issued new, due to my enlistment directly from civilian life. I did not have to buy many new things. But my enlisted status meant that if I failed, I would start my illustrious career in the Army as a Private E-2. Talk about motivation.

While I was awaiting my class start and I was on the month-long work detail around Fort Rucker, I hurt my knee on a run. I limped for a couple of days and then went to the flight surgeon, who wrapped it and gave me light duty. Brown Flight (Class 74-47) started up during this time.

During my second week we watched, amazed, as the TACs raided the barracks early on the day the Brown Flight course started. The TACs raised sand with them, emptying their sea bags onto the floor, tramping on their clean uniforms … and after suitable abuse, moved them into the new barracks.

Start date for Blue Flight (Class 74-49) was coming up, and my knee was not getting any better. I could still manage a run, and I begged the flight surgeon to let me start with my flight. He asked what marvelous cure he should list for my up-slip, and I told him it had better be a miracle. He was a wise guy, and he wrote it on my up-slip, crediting a miracle for my quick recovery. I limped all through flight school (and for the next 17 years) on that knee.

The School Senior TAC was CW4 Warren Case, a crusty old Chinook pilot who tried to be evil but was a great man. Next in line was CW3 Montoya, the only one-eyed warrant officer still allowed on flight status. He had lost that eye in a mid-air collision with another helicopter. He would peer at you with his steely brown eye, and his glass eye would wander off, giving an oddly comical horror to the poor candidate feeling Montoya's wrath. He became TAC Officer for Purple Flight (Class 75-01), the flight after mine.

Later I was flushed to Purple Flight (Class 75-01) with pneumonia, and he had to grind and torture me and test my metal before accepting me as a full-up member of *his* flight. Both Case and Montoya were the ones who seemed driven to qualify good men. Each could stare you into oblivion, and with a word, your ego could be squashed.

There were two TACs over my Blue Flight (Class 74-49). They were CW2 Ward, who had his lung removed and was managing to stay on flight status, and CW3 Jim Fowler, who was coming up on retirement. I heard Ward had died, but five years later I met him in Germany, a CW3 and still on flight status, still flying and still smoking. I was very surprised, and he seemed happy to see me. I did not care much for Ward, but both he and Fowler were straight shooters, and they did well with us.

We became Class 74-49, Blue Flight. Our mascot was Yosemite Sam, the cartoon character. Now, until around 1973, flight school had been conducted with preflight and initial flight training at Fort Walters, Texas. It was a large rural area and a great training place. When the intermediate and senior flight training were moved, all the training was then done at Fort Rucker, Alabama.

The last class at Walters was the previous Blue Flight, about a year before us. About that time, the flight classes were reduced to about one class a month, beginning to start classes of about 32 each, instead of the Vietnam-sized classes of a couple hundred students each. That meant, basically, that instead of a couple hundred candidates training for Vietnam (I believe twice a month), 32 or so started with us at Fort Rucker each month.

In those days, Flight School was quite different than today. I think it is still nine months long, but in those days we were mostly trained in temporary ranks of Specialist 5, unless you had a higher rank before going in. We all wore warrant officer candidate brass for rank. In other words, when in uniform, we were widely regarded as incompetent and completely without the usual military standing. Last time I knew about, a warrant officer flight candidate goes through a month of Warrant Officer Basic, for his harassment phase, then straps on his bars and goes to flight school as a temporary warrant officer. No harassment, no hassle except study. Imagine that.

WHEN FAT MEN FLEW

Flight School Progress

(All you aspiring aviators going to flight school now, forgive me if my summary is too simple or is inaccurate in any way).

Pre-Flight

In those days it consisted of two weeks of classes all day with harassment and work details morning and night. Twenty percent of the starters quit in this period. The candidates lived on post without a break for family, except occasional family visits.

Junior Flight

This training was indicated by an orange tab on your left breast pocket indicating you were actually flying. The schedule consisted of six weeks of half-day initial flight training in the TH-55 (Schweitzer helicopter) and half-day in classes, with harassment and work details morning and night. In addition your uniform had the warrant officer candidate brass. The candidates lived on post without a break for family, except occasional weekends.

Intermediate Flight

This level was indicated by a different tab on your left breast pocket; the tab was orange, with a vertical black line. This indicated you were in actual Instrument Flight Training, the toughest part of flight school. You also wore the warrant officer candidate brass. I recall the schedule was five months of grueling, long days … complicated training … constant oral and flight testing and eval … with even more harassment and work details morning and night. The candidates lived on post without a break for family, except occasional family weekends. This was my major test—a very stressful time. Most of the actual failures occurred in this phase. More on that later.

Senior Flight

This part was a blast. In addition to warrant officer candidate brass, you wore a black tab on your left breast pocket. The balance of flight school was spent in tactical training, NOE (Nap of the Earth, or fast-as-you-could-get-there flying as-low-as-you-could-go) flight, night flight with tactical approaches and map reading. (*Oh yes.* Night and day we used 1/50K maps, taped together in sections marked with course and time ticks. We folded and wrapped the maps carefully and navigated endlessly.) In those days we stuck out our chests and called our night flight operations *Night Hawk*. Scary stuff. We did not yet have night vision devices in our training. But that is why, when the old NVGs (Night Vision Goggles) came out, even with all their imperfections (like zero depth perception and very grainy visual acuity), the popular cry was "Black air has no lift!" This was in reference to the *green* air through which you could see nearby objects fairly clearly in the NVGs but which you could not *possibly* see unaided. Black air was bad; green air was … better.

Our flight class had an odd assortment of newbies as well as vets. We were in the early stages of the major equal rights efforts in the Army, and we had a big black kid and a couple of white southern boys join us right out of high school. While we were still in snowbird status before pre-flight, the black kid bought a late model Corvette. I cannot imagine how he paid for it, and he had no time to ride in it, so it stayed parked in the lot out back.

As soon as we started flight training, he immediately failed two check rides. The rule in those days was no more than two consecutive daily pink slips (failing marks from your instructor) or two check ride failures (from another IP), and you were out. He got a break. They recycled him, and he started over. He failed to make the mark again, and he was gone the second month.

Those two white kids, well, they bought fancy but less extravagant cars … and they washed out right away. They got no second chance, but their failures were not recoverable. Remember here, we were a pretty close bunch. Every failure was a threat to all of us. We all felt it, and we all worked to help each other. But it didn't matter who it was; when they failed, they were gone, and we blew it off. The man who failed was alive. It was okay because life would go on. But it was a lot like a death, because they would be gone. Immediately.

"Too bad. So sad ... what is on the schedule tomorrow?"

It was the attitude you needed to get through that difficult moment. I did not realize it would become the standard cultural response to the hazards of the helicopter world. It is funny what you remember.

I saw all three of those cars on the lemon lot in Daleville after those kids were gone.

In Flight 74-49 there were two exceptions to this callous, indifferent outlook.

We had a natural leader named Steve Van Slyke. He was a former Marine, smart, fit, talented. Skilled. The epitome of all things noble in the Warrant Officer Corps. We loved that knucklehead. There were other good men there too, and I give it all to them. But one day Steve resigned, I believe due to the stress flight school had on his wife. For the entire flight, it was like being gut shot. He departed for the regular Army with hardly a word and, certainly, no complaint. He did not fail.

Not Steve Van Slyke ... a natural leader and exceptional man. I believe he left in the rank of corporal, a rare acknowledgement to his soldier skills. I heard later he was involved in a motorcycle accident and badly hurt. I have not heard of him in years.

The second exception was just the opposite. We had another kid who was sharp, a vet, smooth, talented. And he decided to become involved with another candidate's wife. One day, without any inkling, staff came out to the flight line and took him away. The entire flight felt a sort of scornful mourning and dismissed him from our thoughts. I cannot even remember his name. I am glad I cannot. Life is hard enough without plain, selfish stupidity.

Hell. I just remembered his name. *It is not going in this book.*

And just so's ya know what a real hero I was when I was at the top of my game ... out of 32 starting candidates, we ended up graduating only fifteen.

I, yours truly, was listed ...wait for it ... not yet ... *now* ... as The Goat. I graduated fifteenth in the class order. I thought arrogantly about printing it on the back of my wings, where no one could see it. But I kept quiet, and no one else ever knew until now. I knew knuckleheads in my career who would swear they always knew I was a dud ... but I kept the proof to myself.

FLIGHT SCHOOL PROGRESS

Mark Twain had it right: "It is much better to keep your mouth shut and let folks think you are an idiot than to open your mouth and *remove all doubt*."

Well, I did have an Instrument Instructor once who, being mad at me for something stupid, asked me how the hell I ever graduated from flight school.

I smugly told him George Patton graduated last at West Point.

He knew I was lying. But without accusing me, he slapped me down hard: *"So did Custer."*

Pilot candidate dispositions.

Special Orders #10824 May 1974

NAME	DISPOSITION
Breckens, Sanford D	Completed career
Brown, Wiley E	Army Reserves
Coffey, Charles M	Medically retired in 1977 after being hit by a car
Cooper, Ernest G	Completed Career
Cormier, Steven S	Resigned
Davis, Richard L	Self- elim ... returned to active service as E-7
Graham, David L	Graduated. I think he completed his career.
Hallberg, Christopher	Self-elim
Hicks, Hunter G	Set back; graduated two classes back.
Kiefer, James G	Self-elim
Kingsley, Ernest D	Set back one class, completed career as CW4
Laneville, Edward WI	I believe he graduated
Owens, Larry A	Eliminated.
Purintin, Larry L	Took a commission and retired a major
Riley, Michael J	Retired a CW3
Sanders, Roland E	Graduated and, I believe, finished a career
Schneider, George R	Eliminated
Serrano-Gomez, Tito	Self-elim
Stankewicz. Mark J	Eliminated
Vanslyke, Steven L	Self-elim
Ward, William M	Made CW3 and got out
Weinberger, David III	Eliminated
Perkowsky, Thomas A	Went into the Alaska reserves
Frisby , James A	Went back to the Alaska Reserves
Sims, Hal D	Alaska Reserves

Junior Flight Status

Our first flight training was in TH-55s. Much of our class work and all the initial flight were done at Hanchey Army Airfield near Fort Rucker, Alabama. My first IP (instructor pilot) was Bob Agee. He was a terrific TH-55 pilot, a Vietnam vet, and he had a heap of helicopter flight hours. On our "nickel ride," the first time I was ever at the controls, he told me to lower the collective after he rolled back the throttle. I failed to compensate for the decreased torque with pedal input, and we did a nose tuck of probably 30 degrees. Scared the life out of me to see the earth fill the bubble top to bottom. For the rest of my career, if I was ever in an aircraft with an unannounced nose-low attitude of five degrees or more, it got my full attention.

The TH-55 was a Schweitzer, which looked a lot like a Hughes 300 or maybe a miniature OH-6. It was orange and white and had a large round plexiglas bubble covering the crew cabin, top to bottom. The main rotor system had three fully articulated rotor blades, a stove-pipe sort of tail boom and a very light-weight tail rotor blade. It had ingenious oleo struts on the landing gear skids to compensate for the comparatively poor landing skills of new pilots. The VNE (the maximum allowable speed, or Velocity, Never Exceed) was 60 KIAS (Knots, Indicated Airspeed), and it was powered by a piston engine with a tortuous combination of a *manual* throttle and an *automatic* over-speed governor. Hence, a number of new pilots would parade down the taxiway like little ducks in line to the departure pad, with all the aircraft jerking to the left and right as the governor kicked in and each pilot struggled to maintain a smooth, constant rotor RPM.

During this first phase of flight, we soloed. Once we could hover, we were allowed to fly around the pattern and develop some air sense. This accomplished, more or less, we were given a local area 1/50K map and cut loose to find our way, single pilot, to all the little local landing areas that had been surveyed for our use. The landing spots were marked with brightly painted tires to ensure easy identification by a busy, confused solo pilot.

Bad weather was often a problem and sort of sucked these little hummers in. I remember being caught in a squall with my IP when we were trying to return before terrible weather hit us. He had that thing cranked over to 80 KIAS, and we propped our feet up on the bubble to keep it from collapsing.

The funniest part was that we had some Vietnamese pilots who spoke very little English (*me go now ... me land now ...*), and they drove the air traffic control folks crazy. After we had an all-weather recall issued, this little guy, flying solo, announced, "*Me go now,*" and off he flew, directly into a storm. Two IPs flew after him and finally got his attention so they could lead him back to the airfield.

Now, I was not a natural-born pilot. I soloed at an average time ... maybe 10 hours. I was on my second turn around the pattern when I kicked off the left adjustable (anti-torque) pedal and sent it into the chin bubble, where the accident investigator found it. Unable to stop my spin, primarily because I was too stupid to press the pedal stub from which I had kicked the pedal, I crashed in a spin on approach to Toth Army Airfield. I was grateful it was a flat landing, and the aircraft did not turn over. Lucky for me, the main rotor blade did not pass through either the tail boom or the cabin. But I knocked off the tail rotor.

I was stunned. I could not believe it. After landing, I punched the button and yelled, "Mayday, Toth. Lane 4."

I tried to sound calm, but it came out pretty stupid. You could hear the tower operator laughing as he called the flight commander to the runway.

They sent me to the hospital for blood work and a new up slip. I am pretty sure the accident board labeled it "Just Stupid," but I was flying again in two days. I am not sure, but I think I was the only knucklehead out of Flight 74-49 to crash. But I never got lost. And if not the sharpest knife in the box, I passed all my tests, my flight exams, my rides, and I was promoted with the remaining Flight 74-49 candidates to intermediate status.

Intermediate Flight Status

Intermediate status was a royal pain in the butt. We had four months, I think, of classes and simulator time, then transitioned to the D Model Huey for actual aircraft time. (They were not using H Models for instrument training yet.)

The Army aviation world I knew used the UH-1H (H Model Huey helicopter) for cutting edge tactical and night hawk operations. All Bell Helicopter products (UH-1, the Vietnam era utility helicopter; AH-1, the Vietnam era gunship; and OH-58 scout helicopter, the Army version of the Bell Jet Ranger) had about 2.5 hours fuel capacity. Their cruising airspeeds were all between 80 and 120 KIAS. Because an instrument flight requires a 30-minute fuel reserve, there is simply not enough range to make a regular habit of instrument flight possible. Since there was never a guarantee of clear weather, the primary purpose of instrument rotary wing flight was emergency recovery. If you flew into fog or a cloud, you had to transition to instrument flight and either navigate to an instrument airfield or to clear sky, or you had to call for a ground-controlled radar approach (GCA).

All that said, the simple fact is that if you are in a helicopter, you cannot bump into something (like the ground, mountains or wires) without major concern for your survival. So instrument flight training was taken in deadly earnest, and it was a primary reason for failure in flight school. I was no exception.

I arrived just after the old instrument simulator, known as the Blue Canoe, had retired. It was a blue box with instruments and controls indicating your flight situation, which was pretty much just a procedure trainer. You could see over the top of the box to the floor if you wanted. The box did not move, but it allowed you to manipulate the controls while managing your airspeed, altitude and proximity to a chosen flight path on instruments. You could take the "canoe" through published instrument procedures and landings and maintain interaction with an ATC (air traffic controller) operator. It was cheap. It was cost effective. It was not very realistic because in the canoe, you could only accomplish instrument emergencies, not hardware failures. (Whew ... I feel old.)

The most modern simulator we used then was a Singer UH-1H SFTS (Synthetic Flight Training Simulator). It was a mock-up of the UH-1 cabin suspended probably six feet in the air; when flying, it moved through simulated flight gyrations via hydraulically powered controls. You climbed onto the frame, strapped into the cockpit, and suddenly the rotor noise started and you started flying. You could enter flight at any point, or you could do an ITO (Instrument Take Off) and climb to your flight path.

While you were strapped in, it looked and sounded sort of like a real aircraft. There were no exterior visual options, because it looked from the inside as though you were completely socked in. It had both pilot and copilot seats and controls, and a jump seat was centered behind the flight crew. The jump seat was used variously by the instructor or by the crew member awaiting his turn to fly. The crew could communicate with the ATC operator, who was sitting at the console below the simulator; or the IP could make his own flight following by acting as the controller.

Emergency instrument procedures training was sort of realistic. You could have a tail rotor failure, an engine failure, a hydraulics failure or any number of imagined issues with which to test your rote knowledge of proper procedures. The trainer would buck and snort in a simulation of no-visual-reference flight, and it was the cutting edge of the day. Today we have visual flight simulators that allow you to transition between visual and instrument flight much more realistically.

Anyway, during my instrument training, my instrument instructor pilot was Mr. Schoenfeld. He was a large, pleasant-looking man with the heart of the devil. He drove an emotional stake in my heart, and I can tell you if any single source of frustration made me ready to kill or quit, it was him. Granted, my demeanor did not improve by my very stressful candidate schedule, to arrive daily at the barracks at 0400 to shine, buff and get hassled in the name of discipline. But Mr. S could have done so much better than he did. And I could have been a much better instrument pilot.

I was not a rocket scientist, as I've mentioned before, nor was I a natural aviator awaiting the stretch of my new wings. I had none of the dare devil mentality of Chuck Yeager. I was just a kid trying to be an Army pilot, and I gave it my whole heart. I was never a great instrument pilot, but during my 17 years of flying, I punched in and got home twice.

In spite of his pleasant demeanor, Mr. Schoenfeld seemed ready to slit my throat. (Remember here, for all my moaning, I *passed*. Many did not, and they did not even deal with him. He got credit for my passing, but it was not to his credit.)

I may have mentioned the instrument phase was very stressful. It was designed to be that way, since fear and proficiency are often together in real-life situations. If you couldn't make it in school, you sure couldn't make it in a real emergency. Any time you entered instrument flight in a helicopter, it was an emergency. Much as I support the premise, I loathe the men who, on a power trip and without intent to do good or achieve high standards, twist the knife. So it seemed to me.

Flight School Instrument Training Process

The procedure for flight school instrument training progress was supposed to go like this: as you went through your instrument flight training, you got an IP eval (Instructor Pilot evaluation) each day.

White slip. A good day … safe flight … mission accomplished.

Yellow slip. A bad day … nothing deadly … poor judgment or mistakes needing correction. You'd go home with a sore butt from your instructor's tender guidance.

Pink slip. "Get off my flight line" (*because yer an idio*t … and other sweet notes of encouragement, such as *How the heck did you make it through initial flight training anyway?*)

The world was good—or, at least, acceptable—*if your next flight slip was white or yellow. In practice, this is the way it worked:*

Yellow slip, first or second time. You got specific guidance and training, homework, and another excuse for your IP to make you his slave. It happened, but you were not supposed to be eligible for two consecutive yellow slips.

Pink slip. You got specific guidance and training, a butt chewing, and your life flashed before your eyes.

FLIGHT SCHOOL PROGRESS

Second pink slip. You were automatically given all the above (specific guidance and training, a butt chewing, and your life flashed before your eyes again). Then you were put up for a mandatory Progress Ride (*prog ride*) with another IP, someone not your own. The complete lack of merit in your flying future became clear, and your past stresses looked from afar as a beautiful rest stop on the road to this torture.

Third pink slip. You failed your mandatory prog ride; you were either set back to another class or thrown out of the program while you watched your happy life and your good friends pass from your memory.

From This Terrible Moment: One of Two Actions was Possible.

You were set back to another class for another effort, but under the constant watch of mean-spirited persons of questionable antecedents and dubious progeny.

Or you were cast out and allowed to resume your illustrious career in the Army as a non-aviator in your last rank. In my case, by my conditions of enlistment, my last rank would be PV2. In other words, being cast out would mean... the bottom.

When I was forced to ponder this possibility, I did, in fact, bitterly remember scorning my recruiter over the option of enlisting as a corporal. And I briefly pondered the measurable difference in pay between private and corporal.

WHEN FAT MEN FLEW

My Personal Instrument Flight Training Experience

It was bad enough that my recorded performance in instrument training left a lot of room for me to doubt my successful completion of the training. I was never more than one flight away from a mandatory prog ride. I was up every morning at 0400 to report to the barracks for such tasks as polishing floors and cleaning latrines. I was home at 1100 to start it all over. I was exhausted. I was discouraged. I was desperate. As the pressure increased, I was so tired one morning I set my helmet bag next to my car, got in and backed over it.

In those days the SPH-4 flight helmet was advanced equipment … expensive. Worse than that, I had scheduled Christmas leave and barely had money for it. Now I had to pay for a new SPH-4 flight helmet and had to figure out a way to wriggle out of a 15-6 investigation (DA Form—charges of destruction of government property). I was beaten, and I looked it.

I drove home with my ruined helmet and walked to my kitchen sink and cried. I was ashamed. I was going to be a private in the Army. I was going to fail, and my poor wife would have to bear the consequences. God had to be laughing, because I was an idiot for risking it all, giving up my job in the steel mill and dragging my sweetheart into hell with me. It was the bottom.

FLIGHT SCHOOL PROGRESS

But she came up next to me and put her arms around me. She was silent. She listened. I confessed that I hated it. But I had been a corporal where real men were corporals, and I was not going to quit. They could fire or kill me, but they could not eat me. I would not quit and be a private in the Army.

My first break in all of Instrument Training came next morning. I went to the Survival Equipment Specialist, an old sergeant. I said nothing as I handed him the torn bag and broken helmet. I apologized for his ton of extra paperwork and confessed my sin. I told him I would pay for it, that I could not go home for Christmas now, but that I would pay up and get it all behind me before I got set back to another class.

He still said nothing.

He turned on his heel and disappeared into the back somewhere and reappeared with a new bag and helmet. He tossed it up on the counter and said quietly, "You didn't get it here. Merry Christmas!"

He turned and walked away, probably so I wouldn't get too sloppy. In full credit to me, I did *not* try to kiss him.

My poor wife, who had braced for the worst, now propped me up for the last check ride. Remember here that I was not currently facing another prog ride, with all the threat to failure that would imply. My instrument instructor pilot was being a horse's patoot. That was all, so it could have been worse. But I was simply exhausted and beaten and stressed.

Check Ride Day

So, in this world, your instrument instructor pilot, the guy who trained you, is sort of "the father of the bride" in the process of training a successful instrument pilot.

You, the student, must show up, put up, pay up and shut up. You take your beatings and humiliation in silence. Whatever is said or done is to increase the pressure, to "test the metal" of the aviator, as it were. The student just had to deal with it. I was simply going to have to endure to the end.

On the *big check ride day*, you are supposed to show up prepared for the complete evaluation. That means ready for the oral, any written test, the preflight, the weather brief and finally the actual check ride.

You sit down with your instrument IP and get his morning lecture. Included in this lecture is an estimate of your potential (expected performance) grade, which he gives you in the form of a sort of "pre-check ride" grade slip. This estimate is between 70% and 100%, the minimum passing and maximum scores. (The elephant in the room is ... he has *got* to put you up with a minimum score of 70, or he has to fail you outright beforehand.) Then you are handed off to another IP who gives you the check ride.

This other IP, the official Instrument Flight Examiner (IFE), gives you an entire evaluation and pronounces a strictly subjective score. That is, if you don't step outside the limits of safety and do something unforgivable, the score is subjective and *passing*. Otherwise, it is up to you to sneak over to the snack bar, call the little woman at home and let her know ... "Looks like I'm gonna be a private again, Mama."

This is not funny.

This exhausting rite of passage is normally complete in four hours from beginning to end.

The details

This tradition of real men being tortured and hammered into deadly warriors from the sky starts with an oral exam of all instrument flight rules, instrument approach procedures, aircraft emergencies, a review of any catchy tactical procedures that come along during the exam, a few maintenance questions and whatever the SIP (Standardization Instructor Pilot) can think of.

Then he gives you a mission, and you plan it. You show it to him, including the route you have drawn up, current pubs, maps and flight plan. The SIP who is comfortable with you may review the last time some idiot did something stupid under his tutoring, just for your learning pleasure.

He asks more questions, then you get the weather and you both head out for a pre-flight check. He will pretend to just hang around waiting, but you will be watched, and your log book will be checked. Then you get in and crank it up.

He takes you out for around 90 minutes; he evaluates you in all maneuvers and in your decision processes. Then he gives you a grade between 70 and 100. As I said, the entire process is normally about four hours long, including oral, preflight, mission planning and ride. That grade is added to your instructor's evaluation; it is split, and that gives you a score, passing or failing.

My Instrument Check Ride ... The Torture before the Victory.

The *day of the ride*, my own instrument instructor, *the devil in living flesh*, was sitting at his desk in his usual place when I sat down. He announced loudly that I could not possibly pass the ride. He implied that he was a damn fool for even putting me up with a 70, But he could not recommend me at a lower score. He was going on vacation. He slammed his book shut and walked out.

FLIGHT SCHOOL PROGRESS

I was stunned. His stunt sucked the oxygen out of the room. I was scared. My career, even my brilliant awareness of being a private again, in the Army this time, seemed in jeopardy. I was barely hanging onto my wits. Now this. The other students were stunned. The other IPs were startled.

Being a former Marine lent another dimension to this torment. How could I ever manage as a private in the Army? How could I ever face another Marine after trying and *failing* to be a soldier? How much shame had to go with this torment on top of the stress of being bruised every day, no sleep, and now being figuratively stripped naked and tied to a tree in front of my peers?

Twenty-five years later I met him again. Mr. S still remembered me, even my name. (I am certain it is not because I was one of his shining stars.) Anyway, I asked him about this moment, which he did not remember. I swear he was still holding a pitchfork, ready to stick me with it because… because he could.

So now, shaken to my boots, I met the IFE for my ride. He was pretty quiet about the scene and the absence of my own instructor. He was cautious and indifferent as he started the oral exam. He grilled me. It lasted forever, several hours. But it seemed to go okay. *Finally he gave me a mission.* Thank heaven. Now I could see the end in sight.

When I started, I noticed the weather was still very bad. I finally finished the flight plan, and he grilled every part of my planning and my logic. He questioned me on the alternates selected and the process of emergency landings, and then he went into more emergency procedure questions.

Then he announced that the weather would be too bad to fly today.

"We will have to start again tomorrow."

Oh my gosh! I had endured this day and all the questions—successfully, I thought—only to be put off. I felt a terrible pain in my stomach, an unconscious reflex of nerves and the torment of my uncertain future. But I was still alive. Scared, but actually in fear of the elephant in the room—*either my own instructor pilot would come back with some terrible option tomorrow, or I would start this check ride all over again from the beginning in the morning.* Both seemed unbearable.

Anyway, next day I showed up at my desk. The IFE from the previous day walked in, and I breathed a sigh of relief. *Maybe Schoenfeld was really on vacation.* The IFE sat down, and we started again. From the beginning.

More in-depth questions on instrument procedures. More detail on why I did this and why I planned that on the mission. He changed part of the mission to see how I would do it. Then more questions on publications. The oral seemed to go well again, and I was gaining confidence. He did not yell at me once. And I was just settling into the grind when he announced that the weather was still terrible. We were grounded again. *But instead of bailing out of this torment, he did not even slow down.* The oral went on. He used it to kill the entire four hours of planned classroom time. The bus was late, so he went over a half an hour. It was an eternity. But I was still okay. I went home still alive, meaning I had some hope of surviving this trial. And I was beginning to feel like a veteran of this torment, not such a new guy.

The third day, we knew the weather had cleared when we got off the bus. The IFE and I now knew each other. He was, I thought, going to be fair, but when he sat down he surprised me. We were done in two minutes. We dashed out to the flight line and departed with hardly a breath.

It just happened that ATC (Air Traffic Control) was swamped with traffic because every other SIP, IFE, tactical IP and all flight missions were out trying to knock out the check rides or missions or maintenance test flights they had been unable to complete for a week.

My IFE flew me out on my route VFR (Visual Flight Rules) while I was under the "hood." *The hood was a plastic pie-pan sort of affair that clips over the visor and does not allow the student to look outside the aircraft.*

I flew on instruments, and he played the part of ATC himself. I flew it perfectly. I scored a 92 on the ride, but with the shameful recommended score from my IFE, my final grade was 81.

Hell. I hardly knew how to act. I was trembling with relief, and the post-flight debrief was quick. I went out to the bus and sat down while the rest of the class all sorted out their check ride scores. Some of the heroes were zeros, having barely passed their own rides, but I was sort of the novelty. Nothing was said of the ignominious abandoning by my instructor. I was more like middle of the class now, even with the public flogging I had received from Mr. S. There were other students graded all over the place who had done better or worse. We did not care. I think I was the last questionable student remaining, and we all passed. I did better than average, but I felt as though I had been skinned and hung on a shed to dry.

Like all instructors whose students pass their big ride, I think Schoenfeld claimed some of the glory in this high score. But he did not even see me get my passing grade. And there were no congratulations or smiling moments. I do not recall ever seeing him on the flight line again or seeing him at all for more than 20 years.

So I had made it. That week, I became a Senior Candidate. That black tab on my pocket indicated that all other subordinate candidates had to salute me. I was released from the harassment. No more 0400 work details. No more polishing the floors.

My sweet wife was almost happier than I ... but not quite. I felt unworthy ... to have stewed and worried so desperately for nothing. Whatever motivation that fear had lent me ... it stunk. I felt like that only one other time in my career. We will review later.

Setback

I was exhausted, and that Friday I fell asleep in my room. I woke up burning with a fever, and I staggered to sick call in the afternoon. I was sent home with pneumonia. After all that work, I was set back into the next class (Class75-01, Purple Flight) and spent a week in bed.

It was in Purple flight that my TAC Officer was CW3 Montoya, the grumpy old Mexican buzzard with one glass eye. He was famous for having survived a mid-air collision with another helicopter and being the *only* Army aviator on flight status with *one* eye. I was sure he hated me.

That old pirate jerked me off senior status and made me an Intermediate Candidate again until his guys passed their instrument rides. They went off to their training, and I was kept around the barracks as a sort of errand-boy/janitor. He was duty-bound to test me (*again*) with some sort of torment, just to be sure I wasn't simply another slacker. And I survived it, too. I graduated with them and was eventually an accepted addition to the bunch.

Senior Flight Status

Next we started Tactical Training. We transferred to the UH-1H (the H Model Hueys, stronger but with nearly identical flight characteristics to the UH-1D used for instruments). We had to learn how to handle the aircraft in normal visual flight, perform autorotations and other emergency procedures. We were learning the "new" NOE procedures (fast-as-you-could-get-there flying as-low-as-you-could-go). NOE had been declared irresponsible and foolish in the past, but was now the tactical cutting edge. We also learned night hawk operations (flying at night, unaided by the upcoming night vision goggles).

We were issued 1/50 maps (pronounced "one over 50" because of their scale, 1 = 50,000) and instructed to arrange them to fly any local area mission. Most of us found ways to fold and tape them together so they were a manageable-sized book that could be opened and followed along a flight route to any place in the tactical area. In addition we plotted all authorized landing areas, POL sites (refuel sites) and restricted areas. We used them each day. It was a real contest to see who could develop the best map book, even the best cover.

We also trained in night flight. This was all night hawk, and it was scary. Tactical night flight required a great map recon beforehand. We had to identify and plot noteworthy (identifiable) local terrain, plot a good ground track to our destination, find an acceptable landing area and check enroute obstacles to ensure a 500-foot clearance. Every landing area was set up with a landing "T", which consisted of lights laying in a "T" shape for easy sighting from the air. Sometimes we had a visual glide slope to aid our approach to clear obstacles. Anyway, it was a snap compared to the grind of instruments.

In the end, all the remaining students graduated.

My Conversion to the Church of Jesus Christ of Latter-Day Saints

During my illustrious career as a senior candidate extraordinaire, I was one of the typical coffee drinking, cigarette smoking, beer-swilling pilots. I could not hold my liquor and so did not drink much. But I loved Officers Call, usually on Friday evenings, with beer and chips.

I will spare you most of the details. But a friend of mine, LaBlanc, showed up one day and announced he was now a

Mormon. He said he would be making some social adjustments, such as not drinking. And no more smoking.

Now, I was a Methodist, and even in flight school I was active as a youth group leader in Daleville. I had served a Methodist Mission—a rare and unique resume, believe me. So I considered myself sort of, if not expert, certainly familiar with Mormons, and some of the little known facts of their world.

Ah, yes. The Mormons. Didn't they have more than one wife? Didn't Brigham Young quarterback for some big football team? Didn't John Smith or Jones or somebody start the church and write a book about it? And weren't they just another off-shoot of the Quakers or the Mennonites or some such? Certainly not like the Methodists.

LaBlanc laughed and laughed. I was serious. I wanted answers. No? None of it is true, eh? Well, just what the heck does that mean? *You* really are a Mormon? Yer kidding me, right? *What*? For real? No coffee? No tobacco? And are you sure about that fruit of the hops thing … *beer*?

He brought a Latter-Day Saint girl (Ernie Farnsworth, *one of the first female Warrant Officer Aviator Candidates in the Army*) to meet me and Gail, and sparing you the whole story, we were converted. In April of 1975, I laid my beer, cigarettes and coffee down and was baptized as a member of the Church of Jesus Christ of Latter-Day Saints. My life was never the same. I quit drinking and smoking. I stayed married for 27 more years. I somehow became buried in the children the doctor said we would never have … and I became a much better person. Well, I suppose a good Baptist or an ex-wife might disagree.

But I have learned Mormons are not so much what we do as who we are. You will see it clearly in the rest of this book.

About the time we graduated, my car was rear-ended by another car. That killed my 1971 Ford Maverick. So I did what all new pilots do; I bought a new Toyota pickup, a 1976 model.

Escape and Evasion

After flight school we had our survival training, SERE (Survival, Evasion, Resistance and Escape) training. We went through a couple of days of review concerning our survival skills, then spent two days evading the resident infantry battalion. They would send out search teams, and we would avoid them. But at the end of the week, we had to surrender and endure 24 hours of torment as POWs.

There was some good and some stupid training, but one thing has always stayed with me.

My squad was given a chicken and a rabbit, which we had to kill and prepare to eat. I was starving. There were some carrots and potatoes, but my group was sort of milling around trying to decide who was the cook and who was the boss.

Now, I am an old hand at chicken, but I am not much for the niceties. No one wanted the job, so I stepped up, skinned it and boiled it in an old coffee can with potatoes and carrots. That's right; I skinned it in a minute. I did not bother to pluck that chicken in those woods.

Some city boy tried to roast the rabbit on a spit .It looked darn good, better'n my chicken, but it was a cruel illusion. The chicken was tender, tasty and better than any I ever had before or since, while that good-looking rabbit was tougher than a German boot. My skills were lauded, and the chicken was eaten by all with great appreciation.

We threw away that good-looking rabbit.

10

Fort Campbell 1975-1978

I went home on leave to Holland, New York, in full dress greens. Suddenly my family, especially my father-in-law, was proud. Now the family was not so down on this choice of career. I did not burden them with the narrow brush I had with failure from flight school or very much of my trial there. I never printed the #15 on the back of my wings as I had determined to do. But I was also now a Mormon, so there were some odd looks over that. No matter. I didn't drink, but it was all fun, and off I went to my new assignment.

I arrived with my bright, shiny new bar with the big spot on it (indicating rank of Warrant Officer One) and signed into

the 101st Airborne Division at Fort Campbell, Kentucky. I
was assigned to A Battery, 377th Field Artillery (A/377 FA),
part of the 101st Field Artillery Brigade. Major Schofield
was my battery commander. Colonel S was the division
artillery commander.

A/377 FA was not an artillery battery at all, but a tiny
aviation unit that provided aerial observer and aviation support
for the 101st Field Artillery Brigade. It consisted of only three
UH-1H utility helicopters (Hueys, the utility aircraft of the
Army) and nine OH-58A scout helicopters (Kiowas, the scout
aircraft of the Army). I was quickly checked out in the Huey,
and then transitioned to the OH-58. After that I spent the bulk
of my aviation career flying the OH-58 A and OH-58 C aircraft
in scout missions for the US Army.

Being an Army Aviator

Now, the act of judging an aviator's flying merit is very
subjective and usually conducted by an IP whose ego is much
larger than his ... well ... whatever he could presume to boast
about in the real-man world. Actually, the whole business of
flying requires confidence and expertise, so the art of *being* an
aviator is also usually conducted by an egomaniac whose skills
may not yet be that of an IP, by deduction that should tell you
aviators are ego-bound first, with all other things second.

170

FORT CAMPBELL 1975-1978

It is true. Ask any aviator. Oh … that's right … if you know an aviator, you already know about aviator ego.

So let it be written. So let it be done.

You may be an Army aviator if …

If your wristwatch is not as big as a coffee table, you are no Army aviator.

If you submit to an opinion by someone of lower class (i.e., an infantryman, an artilleryman, or a Marine or some other *non*-aviation type), you are not an Army aviator.

If you ever *admit in public* to being afraid to follow through with one of your aviation decisions, *even though you may be scared out of your wits*, you are no Army aviator.

If on the other hand, you are willing to plan for days and walk a mile to make a 100-yard trip look easy for all onlookers, *even though it may kill you*, you may have enough ego to become an Army aviator.

If you ever feel *insecure because the true shortcomings in that "little" secret*, heretofore known only by your wife and doctor, may be revealed in public, you are certainly arrogant enough to be Army aviator material.

If you ever insist you are right *even though you know darn good and well it can never work out*, and you do it because you simply have to protect your pride, you have outstanding potential as an Army aviator.

If you are an Army aviator with polished boots, you must be a commissioned officer, not a warrant officer. (*Or you could just be lying about being an aviator.*)

If you are somewhat slovenly in appearance but perfect in your knowledge of aircraft, airspace and local watering holes, you could, with lots of work and some mentoring, become an Army Aviation Warrant Officer.

If you can see a man with a dozen medals and barely notice, but see a tiny "Broken Wing" on the back of his hat and *have to march across the room to shake his hand to ask how he got it so you can reveal to him that* you *have one too* ... well ... you have enough arrogance to be an Instrument Flight Examiner.

And yes, I still wear mine.

Now, all this blather is to help you focus on my perspective as a young pilot. It may be slightly exaggerated, but the gist of it is clear. For me, the culture of aviation, pilots and instructor pilots would become a career-long endeavor.

When I checked in, I was immediately taken under the smelly wing of the unit IP, a pain in the neck I will call Mr. Pain (for "in the neck"). There were other IPs who did most of the training, but Mr. Pain did most of the complaining.

FORT CAMPBELL 1975-1978

That guy was my nemesis for the whole three years at Fort Campbell. But that is not all.

The Army was going through a huge culture change at that time. In 1975, the unit had recently returned from Vietnam with the 101st Division Artillery Brigade. The entire culture of the Army was transitioning from the "draftee" Army to the VOLAR (All Volunteer Army). It was tough enduring the constant changes in discipline and training.

The aviation force chaffed under the new restrictions to flight being imposed to improve flight safety.

For example, during the Vietnam era, instructor pilots were allowed to conduct autorotations to the ground, as in real combat operations. IPs returning from Vietnam were restricted to autorotation landings on runways only.

For training purposes, unannounced autorotations were still allowed during any flight as long as the pilot was able to make a full power recovery prior to touchdown.

I was being given an initial transition check ride (in the OH-58) with an old IP, CW3 Dave Price, when he attempted a zero ground-run autorotation just to show me, the new guy, how it should look. It had been awhile since he had done one. He came in a bit fast, held it off a bit long, allowed the rotor RPM to droop a bit too much … and we hopped down the runway on the toes of the aircraft. I was too new to realize our peril, and I was just along for the ride. The IP sort of pretended it was normal. That "clunking" we heard in the back was my first experience with "spike knock," a sort of Bell Helicopter characteristic when the transmission starts to shake a bit. I asked him what the heck that was.

Dave was a man of few words and he couched everything in code. "Just another butt chewing," he said.

You may not understand all this mumbo jumbo but suffice it to say a helicopter has 50,000 parts all built by the lowest bidder. The incident was not good, but it was not deadly, and we got away clean (meaning we were not hurt and the commander did not kill us for doing an illegal maneuver).

Anyway, Dave picked it up and hovered off to the side, telling the tower we were checking something. He got out, peered into the engine compartment (checking the "spike" for unusual wear) and pronounced it good. But we *did* terminate the flight early; we *did* hover back to the hanger, and we *did* whisper something to the maintenance guy to let him be sure to check that the OH-58 would be safe to fly.

We had landed, and I was holding the controls while Dave spoke to him. I could hear the maintenance officer commence to chewing on ol' Dave over the engine noise.

In his inimitable code, Dave commented, "Guess we won't be doing that again."

Quality of the Force

When I arrived in 1975, the Army was downsizing after Vietnam and going through another of its personnel reduction cycles. The transition from war to peace was necessary, but the motive of the US Congress is not always good. In peacetime it was "save money at any cost." In wartime it was "anything for the soldier," at least if it did not cost too much. The reality was that Congress tinkered with money in every conceivable way, but the Army had to manage and motivate the assets (the soldiers) in order to function.

In the face of this unpopular post-Vietnam war, the Army was fully involved in improving its image. That means they wanted the overall Army to be more appealing in order to attract enough soldiers to fill the roster. The concept was to develop the VOLAR, the all-volunteer Army. The only other known option to filling the roster was the draft, and it was especially unpopular after Vietnam. Experience showed that an unpopular draft would *never* get public support.

By 1975, the unpopular nature of the war had squashed the incentive to enlist or to extend a tour of duty. Thus the recruiting pool was really drying up.

On the other hand, the government was shooting itself in the foot by trying to downsize and exercise its post-Vietnam

War RIF (Reduction in Force) option. This reduction happens after every war, I am told; this was my first taste of it.

There were lots of contradictory changes. The rank and file were being discouraged and thrown away as though experience did not matter. While the post-Vietnam Army was being reduced in size, enlisted promotions were being frozen because there were so many soldiers still serving. Skill requirements demanded for reenlistment in specific MOSs were being raised to deliberately improve quality and weed out the slackers.

Oh, no. Did I say that? Political correctness is something else entirely when you are trying to sort out conflicting mission requirements. It may have been an effort to improve the *new* Army, but the soldiers from the *old* Army paid a terrible price.

To save money, reenlistment bonuses were being cut along with other incentives, and the pay was not being improved at all. The Army was still being squeezed to make it a strictly volunteer force. Good men were being passed over for promotion and RIF'd (Reduction in Force) for reasons unheard of until this time.

When they couldn't get the quality volunteers to man the roster, the Army started reducing the quality requirements of recruits and re-enlistments (in things like intelligence, education or felony history) to keep up enlistments. This did not work well. In the short term it helped fill the roster, but it reduced the quality and the capability of the force even further.

In an effort to elevate the career motive and offer a higher quality of life, the All Volunteer Army barracks life was given a facelift. There were better enlisted quarters, better furniture (called VOLAR equipment) and better mess facilities. There was an effort to allow more free time and treat the service like an ordinary job. The fraud in considering the Army "just another job" cannot be overstated. But Congress thought it was a great idea.

These efforts continued to evolve in great confusion. Once a soldier was intelligent enough, educated enough and skilled enough to warrant interest in his retention, there was a concerted effort to encourage re-enlistment based on unit pride and camaraderie as opposed to bigger money or promotions or bonus offers. This means reenlistment might get you a unit of choice, an extension at your current job, or maybe a month's leave. If there was a bonus, it was small and paid out over the duration of your enlistment rather than all at once. There was seldom any discussion of a promotion or a new school or change of MOS. If you were qualified in one MOS, you stayed in it unless you were qualified to change to a more critical MOS.

A re-enlistment NCO was supposed to be appointed in each unit. He/she was a grin and grip personable specialist who did a lot of personal contact work. It seems to me this was more effective when that NCO did not have other big responsibilities in the unit. But in the units I was in, usually there was a busy staff sergeant NCOIC working recruiting for the battalion sergeant major. The S-1 would talk to the NCOIC and point out a person whose reenlistment was coming up; the recruiter would then go visit the target and play the professionalism card. The CSM (Command Sergeant Major) would put in a macho visit doing the "Hey pal, we all gotta stick together" card. The soldier would experience a moment of pride in his fellows and sign on the dotted line. The "soldier pride" motivation was sort of lost in the cloud of, "What the hell is next?"

Believe me when I say these NCOs had a tough time initially. But this increased emphasis on professionalism and integrity eventually resulted in a better force, and it did help improve retention. General Starry actually had a big push on mentoring that seemed to become Army-wide, and I believe it did more toward force recruitment than many other programs. The Army achieved this success in spite of the constant meddling of Congress, not because of it.

Reductions in Force were another personnel management tool that had spotty effect. They were designed to rid the Army of the old hangers-on (enlisted and officer) who were inept, incompetent, irresponsible, overweight or otherwise unfit for duty. These were supposed to be draining the Army's resources without adding to its professionalism. I wish I could say it was always right, fair or accurate, but it was certainly often heartbreaking.

Many officers and enlisted men were tossed out of the Army without real justification. I know many men who went into the reserves after their RIF and managed to get one extension after another as little fights came along to finish out 20 years. Even worse, in the late 70s, the Army (or rather, Congress) started tinkering with the retirement program—not to improve the force, but to save money. Many senior NCOs who could choose to stay or retire were forced to retire. Waiting until later in their career threatened to reduce their future pension. This meant a flood of experienced NCOs retired from the active Army. And some of the folks who should have left … well, they stayed.

So the Army was short of recruits, losing experienced leadership and unable to manage the roster very well. The Army began the terrible practice of pretending that a turnip would suffice when quality could not be found in the line. They called it progress. So there were jobs and units whose efficiency was reduced by this effort. Often, the Cat IV soldier simply did not fulfill the requirement.

I have seen some darn fine Cat IV soldiers, and generally they were exceptional in important ways. The successful Cat IV soldiers worked hard, usually in a physical MOS, such as fuel handler. They had a good work ethic, and most importantly they had good sense and a practical attitude.

Of course, if you get lemons, you gotta make lemonade. But the Army tried to reflect favorably on their quality of force by putting lipstick on this pig and tying a bow on one ear.

To "upgrade the quality of the force," the Army became immersed in an effort to get every soldier a GED (General Education Diploma, a sort of abbreviated high school education certificate). The significance of this fraud is clear but hard to explain. A soldier was pulled out of his assigned active-duty job and sent to class, often for months at a time. The unit was left short-handed, struggling to manage its resources well enough to be effective. The soldier was dragged to class and hammered on until he passed the requisite test. He was given the certificate, and it was placed in his records. He was carried as a high school educated soldier from that time on. When he was returned to his assigned job, his performance and his character were unchanged. The Army did not encourage further improvement in any way, and the soldier fulfilled his potential career based on his ability alone, sometimes doing better and sometimes worse.

In addition to this, the Army established a new standard to its doctrine of training or equipment manual development. Simple manuals were required so every soldier could understand it. So the Army applied a test to all written manuals in the Army—*all* manuals had to be written in fourth grade English in order to be certified. I am not kidding. Each manual had to pass a test establishing its ease of reading and application, and it had to be written to effectively convey accurate information. I have actually written one of these manuals. When the manual is complete, it is hacked apart by an English expert. Sentences are shortened to so many words; there are no four-syllable words unless absolutely necessary; the paragraphs are short and limited to so many sentences.

The Army tried a lot of other things to help with the shortage of personnel. They tried to increase the ratio of fighters to support staff—no more KP (kitchen patrol) duty. Contractors ran the mess hall under a cook NCO. A great number of support element types were shuffled into the reserves and guard units, such as fuel, ammo, supply and water supply, thus increasing the room for more fighters on active duty. The logic was that the reserves could easily be called up during any war, which became a problem later.

Reforger 1976

In 1976 the 101stAirborne Division participated in "*Reforger 76*" (Return of Forces to Germany). Remember, the USA was still committed to defending West Germany (FRG, the Federal Republic of Germany) and Europe from the forces of Communism. I had been trained up to be a PIC (Pilot in Command), which basically meant I was qualified and current to start and fly an aircraft from one place to another and return safely without embarrassing the commander by pranging it in or getting killed.

One of the unique and comforting things about the aviation community is that if you managed to get yourself killed, after cussing about your broken aircraft, the entire lot of them would, in unison, spit on your airplane, and then say with one voice, "Poor, *dumb* Dan." or words to that effect.

In normal civil aviation we have rules that provide guidance for navigating restricted airspace, airport traffic areas, controlled airspace of all sorts and high-density traffic areas. You best not get lost and violate any of that airspace or those flight rules.

In moving American air units around Europe, (e.g., from France to Germany where the International Civilian Aviation Organization, ICAO rules and local rules may not be readily known by Americans), an experienced in-country IP is needed to lead the gaggle of aircraft cross-country from the port into the tactical area. The object is to get all training units in place for the exercise, on time and under budget. Once there, we could maneuver around the exercise battlefield using our own maps and local flight-following.

We were briefed, of course, on emergency flight-following procedures in events such as getting lost, running short of fuel or punching into IFR (into the clouds and on Instrument Flight Rules). And we got a weather briefing and emergency procedures in Europe. We normally did pretty well in this, but we were extra careful preparing for night flight. For you non-pilot types, remember here we were all "night hawk" only, no NVG devices, so map recon was very important to us.

We were also careful to note little hazards like the random "cumulogranite" (mountains) and the legendary smack-u-flat (power lines, strung all over Germany).

Well, our little flight of Kiowas were flying to the German tactical area. It had been a long day. It was hot, it was hazy, the sun was going down, and we were being led by a hot-shot young lieutenant named Kipfer. We were all flying in OH-58-A's, which were not very strong aircraft. In my aircraft I had only myself, a crew chief (Sp/4 Chuck Yeary), a tool box and our kit bags. But Kipfer had three men aboard, with baggage. It was supposedly only at max gross weight, but I suspect it was badly overloaded.

Chuck Yeary was not just any sort of flying crewman; he was a great crew chief and had good sense about him. He had never read a map at anything above four mph, the average fast Infantry pace. In those days, no one taught crew chiefs to navigate unless, like us, circumstances demanded it. I was an idiot. When he strapped in, I handed him a 1/50 map and expected him to navigate. His blossoming map-reading skill was not helped by my elevated (very nervous) vocal instruction. Finally, I had him simply hold it open and place a finger at each identified navigational point.

Note: Knowing where you have been may not be as good as knowing where you are going, but you *don't get lost that way*. Chuck and I finally learned to work together. He turned out to be a great navigator, and he took care of his pilot. I am not sure I ever told him how good he really was. I am certain he could expound on my shortcomings as an instructor.

All Army aircraft had limits, but it seemed that with every few thousand hours, the average OH-58A became more underpowered and required more attention from its pilot. We also had some mystical problems in those days with the old Bell products.

LTE (Loss of Tail Rotor Effectiveness, spinning in some types of hover configurations) was one. The primary problem of this was that the aircraft might start spinning in any high-power hover.

Main rotor droop (the slowing of the main rotor due to low power supplied by the tiny engine) was another. The primary problem here was that as power was applied to keep up lift, the pitch of the main rotor became more severe, dragging down the engine and slowing the blade as it tried to grasp the air, making the droop worse and making the tail rotor slow even more (developing less anti-torque thrust); thus the aircraft lost altitude and directional control.

Taken together, once the aircraft lost power, the tail rotor thrust was reduced, the aircraft started spinning, the main rotor started drooping even more; then the aircraft would start a rotating descent, the anti-torque pedals became less effective, and the terrified pilot over-torqued the aircraft to keep it in the air. That, in turn, increased the droop and the rate of spin ... well, you get the picture.

Back to Kipfer. Poor Lieutenant Kipfer was flight lead with his full load in that little underpowered aircraft. He was very busy.

So, there we were, a gaggle flying along, it getting darker partially from the descending overcast, and partly due to the setting sun. I was chalk two (between lead and trail). We all knew off to port somewhat, there was a large hill ahead, sweetly topped by a tower with a red beacon. No problem.

But then it got darker. It got foggier. That sweetly shining beacon disappeared due to the fog, and now we were all paying strict attention to anything we could still see. In fact, I still think about it. It was my first experience in bad weather, single pilot, and I just did not realize the degree of our peril. Yeary knew. His open mouth, wide eyes and constantly searching look told me all I needed to know, but he said nothing.

We all sort of snuggled closer in formation flight so we did not lose each other. For a while, we could easily make out each other's position lights. Kipfer was senior to us all, and we were certain that Kipfer had a good handle on our navigation. He was odd for a commissioned officer. He actually wrangled a lot of flight time out of operations, as opposed to the usual commissioned guys who spent most of their time on the ground, devoted to other career-enhancing jobs.

It was a good thing we had such unfounded confidence. It probably prevented any extra panic. Yeary, my faithful crew chief, was holding my map and trying to follow along, but he was not experienced, and I couldn't see it well without a flashlight. Doctrine said we used a red lens on our flashlight to reduce night blindness, but you really could not see the map well that way. It was colored in greens, yellows and browns, and the red light did not enhance its visibility. Every time we tried to see the map with a real light, I would go night blind for just a moment or two, an eternity at treetop level at night.

Suddenly the fog got worse. We hit a patch of it, and the lead aircraft was gone.

I have to hand it to Chuck, who still said nothing. He simply held that map and started looking around very carefully.

I punched the radio. "Chalk Two is descending to the right, on the trees."

No response. I was sure I could avoid running over Lead, but I had no idea where Trail was. I wanted him to appreciate my location.

"Chalk Two is descending to the right ... on the trees ... I have good visual." Still nothing.

"Chalk Three ... Chalk Three ... do you copy?" Now I feared he might strike me from behind, and I wanted confirmation of his situation.

Chalk Three was very busy, and all I got was, "Stand by."

Chuck and I actually found a sort of path through the trees, but we were concerned with Trail. Then Lead suddenly called.

"Lead is IFR ... climbing to ... well, I am out. The fog only goes to 200 feet ... wait ... it is clear in a quarter-mile ..." It was good to hear his shaky voice.

"Trail is clear. I have Chalk Two in sight."

We all met up in a half-mile and followed him to the field site. We learned about his adventure there.

It was not good. Kipfer had gone into the soup and panicked a bit while pulling in power to climb. The inevitable main rotor droop started, so instead of climbing, the aircraft started descending. He pulled in more power and the reduced RPM caused the tail rotor to be less effective. The aircraft started turning as he tried not to descend into the trees. He nosed it over to gain airspeed and the spinning was, of course, accentuated.

The infantry captain in the back seat was keenly aware that they were spinning. He was yelling, "Pull up!" He was scared out of his mind. The pilot's shoulder harness in that aircraft is attached on the floor at the feet of the back-seaters, then goes up over the pilot's shoulders to his waist belt. The captain grabbed the front seat's shoulder harness and started yanking on it as though the pilot couldn't hear him yelling into the intercom. And he kept yelling until they were out of the soup. When they landed, he changed aircraft, leaving some unkind words with his pilot. Lt Kipfer, whose whole existence seemed focused on flying instead of career, continued to fly happily during his tour with A/377, but he never was allowed to lead another flight in that unit. I don't think he cared.

Reforger 76 was full of experiences for me.

FORT CAMPBELL 1975-1978

First, we had one week's hard work slammed into six weeks there, and we slept next to the beer tent. Remember here, I used to love beer, and I had just become a Mormon. So my first real test was this trip. I passed without a single beer.

Next, I learned how wonderful German food is, and I gained ten pounds.

Colonel S, the Division Artillery Commander, was supposedly caught in a commo-van sampling the wiles of a pretty little Specialist Four, and in one day he was gone and replaced. Never heard of him again.

The Division Artillery units that controlled us were careless about their aviation assets. They let me be overrun once by the enemy without so much as a howdy-do, and it showed the real merit of the aerial observer assets to the 319th Artillery Battalion. In fact, I heard tanks approaching, ordered my crew chief into the aircraft and had just started to crank when an M-60 turned the corner and leveled the gun at us. Sort of made the hairs on the back of my neck stand up.

The 101st Airborne was scheduled to do an aerial insertion on a massive scale, and we got our butts handed to us because our scouts did not get out and do the proper recon. We had taken a long, circuitous route to avoid detection, when our lead elements began to call out, "We have tanks ... guns in the trees ... more tanks!"

You could feel the tension. The swearing of our Battalion Commander could only be a minor precursor to the response of our new 101st Field Artillery Brigade Commander.

Well, we landed amongst tanks, and it was ugly. Our battle referee, the one who was supposed to come over the radio and pronounce our glorious and victorious insertion, came on the radio.

"This is (so and so). Yer all killed."

I am fairly sure that would have been an exaggeration, but it was bad enough. We got it. The news was not well received at Division. From our perspective, the exercise did not go so well, but the new 101st Brigade Artillery Commander was too new to be fired. At least that day.

The real character of the aviators came out during that exercise. We were completely uninspired by our leadership in this moment, and the casualties that could have resulted were no secret. Seems as though the more scary and more serious the issues, the harder pilots laugh. Nothing is funny when things go that wrong, but we all laughed that nervous, dry-mouth "holy shit, how did *that* happen" laugh. The entire flight did a big U-turn and flew back. There was no panic or effort to avoid further fire, as there probably should have been. It was a silent flight, devoid of expression or feeling. We all knew someone somewhere was getting his butt handed to him in a canteen cup, and we hoped it made a difference. So, the beer tent was swamped that night.

Throughout the exercise, the A/377 pilots were sent out into the tactical area in sections, two aircraft (OH-58s) per battalion, in support of the 319th, 320th and 321st Artillery Battalions. They were all manning towed 105 mm cannon, which were air transportable. We did not do much aerial observing, mostly scouting with or transporting the battery or battalion commanders.

When supporting the battalions, we were sent out in pairs … two aircraft, pilots and crew chiefs with our gear. One day I had a separate mission from my partner. We departed early, agreeing to meet near a particular point that evening. Somehow our crew chiefs ended up at the right spot via ground transport and set up camp for us during the day.

Remember, in 1976 there were no GPSs, no shortcuts to navigation or any easy way to find our way around. For normal missions during early daylight, we would fly our crew chief and gear to the bivouac site and then proceed on our missions for the day. We were handed a 1/250 map for general navigation (covering much larger areas but accurate down to the tree lines in Germany due to forest management laws) and a 1/50 map of the tactical play area.

Night flight was pretty dicey, especially with little local area knowledge. We peeked at the map with a flashlight as we stumbled around the tactical area. When the sky was dark, generally our tactical day was over. We would fly to the vicinity of the landing site, where we hoped our crew chief had set up landing lights (a "T") to help us land. The darker it was, the more challenging it was. The approach procedure began by flying nearby (generally, we could navigate to some proximity of the landing site) and notifying the radio man we were inbound. We took careful note of his winds and hazard report; then came the really high-tech method of air traffic management. The crew chief would turn on the landing lights so we could find him; we would approach and land, hoping we were fully upright and in one major piece. Then the crew chief would turn the lights off.

On this particular night, I had come in at dusk. Yeary and I had failed to contact my partner, and dusk became dark … very, very dark. Yep, it was pretty dark. The winds were spooky, and the trees were tall. This is the stuff that excites helicopter pilots. Not in a good way.

We cooked our meal in silence. We knew even if he had found the FAARP (Forward Area Arming and Refuel Point), he would probably have flown off his fuel load again and be low on gas by now. I pondered over this, but there was nothing we could do. We had received no emergency calls from Battalion, so we assumed he must have landed somewhere for the night. I had to get my crew rest, so Yeary maintained the radio watch, and I racked out.

Around midnight, he came running in and woke me from a sound sleep.

"Mr. K ... Mr. K! Mr. (So and so) cannot locate us. He is out of gas."

Well, he was still airborne, so he couldn't be *quite* out yet.

I jumped up in my trousers, barefoot and no shirt or gloves. I ran to the aircraft. I yelled at Yeary to radio the pilot that he should look around and that in two minutes he would see me.

It was a miracle I had the good sense to untie the main rotor blade.

"Clear!"

I fired it off and broke every rule. I was not fully dressed, and I started without a checklist, no seat belt, and barely had a helmet on.

I pulled it into a high hover, probably a hundred feet ... just above the trees, with every light on. He flew past me almost immediately. I descended and he landed behind me. We shut down, and I commenced to chew his butt for scaring the life out of me. Only then did I learn how low on fuel he was. We discussed the stupidity of pilot-error "fuel exhaustion," but

I did not tell him I regarded this as a direct answer to prayer. He was so short of fuel that next day we did not let him hover out to a nearby road. We made a fuel truck find a path to his aircraft. But I still did not know how much protection I was enjoying until the following morning.

On pre-flight inspection the next day, I discovered that I had failed to remove the exhaust stack covers (made of plastic covers and nylon tie-down ropes) before the panic start of the previous night. They were melted to the engine. But the tie-down straps, which could have wrapped around the rotor blade or main rotor control tubes were lying harmlessly on the engine cowling. They would have made short work of my shiny new (well, old and beat up) OH-58A. It turned out they were clear of the aircraft moving parts, and there was no damage. Whew!

We all survived the entire exercise with no damage or major injuries. The complete exercise was without any accidents, and we were feeling pretty good about it. The day we departed, we joined up for the return gaggle to the coast.

I was sort of mid-pack this trip, in a flight of eight aircraft, being led by another lieutenant. He was determined to find a certain refuel point before stopping. By this time, I had learned a lot about taking charge of my own existence, and I was low on fuel. I called him on the radio, and he dismissed my concern. He was sure we could make it to the next FAARP.

FORT CAMPBELL 1975-1978

Another pilot also called … not as short as I, but he also expressed his need of fuel. The lieutenant did some more waffling.

We all had maps, and we all knew the fuel points were shutting down. And we all knew pretty much where they were located and where we were going. By now my crew chief could find it blind-folded; he was a great daylight navigator. He had packed some C Rations and our cots, so we did not need anything to survive a couple of days out.

We passed a town that had an airfield with a large Reforger FAARP that was shutting down, but we could still see helicopter traffic there. I called our lieutenant to declare a fuel emergency, and I broke off toward the town. The lieutenant was answering me with some stern rebuke of my foolishness, when the other guy called out and followed me. Then another aircraft, and the lieutenant told all of us to get in line, and he would lead us in. We got our gas and flew on.

I learned a couple of really important things in that exercise.

The first was a lot of practical stuff about flying and decision making. Only safety matters, and a pilot must make his own decision when other decisions do not seem to help. We all understood that if we broke the airplane, no matter who said what, it was the pilot's fault. I got more of that here than any other assignment I ever had. And, I did not get killed. That felt like success to me, a new warrant officer. One of those minor but significant achievements you look so hard for.

The second thing I learned from my sweet wife. Having been gone for two months, I fairly expected her to jump into my arms … which did not happen. Two months pregnant, she pretty much shook my hand and asked me where I would be bunking tonight. I got the real idea when she threw up the second time on the road home. I would learn to tread very carefully.

Motor Officer

When I returned to Fort Campbell from Reforger 76, I volunteered to be the Motor Pool Officer. It was assigned to me as an additional duty. I was not familiar with motor operations and wanted something to challenge me. There were no other volunteers. Funny how that works. Instantly, I was the Motor Officer.

I got more than I bargained for. A/377 FA had returned from Vietnam with a few old Gama Goats, several old CUCVs (pronounced CUC-V) (Civilian Utility Cargo Vehicles—old Chevy Blazers with enough bondo and bailing wire to keep 'em running), a few jeeps, one five-ton truck, three "deuce and a halfs" (2 ½-ton trucks), and a secret ¾-ton pickup we kept up for errands. The best running vehicle was the five-ton. The rest of 'em were wrecks, long past their "best if used by" date, whatever that may have been, and a constant nightmare of maintenance. Especially the Goats; all were junk.

I arrived to find a SP/4 running the shop, and he was struggling. We had two actual mechanics, and a couple of extra enlisted men rejected from other jobs. I needed an NCOIC (Non-Commissioned Officer In Charge, a staff sergeant or Sergeant First Class). I did not realize it, but our little motor pool was a microcosm of the problems faced by the rest of the Army everywhere. They pulled out more of our personnel for GED training than we had personnel, and I was not happy about it. My commander, Major Schofield, basically told me to shut up. He was rude but very helpful.

One day Brigade sent a motor NCO down to work our shop. He was a fairly short black guy who had been busted for drinking, according to the scuttlebutt. His name was SSG Cleve Watson, and after I was so ready to believe the bad gossip, he came into the unit and saved my career and my motor pool. SSG Watson turned out to be the best kept secret in the Army. He had been caught up in General Wickham's post-Vietnam anti-drinking drive, barely failed an alcohol test at a random stop outside the NCO club and reduced one grade. I always felt his reduction was unjust, but he never complained, never asked a favor, never drank, and his entire success in our motor pool made me the envy of the brigade.

Watson came into my motor pool clean and fresh and with a whole new attitude each day. The other soldiers instantly respected his expertise. He worked with each man to get his GED done and initiated an optional enrollment in Army training programs. He went through our TAMMS (The Army Maintenance Management System), our other supplies and our maintenance records like a house afire.

After a few days to see the operation, he turned to me and asked me how I work. I told him I would support any effort he made so long as I could keep my integrity, and he simply asked me to sign whatever he put in front of me and speak for the section to the commander. It was the best deal I ever made in the Army. He was a one-man section. When he was not supervising or mentoring, he was under a vehicle or out gathering impossible-to-find parts.

I wish I could find him. I actually located another Cleve Watson—a retired, black, motor NCO—but it wasn't the man I was seeking. Go figure.

Mr. Hung

I arrived at Fort Campbell, Kentucky, as a new pilot, a new officer and without a real understanding of my new place on the social ladder.

FORT CAMPBELL 1975-1978

My sweet wife and I had been assured we would never have children, but I am certain the very day I became a Mormon, she became pregnant with our first child.

We arrived at Fort Campbell in our new Toyota truck. We were broke, so we kept a tight budget. I worked hard, and our extras were few. Did I mention we were broke? We had a favorite Chinese food restaurant, and I had just enough cash to take my sweetie and pay for a sitter and a buffet. She was so pleased, and having just had our first baby and nursing, she was naturally thirsty. Very thirsty. In those days, a soda did *not* come with the meal, and one soda was charged for each drink. She downed three of them before I could throw myself on the waitress to forbid any more. I managed to rummage through my pickup and find enough change from my ashtray and floor pan so I did not have to wash dishes.

Well, we had a garden … we used cheap gas … we did everything to save money, and we were okay. One day I got a call from a Captain Lamb at Division Headquarters.

"Do you know Mr. Hung?"

"Why, sure I do."

Hung had been a pilot in flight school with me, a Vietnamese sergeant, decorated for valor, and sent by Vietnam to flight school. He had graduated with some difficulty, but he was a pilot in the Vietnamese Army, as far as I knew. I did not know what had become of him since the fall of South Vietnam.

Lamb said, "Well, he is at Indian Town Gap, Pennsylvania, waiting to hear from you."

I was thrilled and glad he was alive, but I had no idea where this was going.

I called there immediately and spoke to the powers in charge. Seems that Hung had survived his evacuation to the USA and had listed me as a point of contact—possibly as a sponsor to his stay in the USA.

"Well, just how much room do you have?"

I asked why he would even ask. "Well, he has his sister with him."

"That should work okay. My wife is pregnant, but we have no children yet."

"Well, his mother is also with him."

I told him I thought we could handle that. Was there anyone else? No, his father had been killed, and they are the survivors. So … okay.

Eventually Hung arrived with his mother and sister. We had a point of contact who spoke Vietnamese at Indian Town Gap, and I was sure they would be unnecessary. So the three of them settled in.

FORT CAMPBELL 1975-1978

Hung was a perfect gentleman. His sister was a delicate flower—slender, beautiful and very sweet. But I did not understand the domineering attitude of the matriarch.

She spoke broken English, and Hung had to do a lot of translating. She said Hung was a hero in Vietnam, so why wasn't he treated better here? (Seems *her* living circumstances here did not measure up to the mother of a hero.) Well, I had gone all over and found him a government sponsored program to become a journeyman welder, and he would be paid as soon as he started.

"Oh, no," Mama said. "He pilot. *Pilot!* He fly. Good pilot. You find pilot job."

I kept trying to soothe her feathers, but I expected Hung to speak up, not simply cave in to the shame of her scorn.

"Oh no," he said. He simply could not do that. Daddy is probably dead; Mom had no friends (I wonder why), and he would find a way to become a pilot and please his mother.

Well, it went on for about two months. My poor wife, getting bigger and bigger, knowing our disposable income shrinking to nearly nothing. Mama was bearing down on Gail, though I did not fully understand the difficulty of it all. I even sent Mama to her bedroom once. She was offended, to the terrible chagrin of Hung.

Then on another cloudy, rainy day, CPT Lamb called again. At work. Of course, my commander wondered just why Lieutenant General Wickham's adjutant was calling me.

"Mr. Kingsley?"

"Oh yes, CPT Lamb. How are you?"

"Yes sir," he said slowly. "This *is* Captain Lamb ... *blah blah blah* ... and I have been instructed by General Wickham to speak to you."

"So, sir ... what is this about?"

"Well, this is about the Hung family."

"You mean *my* Hung family?" I was incredulous, and I knew things were going to pop. I could hardly grasp his full purpose, but it was obviously not a social call.

"Yes, Mr. Kingsley. The general has been advised you are not feeding them properly."

I choked off the shriek I felt coming in my throat. "Who is this, really?"

"This is CPT Lamb ... adjutant to General Wickham—"

"Oh hell, sir. I know who you are. I know who General Wickham is. Tell me precisely what you are saying."

"Well, we have been told you feed them only peanut butter and jelly sandwiches."

First I laughed, but the anger quickly overcame the humor. My wife and I often ate peanut butter and jelly sandwiches for lunch and for snacks, but I could see the wheels spinning.

"Sir, just who told you this crap? Surely you know this cannot be true. You know I eat at home at least twice a day and PB & J is simply a quick appetizer."

"Well, it seems Hung's sister has been seeing Mr. (So and so, another Vietnamese escapee who was befriended and evac'd by General Wickham before the NVA could find him). Mama-San has told him you are mean to them ... that you do not respect her son ... and the food—"

That did it. I interrupted him. "Sir, they eat what I eat. Why don't you stop by and bring Mr. (so and so), and the two of you can haul them away with their bags to the general's house ..."

"Now, Mr. Kingsley, I have only been instructed to check up on them."

"Well, sir, don't you worry. My wife has put up with that woman for months. Gail is pregnant with our first child, and after today, there will be no more complaints."

He sputtered and choked and hung up. I left work and went home.

I arrived to find Mama-San lording it over my wife, and I stopped her with a cold stare.

"You are leaving. Go pack." She pretended not to understand. Hung came out. He understood very clearly. She tried to refuse, and he calmly explained that I was in charge ...that this was not her option.

I picked up the phone to the point of contact (POC) at Indian Town Gap. I spoke clearly and carefully.

"Sir, I am at the end of my rope here. Mama-San has successfully convinced the Commanding General of Fort Campbell that I am not feeding them."

"Now, Mr. Kingsley, we can send you some help if you need it. Perhaps some counseling—"

"Nope."

"Nope?"

"No. I am going to give you six hours. In six hours, more or less, they will be at the airport in Nashville, Tennessee. Hung, and sister, and Mama will all be there with their luggage and whatever they can carry. They will need a ticket ... wait. If you do not call me with a flight number and a way to pick up a ticket within three hours, I will take them to the Greyhound Bus in Clarksville, and I will send them to you myself."

I gave the phone to Hung, and they spoke, then hung up.

They all got plane tickets. I called the POC again later to made sure they made it. Then I ensured he understood what we had been through, including the rejected offer as a journeyman welder. He listened quietly and sighed.

"There is more."

At first my heart sank, and I could see my commander stripping me of my rank and dropping me at the gate.

"Seems like Mr. Hung, the dad, is still alive."

"No!"

"Yep. He evacuated in a boat. It was a slow ride in a big boat … took him around the world apparently. He was sad. He was lonely. He was sure his family was dead."

"Oh, yeah?"

"He met another woman. And married her. He is here in Indian Town Gap."

He was clearly hoping I might volunteer another sponsorship.

As I started to laugh, I wondered how the poor bastard was going to survive Mama-San's wrath.

The last I knew, Hung and his sister had found a church in California to sponsor them. I never heard what happened to his mama or his poor father.

Mentoring in the Army

One of the sweet things about being in the Army is that you are expected to mentor your subordinates. I took this mandate seriously, and I tried to coach, coax and encourage them to professionalism and honorable careers in the Army. That is the way the professional Army is built up, by bringing men along in the image you can cultivate.

Along the way I mentored three fine men into the warrant officer ranks—Paul Kemp, Mike Foley and another kid whose name slips my mind—while I was at Fort Campbell. In an odd coincidence, two of these men were killed flying Army helicopters.

Paul Kemp. I met Paul when he was a Specialist 4 in A/377 Field Artillery with me at Fort Campbell around 1976. He was an enlisted man who showed up in church with his sweetheart, Glenda, and a couple of kids. He and I shared the Melchizedek Priesthood, and both of us had responsibilities in the local ward. According to US Army protocol, as an officer I was not allowed to socialize with Paul, a lowly enlisted man, but we remained fast friends from the day we met.

Even on field exercises, our friendship was respected for its professionalism, and we were allowed to bivouac together.

Paul and I shared many things, mostly in our church activities, and he was clearly a cut above the average. He adored his wife and children, and his example was sterling in his personal and professional life.

I immediately started grooming Paul to go to flight school. If memory serves, he left for flight school in 1976, finishing in early 1977. I stayed in touch with him throughout flight school; he did well. He graduated and went directly to Germany as a UH-1 pilot.

I received orders, first to Cobra training, then to report to Germany on 1 July 1978. Paul was scheduled to sponsor me in-country and meet me at the Frankfurt airport. How we looked forward to that—he and I as best friends, and Glenda and Gail as our matched pair.

Warrant Officer One Paul Kemp was killed around 26 June flying an artillery battalion staff into Wurzburg, FRG. He was copilot with another WO1 whom I did not know. They were descending out of instrument conditions when his Huey suffered a 42-degree gearbox failure, and then a partial tail boom separation. They controlled it all the way to the ground, and in an apparent effort to avoid a house, lost control of the aircraft. It hit the ground upside down. All the men were killed.

My wife flew home to Paul's funeral to comfort Glenda in Wisconsin. I went on to Germany. It was a great personal loss.

Mike Foley. I met Mike in church in Clarksville, Tennessee, around the time Paul Kemp left for flight school. Mike was also a Specialist 4, as was his wife, both having a Military Intelligence MOS. They were a handsome couple, and we became very good friends immediately. They were newlyweds, and they were new converts to the church.

Mike and I were in different units, so our friendship caused no problem. Remember here that the Church of Jesus Christ of Latter-Day Saints has no paid clergy, so most of the time everyone has an assignment, and participation can be in every conceivable form of service. He and I were young and strong, and both of us held the Priesthood, so we were often on assignments together. I remember keeping bees and digging drainage lines for a parking lot behind the church building. Gail and I had many personal service moments with Mike and his sweet wife, Sharon. I do what works. I started mentoring Mike to apply to flight school.

Mike was accepted immediately, but things did not go well for him. While in flight school he was sitting in the jump seat, behind and between the instructor and the student pilot flying the aircraft. The student pilot panicked in a hydraulics-off maneuver and pancaked the aircraft on landing. They hit so hard the student pilot was killed, and the IP at the controls got badly banged up. Mike was ripped out of the aircraft and thrown through the "doghouse," the small window above the pilot's cabin. Alive. Still strapped into his seat in the middle of the runway.

Mike recovered, graduated and went to the Panama Canal as a UH-1 pilot. I stayed in touch with Mike for several years. More on Mike later.

On The First Kid

My wife and I had married with the absolute understanding that we would have 10 kids and a Saint Bernard. (She allowed that we would *buy* the Saint Bernard.) She made me promise this agreement would be unquestioned, and her parents thought she was kidding.

Anyway, we married, and my sweet wife immediately became "with child." We were closer than we had thought. We managed to be sick in concert, even when we were apart. She would feel queasy, and I would throw up. It was a great arrangement. Food was reduced to mere necessity. And it had to be bland, boring and cold. There was nothing like a little grease or cheese and asparagus to get the old churning started.

It was a tough pregnancy, the toughest as far as our pregnancies have gone over the years, and we lost our first child. There were some serious complications, and my wife continued to be sick for more than a year.

Now, in those days we went to an old family doctor, the same one who had delivered my wife. He was a great old guy, not given to the usual wisdom of the modern medical community. Dr. Stewart loved his patients, and he did not often burden them with unnecessary details. Life was life, and whatever the personalities, he never forgot: his business was the *practice* of medicine, not the answer to all things.

Anyway, my wife did not recover quickly. One day Dr. Stewart confided in my father-in-law that we would never have children. They decided not to let us know it, and probably they felt it was for good reason. I don't think there were any long-term bets on our marriage anyway, and even if it did work out, what difference would it make? (I don't think I could buy this line now days, but it worked then.)

We went on to have two blissful years during which we discovered that the baby plumbing simply would not work. We went along very happy in our ignorance and really did not think much about it until one day in mid-1975, when the lady of my life woke up and got sick. She came back to bed, and I got up and got sick. When I came back to bed, I felt better, and my wife was very sympathetic.

"You wimp—"

FORT CAMPBELL 1975-1978

"Hey, you don't suppose …?" I mumbled.

"No, Dan. I'm sick and you're a wimp. That's all."

Right. So the promised arrival of my first child was a pleasant surprise to all of us. I was very happy about this arrangement, and so was my father. I had the distinction of being in the 101st Airborne (Dad's old division when he was at Bastogne in WWII), and the advent of a grandchild just topped off our relationship with a cherry.

I became part of the pre-natal care package. They showed me films to shore up my constitution (I had delivered calves with less trouble), and they graduated my sweet wife and me from the class on the helpee-selfee method of childbirth. I could breathe, blow, coach and whistle my wife through all the parts of labor, and I had stood up to the most difficult tasks as though I were born to it. I was the pride of the clinic. Until *he* was born.

It was a beautiful Sunday, and for some reason, though he was nine days late, I was surprised. I was required right alongside to coach and support my wife. I was pretty good, until he arrived. The doctor was a real sport.

"It's a boy! Wanna cut the cord?" I was delighted. Let me at 'em!

Then I got my first good look, up close and personal.

"Whoa … geese, Doc, isn't it … I mean, a bit purple? Is it okay? Yeah … yeah … *he*, then … isn't *he* a bit purple? Wrinkled, too, if you ask me. What? <u>Hold</u> it? I mean, *him* … I mean, he's so … so … *naked* … and what if he … you know … pees … or worse."

I felt guilty. I was in shock, and my sweet wife was so happy. Now I had her … and this little … rat-like, naked creature … to love and take care of.

I was confused. Bewildered. I was sure I would get over it, but … gee whiz. If I had only known then … *I had only five more little rat-like naked creatures to go.*

Orders to Germany

It is funny how career decisions go in the Army. I decided I wanted to fly Chinooks, the CH-47, heavy lift. I noised it abroad, but in discussing this with a Department of the Army Warrant Officer Manager, I told him I would be happy in anything but a Cobra.

Presto. I was on my way to Cobra school.

So in late 1977, I received orders to an attack helicopter battalion bound for Germany. I was to be cross-trained in the Cobra (the Army AH-1G helicopter gunship) transition and TOW training (the anti-tank missile system) at Fort

Rucker, Alabama. I was scheduled to arrive in Germany sometime around July 1, 1978, with orders for some time around April-May 1978. I applied to my commander to see if I might stay at Campbell, since I had a new home there, but he couldn't manage it. There is just no such thing as an indispensable aviation warrant officer.

WHEN FAT MEN FLEW

11

TOW Training:
Fort Rucker 1978

I returned to Ft Campbell, Kentucky, to drop the family
and go on to Fort Rucker, Alabama, to begin my Cobra
transition. Ever the good Army wife, poor Gail packed all our
stuff alone and shipped it to Germany. When she was ready for
the move, she jumped into our old Suburban and drove down
to Fort Rucker to join me. She was stressed with the move
and exhausted, dealing with our two young sons. I remember
waiting for her out in front of the BOQ (Bachelors Officers
Quarters). When she arrived, it was dark and not well lit. She
entered at the far end of the parking lot, and she simply headed
across the parking spaces with our old Suburban. She drove

over every bump and parking marker until she arrived in front of me. She got out and started crying, allowing me to rescue her for the night. We got an efficiency apartment in Ozark and spent two wonderful months at Fort Rucker while I was in training.

I enjoyed the Cobra transition but especially the TOW missile. I got to fire that thing. I was serious, competing for the privilege, and a couple of guys made fun of me. But it was still a blast. I hit the target, an old M-4 tank.

Now, the chronology here is a bit rough, but as we were near end of training, we took a trip down to Florida to visit my in-laws. We traveled in a pop-up trailer and were there when we were notified that my father had died.

We drove through Fort Rucker to drop the pop-up, then on to Fort Campbell to take care of our moving paperwork, and finally we drove home on leave to Holland, New York. That was Gail's family home. It was convenient to my father's family in Wyoming, New York, and we were spared extensive travel and hotels.

The Day Dad Died

I had a peculiar relationship with my father. He was an alcoholic, but not a bad man. He loved his family as well as he could, and he gave us as much as he was capable. He worked hard and cared about many good causes. But as with all alcoholics, there was a lot of fantasy and untruthful things about his life.

When he told me he had cancer, he was clearly expecting me to be upset. I had become completely numbed by our relationship, and I pondered over his fate for several days before calling back. He had been "dying" for 20 years, and I didn't see how it was any different now.

When we had flown out for Christmas, Dad had looked terrible, but not a lot worse than usual. He was awfully thin, and he was more impatient than ever. Part of his impatience was shown in his having little interest in my wife and less in my children, as I've mentioned. He was always in pain, and I did what I could to be around without wearing him down. I still could not relate to his suffering or his illness.

The doctor had been absolutely unwilling to speak to me in reference to Dad's real condition, though I asked several very specific questions about "How bad" and "How long." Dad had a lady friend who wouldn't talk about his dying, and Dad was pretty vague, except to say he would be cremated. So I left there feeling wasted, as I usually did in our relationship. But it had not occurred to me that he would really die. I just could not believe it.

My poor pregnant wife and two babies had a miserable stay. I had been glad to leave, and we were happy to get back into the busy flow of Army business.

Four months later he died at age 54. Because I was on leave enroute to Germany, it was easy to get away. I raced home to western New York, where he was to be buried. The entire process was a continuance of his life, as though the Great Practical Joker simply had to wring this out into one last gasp of anguish shared with all who loved my dad.

A woman who knows me and knows we do not believe in cremation asked me how I could let that happen. Without explaining, I was rude and told her to butt out. I never tinker with a dying man's wish. And I don't tolerate anyone who presumes to provide that guidance to me.

On the day of his funeral, I ordered flowers from a great florist who had a minor problem … one I did not know about at the time. He was a binge drinker. I arrived to find his wife frantically trying to "finish" my arrangement. I waited an hour, and she was in tears when she handed them to me. I told her it was okay, that I understood. I didn't lie. I hated it, but I did understand perfectly.

I drove the 40 miles to the place of the funeral, late, where the funeral director had not yet located the urn. It was lost in shipping. I tried to ask how that could happen. The funeral director treated me like any other inept moron and was deliberately vague. But he assured me they would get it there.

The funeral started late, shortly after the urn arrived. When it did get there, it came absolutely without ceremony, or even dignity, enclosed in the strange little pine box (like a tiny orange crate) in which it had been shipped. It was smaller than a shoebox and came complete with handling tags, address and postage markings. Did I say it arrived without dignity?

A pale, sweaty little man with a spade, in a brown suit with black shoes and white socks went up to the place directly in front of Dad's marker. He eyeballed the little box and quickly dug out a chunk of dirt in front of the stone, leaving a hole just large enough for the box but not really deep enough to hold the box and the dirt. He placed the box in it and topped it with the chunk of dirt. The dirt stuck up obnoxiously, and the man was in a hurry. He stepped on it, jumped once and crushed the dirt into a less formidable chunk and tried to smooth it down.

When that clod burst, I could feel the bones in my chest break. It was the nearest thing I had to honest pain the whole day. I felt tears rush to my eyes. I was afraid I would cry. I thought about getting that guy by the throat and inspiring his social skills when a funny thing happened. That batch of tears stuck right behind my eyes. I couldn't see well, but I would be damned if I was going to let this get the best of me.

The day was not over. There had been an incident with my dad as a young man in Arizona, when a young pilot had been killed in a crop-duster accident. The coroner had signed his death certificate with a pencil, rather than a pen, a sin about which my father mourned his whole life.

"Hope someone thinks enough about me to sign *my* burial slip with a pen, he would quip from time to time. I had thought about this several times. When the driver of the delivery truck came up to me, as dad's next of kin, to have me sign for it, he offered me a pencil.

I took it … broke it … ripped the receipt out of his hands and signed it with a pen. And then I gave him the pen. And I cried. It was a wimpy, drippy, stupid flood of feelings. It was for me, to miss whatever he was to me, and it was for him, that he had swung so hard and missed so clean on the important things in life.

I loved my dad, but nothing about his family seemed normal. There was no sorrow, no mourning. Nice people came to pay respect, lots of honest, hardworking people who knew him and loved our family. What was left of his family was there … but there was no closeness. There are other indicators of unhappiness there I won't go into, but it is sufficient to say I have been back only once, to visit my Aunt Issie, the only person at that funeral who really loved him. And to visit his grave. I am ashamed to admit it … but when I went back, someone had to show me where it was.

It was while we were attending to Dad's funeral that I got the call from Germany with the news that Warrant Officer One Paul Kemp, my dear friend, had been killed in a helicopter accident.

WHEN FAT MEN FLEW

12

Illesheim, FRG, 1978-1981

Deployment to Illesheim, FRG

I arrived in Germany in July 1978. I went to Illesheim, Federal Republic of Germany, assigned to 2nd Platoon, C Co, 501st Attack Helicopter Battalion, the Ghost Riders. We were actually one of the old company-sized attack units. Seems as though we had 12 Cobras (modified G Models, called "S" Models now), nine OH-58As and three UH-1Hs. The airfield was located south of Wurzburg and between Heidelberg and Nuremberg.

I was assigned the MOS 100E, Cobra pilot. During my tour my "additional duties" were usually the *assistant safety officer* and the *COMSEC (Communications Security Custodian)*. My career goal (my choice of aviation warrant officer specialties) was to become an aviation safety officer. There was no way I could become an aviation safety officer until I had the school, so I volunteered to be the keeper of classified documents and be the errand boy for the company safety officer.

Our unit was located south of Würzburg, in, Illesheim. It was part of the 501st Attack Helicopter Battalion with B Company out of Ansbach. Our wartime mission was supposedly to fly east on alert to fight armored forces moving our way. The obvious truth was that armor would be hard pressed to get past any infantry in our area due to terrain. We expected to be sent up around Fulda to do what we did best— kill tanks.

I was a catch-all junior warrant officer and did a lot of odd stuff. As a new AH-1 pilot, I was expecting to do a lot of gunship training, but in those days it just did not work out. I was experienced in the OH-58 and the scout mission, so I did that whenever I could. But the primary issue of the Cobra in those days was that these were mostly rebuilds from Vietnam, old D model Cobras upgraded for use in Europe. The bigger engine helped; the transmission was "ball peened" to strengthen the operating limits for a bigger load, and the tail rotor was bigger. However, they added a hundred pounds of wire and equipment, so the increased power did not yield much in the way of improved performance.

During this time they discovered a problem with the rebuilt Cobras. The transducers, electrical sensor transmitters that were supposed to transmit readings from transmission or engine to the cabin gauges, would be rendered inoperable in a good rainstorm. So we had a long period when we did not fly as much as we might.

Bad Moments

I had a few unique experiences while flying in Germany, and all my real challenges were in the Cobra.

One day while pre-flighting a Cobra for a flight to a distant firing range, my pilot noticed a broken safety wire on the top part of the transmission. He had a TI (technical inspector) check it out, and the TI thought it was odd but determined it was a wire flaw and not an actual torqued bolt coming loose. He rewired it, and we took off.

That evening after we landed, and after the throttle was rolled off, the blade swung around about four times and stopped. I had noted an increased torque reading but had no indication of problems until the main rotor blade just stopped. When they took the magnetic plug (designed to collect metal shavings from the transmission oil) out of the transmission, they discovered it was filled with shavings. The Cobra was in the final stages of transmission failure, and we got off easy. The normal catastrophic failure had been avoided and the training continued with one less aircraft. No damage and no injuries.

During another training flight, as I was out with my favorite IP doing tactical training, we hovered around a large field of small flowers (mustard?) and did some tactical maneuvers. We pulled pitch to take off from a low field and had an engine failure; we landed beside the only tree in a mile. When we shut the aircraft down, it was obviously hot and acting oddly. Those little flowers had plugged the engine intake filters solid. We discovered that everywhere we had been on that field looked as though a large vacuum cleaner had cleaned off the flowers in a long path. Another lucky day ... no damage, no injuries.

On another flight, a day departure, night arrival from a distant field site, I was lead of three Cobras. I had done a careful map recon, and I had been briefed on the various high-tension wires, which are always a problem in Germany.

The Cobra is a tandem seat aircraft, one pilot fore and one aft. So you could not just glance over to see the map. I was the pilot, not the navigator on this flight, and I kept trying to get my navigator to pinpoint our location, with the intent of avoiding wires.

The flight was uneventful and the aircraft were operating perfectly when the little hairs started up on my neck; I did another check with my navigator. We were actually on an administrative flight, so it did not matter so much. But I turned on my landing light and aimed it ahead. I probably had altitude enough to miss them, but there they were—high tension wires right in front of us—and we all started chattering instantly while gaining more altitude.

Even today, when I have bad aircraft dreams, that is the dream I have. I never had a crash or near miss that really haunts me. But wires ... they are sort of like a giant spider waiting in its web ... to gobble you up.

Career Development

During those days—1978-1982 and beyond—there were three specialties warrant officer aviators could choose, in addition to their pilot duties.

Instructor Pilots (IPs), which included a variety of responsibilities such as company, battalion or brigade level IP, instrument flight examiners (IFEs) and specialty trainers in various aircraft.

Maintenance test pilots, which would generally include qualifications in all the aircraft in the unit and extensive maintenance training.

Aviation safety officers, a specialty requiring the officer to track and stay current on the Army safety policies for training, explosives, petroleum handling and all other operational and hazardous materials tasks.

Now in the real, competitive, aviator world, when everyone is a pilot, something needs to reflect the "value added" in a warrant officer to ensure his promotion. He is trying to display his skills as well as become more proficient. And I did that, too.

I had made up my mind that safety was my thing. I was determined to get into the US Army Aviation Safety Course (USASC) at Fort Rucker and get a safety officer assignment on my next rotation. I was a sort of assistant safety officer in the unit, to demonstrate my interest, and I was always volunteering for odd stuff to show some other skills. So I was also the unit COMSEC (Communications Security) officer, and I enjoyed it.

Education Requirements

There was a catch-22 issue for warrant officers. The educational requirements for promotion continued to increase after the Vietnam War ended. When I got to Germany, the requirement for promotion to CW3 was associates degree in any discipline. Like all warrant officers with an eye to a career, I spent my entire tour in Germany trying to improve my skills and better myself for promotion. Better to have more than settle for the minimum required.

In those days, warrant officer promotions were awarded to aviation warrant officers in this order: CW2 after two years in grade as WO1, CW3 after six years in grade as CW2, and CW4 after six years in grade as CW3. I made CW2 in 1978, CW3 in 1984, and CW4 in 1990.

I arrived in Germany a fairly new CW2. I had worked to achieve a promotable advantage in my education by the following subterfuge. You can scorn the method, but the degree was achieved from a real university, and a single promotion won in this fashion seemed to justify the effort.

I had taken a number of significant courses at:

Arizona Western College, Yuma, Arizona. I had obtained a real year of college before my experience in the USMC, covering courses such as math, algebra, some calc, vocal music, English, and physical training. Music appreciation was especially valuable.

USMC Correspondence School for binary math and correspondence NCO Academy. I had also enrolled in but not completed a correspondence course in electronics repair.

Embry Riddle Aeronautical University (an icon in the aviation community) in things such as aviation history, flight planning and the E6-B Flight Computer.

Eagle University (another icon in the world of awarded credits for "life experience," including sponsorship by half a dozen local colleges) in gardening, accounting I and II, technical writing and the like. I cannot tell you how valuable the gardening was for my career.

BYU correspondence course in the Old Testament, New Testament and, I think, a course on the Book of Mormon

New York State University (NYSU External Regents Degree Program) for a summary evaluation of my odd credits and life experience, my end-of-course exams and their award of 36 hours for successful completion of the Graduate Record Exam.

End-of-Course exams were available and were a quick way to gather credit if you could pass the tests.

At NYSU, when you enrolled to obtain a particular AA degree, you sent money. You listed your name and a copy of every course and grade you had from every school you had ever attended. They charted this information on a sort of "bank account" form showing what credits you had and what you needed for your degree. I had already achieved this before my arrival in-country.

ILLESHEIM, FRG, 1978-1981

The next stop was the local Army Education Office, hat in hand, to apply to take whatever end-of-course exams I could pass that would help me get my degree. You and your education counselor would estimate precisely what you needed to graduate. When you took all the exams you could find, you would then submit the documents for an evaluation. They would tell you exactly what you needed to graduate, and you could choose end-of-course exams, other special exams or the courses necessary.

So I submitted my completed requirements. I had already completed my Associates of Science in Sociology. That degree had placed me ahead of my peers in required education. But it wasn't much.

In 1978, when I arrived in Germany, I was a young warrant officer busting caps to advance my career by any means. When I had pretty much recovered from Paul's death and settled into the unit, I headed down to the Army Education Counselor to see what he could see. This guy was different … and he had some enlightening insights for me.

The most important one for me, seeing how I wanted so badly to get a Bachelor's degree, was that the NYSU program had a Bachelors program, and part of it allowed 36 upper-level credit hours for a single test. That test was the Graduate Record

Exam (GRE), and passing would bring the achievement within reach for even me.

That counselor did a more detailed evaluation of my educational status than my previous education guru. I had to choose between some of the softer degrees—history, English, sociology, and a few others. It did not take long ... sociology was my pick. He started lining me up for some advanced end of course exams, which the Army gave me without cost. When we thought we had enough other credits for this degree, he signed me up for the GRE.

The GRE was a specialty test used to measure the knowledge of a person attempting to enroll for a Master's Program. I took a leap of faith to invest the study-time and the money. But I had a bizarre plan; if it worked, I would be crowned king.

NYSU sent me a little summary showing the topics of the test and the percentage of questions on the test. For example, 15% on modern prison science, 10% on certain social issues, 8% on inner city cultural problems. (I am writing this from a 35-year memory, so give me a break if it seems sort of weird. It *is* sociology, after all.)

I got the index of the Encyclopedia Britannica and copied every reference topic, then copied everything listed under each topic.

I had created a 200-page study-book of the most boring data you ever heard of. The test was all multiple choice, and I planned to give it my best shot. I even considered postponing the test once, but my deployment schedule was too hectic, and I took it straight away. It was stressful. And it was cheap. And I passed. The contact there asked if I wanted a Bachelor of Arts or a Bachelor of Science, and I told her she had to be kidding. I took the Bachelor of Science and framed it before they could change their minds.

My education counselor was ready to run down the road with his hair on fire. He had never persuaded anyone else to do it, and he had sort of limped along lining up courses for students who came from the local line units. *Now* he had an example, and his business trebled. I never told him about my little book; he just thought I was a genius and got really lucky. The other guys, though, actually wore that thing out.

Germany Instrument Ride, April 1979

Every year an aviator had to renew his instrument qualification. The only one equipped for instrument flight was the UH-1. In fact the instrument simulator was called a UH-1 SFTS (Synthetic Flight Training System) and was actually a simulated Huey cockpit. It was the same model we had used in flight school. The simulation center was located in Heidelberg.

The simulator consisting of several Huey cockpits was
next to a controller's console. They were each mounted on a
hydraulic platform about 10 feet above the floor. It moved,
sounded and felt more or less like a real aircraft with no
reference to the horizon except for instruments. The controller
at the console normally gave all the radio clearances, flight
following and GCA instructions during the flight. Usually.

Now, all Army rotary wing aviators were UH-1 qualified, and
we were required to get most of our annual instrument training
and check rides in the simulator. But we were required to fly a
minimum number of flight hours each year to maintain currency.

Whew. So I arrived in-country as a new CW2 (well, I
had been in grade for a year, but I was a brand spanking new
AH-1 driver). I had spent the previous six months learning
all the rules and regs for ICAO (European flight rules) and all
the local airspace rules and checkpoints. I had our local IFE
(Instrument Flight Examiner) grill me on the rules and regs,
and I was marginally catching on. As a Cobra pilot I hate
instruments anyway, as every good Cobra pilot should, and
the IFE, well, he was trying to be helpful and *not eat me*. He
was concerned enough to discuss my progress with my platoon
leader. I was never very excited about instruments, and he was
not very optimistic about my upcoming ride.

ILLESHEIM, FRG, 1978-1981

April, my birth month, came along. All renewals and semi-annual rides are scheduled on your birth month, and I got a date for my instrument ride. If I weren't proficient, I was determined to at least get my training without someone chasing me to do it. The simulator was far away ... a long ride. My platoon leader, a captain who was proficient and respected, was going my way and offered me a ride. He was a competent, capable guy who had made a life hobby out of fixing old BMWs. He was going to do his bit to grill me on my training while we were enroute to the simulators. He was trying to be uplifting and still give me a sort of informal oral exam. I was still pretty raw about my flight school instrument training experience, and I had dark visions of this informal grilling on my ride to the simulator. He might be good, but he was not an IFE, and this grilling might not be profitable, especially if he, my rater, took this to heart in an adverse way. Sort of like a conflict of interest.

I liked him, but I was not ready to kiss this guy, if you know what I mean. He did not know me well, but he had been getting an earful of my faults from the platoon IP who had made this new CW2 into a personal project. He was going to polish my skills if it killed me, and it became ugly. I knew the captain had heard unflattering commentary from my IP about me, and it had been often and frequent. I felt as though these discussions ranged widely from my personality to my professionalism with just about everything else the

IP could throw on the fire. I had been harassed by this guy on several rides, all resulting in a pass but with zero flattery about my proficiency.

In the meantime, I had started riding with various IPs around the unit, and I kept doing well. My favorite IP got sort of nasty; I was in his platoon, and I was stepping outside the lines. I put on my arrogant attitude and demanded a surprise ride, *which happened that day.* I was very happy to pass it, but he was embarrassed, and he continued to harass me. I demanded another unannounced check ride by another IP and passed *that,* and now the chain of command was trying to figure out if I were a troublemaker or if Strick (my IP) was trying to be even more arrogant than usual.

As a good platoon leader, the captain was concerned about lots of stuff, but for me, his newest charge, he was more worried about the instrument ride than the rest of it. The theory was that we could handle all the personality stuff in house, but the instrument proficiency had to come first. We had lots of tactical aircraft to fly, but the limited fuel load simply did not allow much real instrument time. So whatever we could get, we took.

Anyway, my captain told me I could not ride up to the simulator (seems as though it was in Heidelberg, 90 minutes away) with the Instrument Flight Examiner (IFE), because it would be a conflict of interest. *He* would be giving me a ride up, and by the by, *he* had an instrument ride that day, and *he* would be my copilot, and *he* would help me successfully fly this test, "S*o don't worry, Dan, 'cause we will get it all done.*"

I was pleased by his confidence and his personal interest. He was not convinced I was the brightest bulb in the box, but he loved my Marine Corps attitude. So after a month's encouragement and mentoring by this guy, we met and did our 90-minute ride to the simulator. We discussed all the fine points of instrument flight he could think of, and we arrived just as the IFE got there.

He was a nice guy and did not appear ready to pounce on me. We had a relatively thorough oral exam, and I did okay. I was feeling pretty good. The captain, who presumed credit for my success, was still concerned. But as my copilot, I could count on his alert nudge in the cockpit to keep me focused.

Then the IFE dropped the bomb. *He* would be the copilot, and *he* would be acting as the instrument flight following. Now, normally, the IFE sat in the jump seat behind the pilot; the copilot sat in the left seat, the pilot sat in the right seat, and the flight following was conducted by a specialist sitting at the console.

The IFE then announced the captain would take the first ride; the flight following would be entirely internal, and I would be second. I would be alone. With *him*, the illustrious, all powerful, confident IFE. The captain moaned but remained silent. The IFE then told me I could take a break. He told me to go relax and get some pokey bait.

Unbeknownst to them both, I grabbed a headset and sat at the console below the simulator. I listened to the entire flight. I watched the monitor displaying the flight path, and I saw the entire ride go south on the "holy shit" express.

The captain started out well, but he turned the wrong way on an instrument approach, busting airspace, and not recovering because he did *not* realize he had turned the wrong way. As he flew off into the ozone layer, I had more dark visions of my own career.

Suddenly, the captain came to life and tried to correct the ride but failed. And the flight was terminated early.

They came down out of the simulator and the captain looked … well … awful. He sat down near the console, wearily, without a word.

The IFE called me up into the simulator. I still don't know who I was that day. I planned it. I flew it perfectly. I flew the pattern perfectly, I made the approach perfectly in spite of an emergency procedure, and he gave me an engine failure on short final that went right out of the book. I made the calls, timed the time, danced the dance and sang the song. I had an awesome showing, and I could hardly contain myself. But I shut up.

ILLESHEIM, FRG, 1978-1981

I climbed out of the cockpit, and there at the console was my captain, wearing my headset. He was slumped down in his seat.

We drove home in silence. Usually on a trip like that, we stopped for a McDonalds or some special (rare in Germany) treat, but he was not in the mood. I had expected another ride with my difficult IP friend, and I happened to mention it to him.

"Don't you worry about him. I will take care of that."

Every new guy must overcome the new-guy status in his new assignment. But my entire place in the unit changed that day. The captain and I got along famously after that. My OER ... the Officer Efficiency Report ... was good. My "new guy gets the coffee" status seemed to be upgraded. And when there was any required unannounced rides scheduled in my platoon, I got half of them.

I never failed one of those unannounced rides, but my favorite IP complained about it every time. He later became a very good friend. But it took awhile.

In the End

Years later, Strick was the IP in an Apache when he landed with a student pilot, and the tower alerted him to smoke coming from the engine. When he touched down, the student panicked and dove out of the front cockpit. He kicked the cyclic … overpowering the pilot's cyclic due to mechanical advantage, and the tip-path plane knocked off the forward apparatus on the nose of the Apache (TADS/ PNVS).

The commanding general made loud and rude public comments about pilot error, and Strick retired. His family fell apart; he moved to Florida and committed suicide.

The issue in this tragedy, I believe, is *resilience*. The Army is a political game, and every now and again a soldier (pilots more especially seem stuck in the image game) will make a mistake. It could be in his personal or professional life. When he does, he has to suck it up, deal with the consequences, and move on. Strick's primary problem was his lack of resilience.

Strick actually did nothing wrong … he was just there. The accident board investigation can point out the error, the accident, the complete lack of injuries (to his credit) and demand more training, more diligence, perhaps a change in aircraft procedures. But a gorilla could not have held that cyclic more effectively. He was misled by the warning from the tower. The aircraft was not actually on fire, as he was led to believe; the student was panic-driven by his own fear, and Strick landed safely. But he looked pretty foolish when the TADS/PNVS was knocked off, and I am certain that his personal pride was crushed.

I believe that with his professionalism being publicly criticized and his family disintegrating, he could not bear it. I was his friend, but not a pal. He did not come to me. He had lots of options to get help, but he simply could not bear to ask. Just another ounce of resilience might have kept him sunning on the beach or fishing off south Florida.

The Army does not teach resilience very well. We lost him when he retired. But we let him destroy himself for pride. Anyway, he was my friend, and I miss him.

15-6 Investigation in Germany

In Germany around 1981, a young captain, the commander of the maintenance company of 501st Aviation Battalion, had departed country to return to the good ol' USA. Now, as commander, he was responsible for every nut and bolt, every aircraft, and every tent peg in the company. He accounted for that stuff on a hand receipt. The dirge of all commanders is the confounded, blasted, good-for-nothing-but-headaches hand receipt, and his hand receipt was not ever cleared. The hand receipt is a monster, and all of it, every piece, is signed for on subordinate hand receipts. That is a lot of paperwork in a 300-man company of mechanics, pilots and miscellaneous staff. That says to me that, while he was supposed to be clearing up his paperwork prior to departure, Headquarters probably had him jammed up doing every dirty detail in the battalion. His replacement was already here, you see, and so *obviously* the outgoing company commander had nothing better to do but busywork details for the battalion commander.

Anyway, the hand receipt had never been cleaned up. It was a lot of money. It was important. But no one bothered to help.

The company commander's supply sergeant should have finished it … but no such luck. And I was certain that all those subordinate hand receipts were around somewhere. So, the new commander refused to sign for the "missing" equipment. The supply sergeant was just not gonna get out of his chair. And after dragging their feet for several months over $7,000 worth of missing equipment, the battalion commander called for C Company 501st (we were a separate company at a separate location) to conduct a "15-6" investigation (pronounced fifteen dash six). I was assigned the job.

The investigation for equipment that is stolen, lost or missing for some reason uses a "15-6" form and is called a "15-6" investigation. It is a dreaded method of financial accountability amongst the officer corps, though any hand receipt can be run through this process. It is used to account for the public's hard-earned tax dollars.

This investigation was to be conducted in Ansbach, Germany, about 20 miles away from Illesheim, my unit location. Since I was tasked to do it and I had regular duties of my own to perform in my unit, my platoon leader was concerned that I do it quickly and get back to work.

The first thing I did was advise him I would need at least a week. It was pure speculation made in a bold attempt to impress him with my newfound importance. He did not act as though he heard me. He was adamant that the hand receipt could not be accounted for, and that I was to stamp it and return it. Something was said about "a mission passed is a mission complete," and I was suddenly inspired to dig in. I thought at first he had been smoking some sort of funny weed. It was like talking to a tree. I spoke, and he responded like the wind through the leaves. He barely heard me. I told him I would advise him each day. He babbled on about my being back in a day. But when I left the next day, he knew better.

Being no expert in supply accountability, I went to my own supply sergeant, a superb watchdog of our own company hand receipt, and asked for his counsel. He was a good NCO, and he had some good comments.

He advised me to make a working copy of the hand receipt but not surrender the original without someone in charge signing for it.

He told me to determine what they had found and what was missing item by item and use a pencil on the copy.

And he told me to start searching the work site. The minute I got there I should start to look around and be obvious with my wandering eye.

Sounds simple, but … you just had to be there.

My sergeant was pretty savvy, and he understood that the new warrant officer could be a hero or a villain here. The sergeant was surprised some senior NCO had not been given the task to work with me—to sort of hold my hand, I suppose. But I had been a Marine NCO, and I was listening carefully.

"Be coy to start out," my supply sergeant said." Yer their pal, gonna help them stick it to this chump what lost it all … and they will hate to be embarrassed by something really stupid. Remember, you're clearing up *their* paperwork … and while you are busily going over it with them, look around casually for some significant "missing" piece of equipment. Look for something kinda big … obvious. Nearby, you will find other missing stuff too. Then don't let up until the real keeper of the property (the knucklehead who is actually in possession of it) 'fesses up."

He continued, "The commander *never* really knows where his equipment is. Just too much stuff. That is why we have all these little hand receipts. This '15-6' is just someone unhappy with the captain, and he is trying to let the system whack him."

He looked quickly down at the receipt with a steely stern look. His expert eye missed nothing.

"Who," he asked indignantly, "would steal *four old buffers*? See here … nothing is high value … just a lot of little stuff. Nope … this is just a set-up to sting him."

So I drove to Ansbach without calling ahead and found parking. I had to walk through a couple of barracks and noted a lawnmower in the front foyer. I was sure it was a missing item, and it was not secured in an authorized area.

I went to the supply room and found my soon-to-be-favorite supply sergeant holding court around his supply desk. He was surprised, but he had been told I would be coming. I chatted a bit, asked him about the hand receipt, which copy I conveniently pulled out for his perusal, and he shook his head sympathetically.

"No," he said, "I *told* him to clear that thing. We just can't find any of it. He did not listen to me."

He tried to act offended like an NCO whose service was not truly appreciated. But it seemed as though he wanted vindication.

I asked him if I could look around, and he was immediately on guard.

"Well," he said, "the new commander isn't here right now."

I had to pop his ego early. I did not need to talk to his new commander.

"Gee ... that is too bad. See, I am the 15-6 officer. Here... my orders." I flashed out a crumpled sheet of paper before his suspicious eyes and returned it to my pocket.

"Say ... how about Private *Snuffy* (who was standing there). Let me take him, and he can show me around. I won't be in the way."

I smiled and winked at him.

"And I won't take anything I can't carry away."

I had his attention now. His eye furrowed into a focus heretofore unknown in his current assignment, and Private Snuffy, my suggested guide, was confused.

"Oh yeah ... by the way ... I saw a mower back there parked in the foyer." I nodded back toward my entry. "I did not look, but I bet it is part of the missing stuff ... see here?"

Sarge looked directly at me. "Now, sir—"

"Say ... lookie there ... the captain has lost four buffers. Whaddaya suppose he could do with *four* of them?"

"Sir?"

"*Sarge* ... keep up with me here. I cannot remember the last time I saw a captain stealing a floor buffer with 10,000 buffing hours on it. Hell, I solo'd on one of those things in flight school."

He said nothing, but his demeanor showed concern. He was trying to look indifferent. I suspected this was the look he gave his most recent, hand-receipt-holding commander. But I could see his neck getting red.

"Now ... Top." I looked at him innocently, but this was a sort of slap. He was only a sergeant. The term "Top" is usually reserved for a master sergeant or first sergeant, someone with authority. Someone who makes a difference.

"There are four sleeping bays and day rooms in the barracks. There are four missing buffers. Whaddaya suppose we might find over there?"

"Sir, why don't I go along." Not the enthusiasm I had hoped for, but the offer was priceless.

"Hey ... thanks! That is a swell idea. Say, didn't you say you couldn't find that stuff? Oh ... and tell Private Snuffy there to take a seat. You need someone to answer the phone, and I want to go over there unannounced."

"Well, Sir ... you know, I didn't actually look for that stuff myself."

"*No kidding.* Well ... that's okay. I get it. I haven't actually looked over there yet, either ... and you know, I could be wrong about this stuff."

So, the hesitant sergeant came along. He tried to take point, but I stepped out first. I did not want to be led on some sort of treasure hunt.

The first barracks was right next door. We no sooner got the door open than I saw it.

"Say, Sarge. Take a look at that."

The very first thing we saw was a buffer in the middle of the floor. It had a missing serial number tag, to his great relief. But unfortunately, it had all the markings of the unit that was missing one of those buffers. And the next two buffers had numbers matching two of the others missing on the hand receipt. I decided I would let the sergeant find the last one.

"Holy cow!" In a closet, I had spotted a pile of tools.

"Sir?"

"Now, look at all those tools. No tool boxes, no manuals … but lots of pieces. That just stinks. I bet there are some sub-hand receipts out there we need to find … you know, just to document these things. No sense letting them lay around."

I went home. He went to work.

Next day I came back. He was rather pleased that he had cleaned up part of the hand receipt. He was very unhappy when I informed him that today, a bright and shiny (rare day in Germany), we were going to the flight line to do some more searching. It was, after all, an aviation maintenance company, and the flight line was where the maintenance company did most of its business.

It didn't take long. We found a battery charger, a couple of specialty tools, and a bunch of brooms. We found conexes (large container boxes the size of a 2 ½ ton truck) with tools … gas cans … TA-50 (field issue) items, and more.

I pulled my now-favorite sergeant aside, out of earshot of his minions. I explained to him that I was done playing. I was not sure and did not care who had put this together, but he had 48 hours to figure it all out or I would prefer charges on him.

"But, sir …"

Poor Sarge insisted he had nothing to do with the hand receipt before the captain left … and I told him that not only did I not care, but that he was the supply sergeant assigned before the captain's departure. Sarge was still the supply sergeant, and this was his problem. I mentioned that his boss, the new commander, and his battalion S-4 (supply) would be able to provide sufficient motivation if he could not manage this. Further, I would file charges of fraud in the number of things I had already found and could show intent to do harm to a good officer. Even further, if the number of hand tools seemed to be inordinately large, I would investigate the possibility of theft, and the dollar amount seemed to warrant felony charges.

Two days went by. I arrived to find a pile of items with fresh hand receipts per item ready for my inspection.

Now, I was only a CW2, so my swagger would only work on a sergeant. I knew I could not dictate actions to the battalion staff, but I might create an idea and make it *their* idea. So I wandered over to the battalion S-1, the admin officer.

I sat down with that hard-charging lieutenant to point out the obvious. I was sure the battalion S-4, a major, might not smile on my work, but I had enough issue with this file to clear the captain of wrong doing. I asked if he might take this paperwork and make it gone. If not, I would be willing to see the battalion commander and tell him what I thought in person.

The lieutenant took the paperwork into the commander's office and came out empty handed. He thanked me for my time and told me the hand receipt would be accounted for without delay. And did I need anything else? Yes, would you advise my commander of what I had been doing for several days and release him from accounting for this work? Yep. It was a done deal.

I got a post card from the grateful captain.

The card wasn't worth $7,000, but it was from the heart.

Change of Commander

During my tour in 501st, I had a commander who was infantry. He was a stallion, good looking, arrogant and a man who loved all who would walk the edge for the unit. He was a Vietnam vet, decorated, had a gorgeous wife and perfect kids. We all loved that guy.

He did a lot of stuff to spark the unit including jabbing the commander of B/501st in Ansbach, our sister attack unit, and we did a lot of friendly competition stuff.

Well, the commander there was another stallion, and he was as arrogant as our boss. He suddenly got cancer … and he was gone. I am not sure how he turned out.

Then one day, our commander was gone. He is still alive today and living in France, but he is out of the Army.

This is one of the rumor things the Army does … and it left us all stunned. He had been up for promotion to Lieutenant Colonel, and rumor was he had pinned an unauthorized medal onto his official photo uniform. The care and work attending to every thread, every detail of a uniform for a professional photo for a promotion board … well, there are people paid to ensure it is perfect. I believe it was a Bronze Star with combat V. It is too important to be a mistake. At any rate … it could not be allowed.

I was very disappointed in this, a sort of act of cowardice. Loyalty is my forte… a good commander is a wonderous blessing to any soldier. And he was well respected. We all missed him. I cannot even remember who replaced him.

A Little Problem

Some of my family stories are uncomfortable. This is one of them.

My youngest son came running up to me at church all excited because his brother had fallen down on the floor and would not move. I expected Jeff, my oldest, to come running up, but he did not, so I went into the bathroom and found him curled up on the floor.

For your information, German toilets are probably three inches taller than their American counterparts, and a little boy looking to do his business had to really work at managing that elevation, even on his toes. I never gave it much thought until this moment.

But I was a careful and patient dad. I tried to do some very personal training beyond leaving the seat down for Mom. Little men have surprising issues. I have seen little boy back-pressure. Heck, all my boys could squirt a frozen rope across the toilet, and that initial release of pressure, why, you never could tell just what the impact zone of that little jet could look like. Especially when some careful effort is required for a tall German toilet. So I taught them some rules. Pardon me if I use common artillery terms.

First ... wipe off the firing platform (rim). Cleanliness is next to ... well ... you get it.

Second, stand in close and tip toe to the rim. The more elevation you achieve, the better your options during the operation.

Third, get a firm but gentle grip.

Fourth, stretch that little pecker over the top of the rim and aim carefully. Elevation and windage should be carefully considered. We can't make this a career, now. It is quick, painless and necessary.

Last ... fire a test round. Do *not ever* release that thing to the full-automatic mode until the target has been *acquired and properly engaged.* Initial impact should be obvious to the casual observer.

Be prepared for the unexpected. In event of a "lost round," carefully squeeze it off until the next attempt. Adjust fire immediately and try again.

The unexpected straying off-target still requires immediate follow-up. Cleanup is *not optional.* We do it always forever

... and just to be certain, we take an extra wipe to be safe. I always felt it was terribly tacky to leave a bathroom with urine sprinkled on the toilet seat.

Now, in this, my special and very personal instruction, some specific issues were never addressed. For instance, German toilet seats are made of oak ... heavy, durable and ... well ... intimidating. They are bigger than American toilet seats. Anyway, the issue of falling timber and its associated injury ... well ... it was never brought up before. Heck. It never occurred to me.

Anyway, the basic technique in this instance was clear-cut. Stand in close and do your business, keeping a firm grip on the aforementioned pecker and a sharp eye on the target. You must ensure that the impact zone is *in* the toilet.

It turns out that this toilet seat, one of those large, German, oak-painted black lids weighing at least 20 pounds, would not stay up on its own. It sort of teetered upright for a moment, then would fall down with a heavy clunk. I recognized the problem in a second, scooped him up and headed for our medical facility with visions of vastly diminished numbers of progeny dancing in my head.

The doctor there saw us immediately, but was sort of choking back her giggle. She coughed and stammered something conciliatory.

"Well … I just am not equipped with this sort of plumbing …" and she called in a (male) physician's assistant. They made a picture … with my little son, pants down; they peered at his tiny manhood further shrunken by his trauma. He had stopped crying, but even *he* felt the complete lack of dignity in his injury.

They conferred.

"Well …" She coughed. "It isn't broken."

I was incredulous. Suddenly she figured it out. I was mad as hell, and this was going to go ugly early if she did not pull something out pretty quick.

"Look, you watch him a couple of days. Bring him back Monday. Sooner if he has problems. We can send him to Nuremberg (Hospital) to a urologist if there are any other issues. I don't see any bruising." She paused and looked over at him sympathetically.

She seemed to let out a little shiver, and as she winced, she subconsciously closed the thumb and index finger on her right hand until they were almost a half inch apart. Then she drew a deep breath.

"And frankly …,"She paused deliberately. "There just isn't much to look at."

Suddenly it was funny, and I started laughing. Soon we were all in stitches, trying to comfort little Jeffy.

And except for a few careful baths, there were no side effect except for a little flash of what I call … well … *PTSD*.

The very next Sunday, his little brother Donny was preparing to perform *his* aim and squirt when Jeff ran over, yanked him away and yelled, *"Watch out Donny*! That thing *bites!"*

Branch President

During this time I was active in my faith, and I became the founding Branch President of the little Illesheim Serviceman's Branch of the Church of Jesus Christ of Latter-Day Saints.

There were a number of special moments during my nearly 18 months in this calling. Since the Church of Jesus Christ of Latter-Day Saints has no paid clergy, I stayed busy all the time. And so did my staff. I was not very good at it, but with my church, my career efforts, our three children and being away from her parents, my wife and I had a very hard time. She actually left before my normal departure date, and I was not sure how well we would recover. To her great credit, we did, and we enjoyed our following year at Rucker.

The church had a great relationship in the community, and we were appreciated for our practices. Our habit of not smoking or drinking made us unique, but our work ethic and integrity were a great command asset. The Army treated us with great respect.

CW2 MIKE FOLEY

Mike Foley Missing In Action—the rest of the story to this date, 2021

Remember, Mike disappeared more than 40 years ago, and if my chronology is slightly off, the events are real. But do not write me to tell me I am cuckoo.

In 1980 I received a call from Sharon, the sweet wife of my pal, Mike Foley. She had been visiting stateside, and Mike had remained in-country to work a border assignment. The first Sunday in February 1981, Sharon called him to tell him she would be back and then learned he would be out of country for three weeks. They agreed she would leave school in April and return to Panama, then, to join him.

Mike departed on a recon mission along the hostile border between Peru and Ecuador. It was some sort of assignment designed to keep the peace between two difficult neighbors. The crew and aircraft disappeared over triple canopy jungle somewhere on the flight route along the border. At that time, they were the only missing aircraft since the Vietnam War. There was no foul play suspected, but a final radio call indicated they were having trouble maintaining continued flight.

There were a lot of odd questions I learned about quickly.

It was an odd crew.

The PIC (pilot in command) was CW4 Sooter, a former Vietnam POW of seven years, if I remember correctly, nearing his retirement.

The regular crew chief of that aircraft was deathly ill on that day, so a Special Forces crew chief who was visiting the unit volunteered to take the flight.

WO1 Mike Foley was the copilot.

There was also $15,000 on board, I believe to cover some sort of payroll.

This is one of those spooky mysteries that just keeps getting spookier. The helicopter went down on February 17th. Sharon returned to their quarters in-country in April. She remained there for a year before they finally declared him dead.

Sharon later went to Washington DC to discuss the incident with the Army. According to the officer she saw in June 1981, the Army had conducted a second and third search with nothing to show for it. There was no evidence to believe Mike could still be alive. They marked him "presumed dead" as of 18 February 1982. They backdated it, but he had already been promoted to CW2 in his absence.

In 1981, my family and I picked up Sharon as she returned in-country and took her to Utah. Then she flew home to Fort Campbell, Kentucky.

So ... now it gets weird. I don't need to hear about the little men in white coats. This all happened to me, and I can document what I report.

Some time in the interim, I happened to go to Fort Campbell on a safety inspection and was billeted in a hotel in Clarksville, Tennessee. I went out for a run one evening, a normal routine of mine. I experienced a sort of epiphany ... a vision of some sort, and it was not one I was prepared for.

Mike and I had been very close. We had discussed his marriage and his career often, and we were fast friends. Sparing you a lot of the detail, in this experience—this vision—I spoke to Mike, who asked me to take care of Sharon. I was pretty quiet, and when it was over, I started to run again, when it occurred to me I should ask where he was. I sort of summoned him back, and I was shown the aircraft. It was three-quarters overturned onto its right side, skids up, crashed onto a slope in heavy growth. I could see that the slope was steep, and it seemed I could get the lay of the land viewing it from above. Then it was gone.

I immediately made extensive notes and put it in my journal. I stewed over this for a short time but decided to write a letter about this and send it to the USASC (United States Army Safety Center), Fort Rucker. I was afraid they would chalk this up to hysteria, and my career would be in jeopardy. But Mike was my pal, and it was my integrity.

I have since learned that the United States had an old program (supposedly abandoned now) studying the merits of a sort of telepathy, called remote viewing. I have only speculative knowledge of this program, which is now treated with contempt and derision among intelligence sources—government funding sources in particular. But when that program was disbanded, the participants of it became able to discuss it freely and produced the modern documentary copyrighted in 2019. It is called Third Eye Spies. *It can be found on Amazon Prime. If you search for details of telepathy or remote viewing, you will see this program name hidden and camouflaged amongst bizarre and unbelievable tales of the strange and stranger, space invaders and the like. Any sensible, rational person may be put off by this radical idea, but this documentary must be watched to appreciate its implications. I can only say if I do not know all the mysteries, I am convinced that there is too much truth here to be ignored.*

Anyway, it seems it was about two months later when I got a call from the forensic pathologist at USASC. He had received the letter, and I braced for the usual questions a shrink asks a wacko, but I got nothing of the sort. He was very happy to hear from me, explained that they had *actually found a couple of aircraft this way*, and he wanted all the details. I told him all I could, and I promised to send him a copy of my journal drawing. He hung up with the promise to call when Mike was found.

Now, I had met this pathologist earlier in my career, and I trusted him. I had been impressed in a class he gave once, where thinking outside the box led him to discern the cause for an accident. He had been the only dissenting vote on the accident investigation team and the USASC denied his version. To me, it was the only logical answer. So, as you will see, when he contacted me years later, I wanted to hear his comments.

I was a new CW3 at this time, and I was making my own career as an aviation safety officer. I had a reasonable name, and I stayed in touch with folks around the Army and at the Safety Center. In the Panama Canal Zone I had friends who kept me up on rumors there. As these friends moved around the Army, they would periodically let me know this or that in reference to the accident. But nothing much ever panned out.

Over the years, I heard lots of stuff.

I heard a rumor that some old salty dog had recovered the engine identa-plate (a small metal tag attached at the time of manufacture, with identity and model number, date of manufacture and brand), from that Huey engine. I tracked the guy down, and he denied it all.

I heard Mike was in hiding, teaching somewhere in California, in some sort of witness protection affair. I couldn't find him. But anyway, crew on the downed helicopter had no reason to intentionally disappear. The Green Beret crew chief had a new baby, and Sooter had already paid full measure for his well-earned retirement as an old POW. There was never any logic in that idea that the men wanted to vanish.

The money was not really enough to steal, and the Army supposedly placed a $100,000 reward on the aircraft, a fortune to any peasant in South America.

Around 1990 I was having dinner with a friend—an officer, a mover and shaker guy who was being marked for advancement. He was a West Pointer having just made the LTC list, and I happened to tell him this story. He casually said it was too old. I asked what he meant. He said to me that the aircraft was found, but it was too old to go down there and spend money to retrieve and investigate.

I asked him what in the hell he was talking about.

"Oh yeah, we found it a year ago."

I looked him dead in the eye and asked him quietly if he might want to advise the *wife*.

I choked back all the other questions, but he was stunned when he realized the gravity of this comment. He got up and left. I saw him next day.

"Dan, you're not going to believe this." I knew what was coming, sort of.

"They are denying it ever happened (that the aircraft was found and then not investigated). They are telling me I am mistaken. I went to look up the records and there are *none*. Only the PRAM data are still listed. The accident investigation files are missing."

(Let me sort out some of this "Army-speak." The Army Aviation Safety Center uses a computer to compile all the data of every accident. The Preliminary Report of Aircraft Mishap, or *PRAM*, is the first abbreviated report submitted to the Safety Center after an accident. It lists the name of the participants, the aircraft number, type, date and mission—the bare bones description of the accident, the level of damage (Class A, B, C, D or E) and the assigned accident number for future reference.

I made calls. He made calls. Nothing. I called Sharon and asked if she had heard anything. Nothing there, either. Another mystery. But there is more.

A little while later, my pal the Major came into my office and closed the door. He was nervous. He said he was in the basement near the burn facility they use to destroy classified and outdated papers, and he looked and discovered this on top of the files. He asked me not to attach his name to this, and then he threw a pile of papers onto my desk and left.

It was the full investigation of the first complete search for the site of the accident. It seemed to be the entire paper report. And it is not like any investigation I ever saw.

First of all, they never found the aircraft. They sent in a battalion of Peruvian Infantry to do the search, and they sent in some helicopters to look around. This is pretty rough stuff in triple canopy jungle. The troops suffered a significant amount of frost bite and were pulled out as soon as they could be retrieved safely. The weather was terrible, and the search aircraft seemed to fly in when the fog lifted and left when it came back. In other words, they looked where they could, but they did not find anything. They *did* find an airliner on one mountain. It had apparently flown at the published altitude on a very poorly marked flight chart when the plane suffered contact with a mountain top and had never been found before.

The last radio transmission of Mike's plane was listed. A map was in there, but there is some doubt that the crew knew their location. And the name of the town they said they were near ... well, there were several towns in the area which, in the South American tradition, are named the same—something like St. Marie, stuff like that. There was known to be a lot of fog around, and it was common knowledge that the UH1 had to follow valleys along the way and climb over ridges in passes where it could get under the seasonal fog.

I was able to do a terrain analysis showing the most likely places they had to cross. It was simple enough. The high places had the thickest fog most of the time. So the passes that cut across the mountains were generally where they had to cross, and the crews were familiar with them.

Still, no real answers. Taking all I knew, including my drawing of my visionary terrain map, and all I could learn and all I could find, I xeroxed a page of a map with a tiny "x" marking my suspected spot. And it sat in a corner for 10 years.

The last chapter of this story (so far) occurred around 1994, I think. One day out of the blue I got a call. It was from that forensic pathologist, who had retired in Ozark, Alabama, five miles from my home. He made sure I was the CW3

Kingsley he wanted, and then he asked me over. He had been sick, very sick apparently, with equine encephalitis. It had left holes in his memory, but he remembered Mike Foley, and he wanted to discuss the case. I had my little page with my little "x" on it, and I set it on the table. He took one look at it and jumped over to it, demanding to know what *that* was.

He pulled out *his* little map sheet, with *his* little "x" on it. They were nearly identical.

To this day, the aircraft is still missing. If I could find some hope in it, I would squander a fortune to find it. I actually called "Unsolved Mysteries," and they laughed at me.

One last strange story to go along with this. One of the other pilots flying the same missions Mike had been on is rumored to have located the downed aircraft but then was unable to find it again. I cannot find any documentation to support this. He was CW4 Tuttle, who was later reported missing on a mission in Grenada.

Death of a Soldier's Wife

I was notified on 9 Nov 79 that Tamorah H, wife of my COMSEC NCO, Sgt H, had died. She was 17 years old, six months pregnant and seemingly healthy. I am recalling this cold; I cannot find my written record.

ILLESHEIM, FRG, 1978-1981

I was notified of her death in the late afternoon. We had left work on time, and Sgt H had headed home to an apartment on the economy in town. He found her deceased in bed, he said. I did not really understand what he was saying. He was not himself. She had been sick, he said, but she was fine this morning. I was asked to accompany him back to his quarters to confirm identity of the body, which I did.

We were immediately joined by the unit physician, whose name I cannot recall. The doctor started acting strange—professional and all, but obviously rattled and checking all the circumstances. I identified the girl while the doctor started examining her. The doctor tried to find a knife, but she finally settled on scissors to remove the fetus; As far as I know she did not detect any life, and I am not sure if she took the baby or they took it later. At any rate, I did not witness the surgery.

She got me aside and asked me how the couple was getting along, and I told her they were a sweet young couple, newly married and expecting. She asked me to stay with Sgt H until they had determined it was a natural death. It worked out that the autopsy could not be held until after the weekend. I told her I would put him up but I would not hold him unless I was ordered to. The 1st Sergeant and I maintained contact with him until this was all settled.

Sgt H rode back to my place and walked over to the PX-tra where he had previously ordered a new stereo. He carried it to my house and asked to set it up in the living room. Then he took it down and told me he wanted to go back to the barracks. He went there, was put in a room and allowed to set up the stereo there, and then take it down again.

I think the autopsy was not conducted until Monday, and the bruises the doctor had seen on the body were only the post-mortem pooling of blood after natural death. The young woman had died of pneumonia. And Sgt H was free to go.

The mortician was a creepy but friendly guy ... tall, thin, gray complexion ... long boney fingers ... the stereo-typical image of the undertaker. He made a big point of showing Sgt H that the baby was perfect, and that they had placed the bodies together in a nice casket with a tiny baby outfit for the baby.

I noticed there were several odd-looking photos in his office. Turned out the mortician had been involved in body identification in Vietnam, and he noticed my interest in the photos. He showed me his work. Seems if you have a perfect photo and a precisely sized x-ray of that head, you can lay them together and they will look like a shadowy face, with all the parts fitting. All other things being equal, that was considered proof of identity. His negatives were all overlaid on pictures in a slide so they could be slipped onto and off the picture … very interesting stuff. Spooky, but interesting.

If I remember right, CW3 Stan Berg and I flew the widower to the hospital at Heidelberg with his bag. He was united with the bodies (wife and baby) for the trip to the USA.

Stan and I knew the weather was bad, and we left very shortly after dropping off the bereaved young man. Almost as soon as we departed, we punched into the clouds and did an emergency instrument landing. When we called to advise the commander, the only thing he said was our funds would cover only the room, not any partying.

After going home after the funeral, Sgt H was returned to the unit, and we stayed in touch for many years.

The Scardest I Ever Was

I spent a career as a line-unit attack helicopter pilot, AH-1 (the Army Cobra gunship) and OH-58 (Army Kiowa scout helicopter). For the layman, that means I was always in a company-level attack unit, and when we rolled out for a war mission, I was flying.

I spent my career in one of the quietest periods of our US Army history. Compared to some old timers, especially old Vietnam pilots, I did not rack up a lot of flight time. It was a cold-war, peacetime Army. My first assignment after becoming a Cobra pilot was to the Federal Republic of Germany. At that time, we were working all the bugs out of the new engine and transmission sending-units on refurbished old Vietnam G Models Cobras. If it rained, they were not dependable, so they spent a lot of time on the ground. I got a lot of OH-58 time to get my minimum flight hours.

During this period, we were transitioning from the old Vietnam G Model Cobra to the S Model. That means that in upgrading the old Vietnam Cobra, they went through the Mod, the Prod, the ECAS, the Modified, and finally the finished S Models. It was the Jimmy Carter Army, and we did not have a lot of faith in our upgraded equipment. I can give you examples, but the gist of it was that this lack of faith in the equipment weighed on us when we had a mission—any mission, including the range, an alert, or any sort of unit movement.

Keep this in mind while I try to build the story for your genuine understanding of my cowardice.

One of the clear questions on the mind of a young, aspiring soldier is, *Do I have enough courage? How much do I have? How much should I have? How do I measure it?*

That soldier may not ask this openly, may not even think of it directly, but every new act, every new action in his career

270

requires some nerve to get through it, some resolve to be successful.

Any new career progresses through some steps. In the case of a military career, first comes the thought and discussion of entering the service, then the preparation, if necessary. Then the enlistment or the contract—some recruiter makes his pitch and paints the picture of rosy success, free time, spare money, free room and board or battlefield prowess, glory and manly recognition. Following that, the new soldier commits to a period of time during which he will serve. Then he or she completely surrenders to the military orders dictating his life.

Still he will wonder, *What is courage?* In my case, all this adventure was easy because my upbringing was completely dysfunctional. The Marines was just … fun. Anyway, you figure it out. Then I joined the Army.

For this treatise, courage may be a completely separate issue. But today, I am going to describe only the scaredist I ever was. There is bound to be a connection.

I have been startled; I suppose that can be scary.

I have had a bully threaten me. More than once. But it was just a bump on the road of life. Sometimes there were lengthy periods of stress over it. That is all.

I have been afraid my misinformation has caused harm or injury to others. The responsibililty can be hard to bear. But not really frightening.

I was in a head-on collision accident (not my fault), and once I was crushed against a loading dock. But these happened so quickly that instinct took over. I was lucky, but not really afraid.

Then I once had a transmission seizure in flight. If it had completely seized it would have caused an inflight catatastrophe that would have killed me and my copilot, but we managed to land, and only then did I get scared. It was not traumatic, but it was so important to me that I always checked for those issues afterward.

Once I was flying lead for a flight of three; I mentioned this experience earlier. I had flown a day mission enroute to the range, and I was certain I had marked, measured and checked route and altitude of all obsticles, especially wires and towers. I led the return flight that night, but something was wrong. I had felt a chill in my bones, a sort of sixth sense warning. I turned on the landing light. Dead ahead were wires I had missed … dangerous, tall, high tension wires. We were easily able to avoid them. I felt real fear that time. I was really scared, but it was not paralyzing. It was not terrifying, but I never forgot it.

ILLESHEIM, FRG, 1978-1981

And there was the time I had an engine failure at night, riding with a man who felt very little professional duty to me. As I wrote when I described it earlier, I was very scared and felt very alone. Very scared indeed … so scared it took me a couple days to shake it off. I had not only felt alone in that emergency, but responsible to make all the decisions. This was real fear. I did well and landed safely. But I was ashamed when they gave me an award for it … because I did not dare tell anyone how scared I had been.

But that was not the scaredist I ever was.

Once, at an Italian beach, I became convinced my little son either had been kidnapped or drowned. For 30 minutes, I lived in that hell where only parents who have blinked in a child-watching moment can go. Then we found him. It was terrible. He had run away, and a fluke kept him from our view. I never let it happen again. I did not even kill him.

Anyway, finally this is it. *Fasten your seat belt.*

In the late 1970s, there was a terrible angst between the military forces of East and West Germany. While I was there, as a US Army Warrant Officer aviator (Cobra pilot, flying the aircraft most expected to engage enemy tanks on the ground), I met a West German Armor officer. He was a hungry wolf, an experienced armor officer familiar with his and our tactics. He was smart. He was candid.

He engaged in our conversation as the polite host-country's representative. He spoke correctly, and he was polite but clearly was tolorant of Americans as only a well-supplied (but combat-untried) ally, not necessarily a battlefield asset. He spoke with me as a courtesy, only as an American on his side, perhaps as something that might provide him a battlefield advantage, but without any enthusiasm for our skills.

I happened to bring up the rancor between East and West Germany, since it seemed to be a catylist for American tension, and I asked just how bad it was.

He coughed up a hollow laugh. He adjusted his tankers badge, with the crest of the tank on it, with its gun pointing to the right side.

"See that?" he asked.

I nodded.

"If there is a war, we do not worry about the Russians. We can beat them. But the East Germans ... they are very good. We hate them. *Their* badge looks exactly like this ..."

He pulled off his nomex gloves and pointed a boney finger deliberately at the tank on his badge, with its gun pointing to the right side.

"*... except their tank is pointing left.*"

ILLESHEIM, FRG, 1978-1981

Now, I never was able to see an East German tanker close up, but this conversation was chilling to me. It means nothing now, but the preparation for war in those days was real. And serious.

The C/501 AHB lived with our families in a little kaserne (army camp) in Illesheim, Germany. The normal procedure in those times was that when the East Germans or the Poles or the Russians or other Commies started rattling their sabers, our families would pack up and be sent to the rear, wherever that might be. We would deploy and assume defense of the front line. Just in case.

Normally, alerts were just practice. Regular practice alerts would be whisper-announced the day before and sounded around dawn. For the command, all practice alerts had to be correct and proper. We would all rush to our helicopters and depart into the local countryside around sunup. There we would land, have breakfast and wait with our aircraft for an "all clear" and an RTB (return to base) radio call.

In the meantime, back at the kaserne, our families would all go through their part of a mock drill (which allowed the unit to bring all the admin paperwork up to date). They would all sit around the company headquarters drinking pop and eating bratwurst … and maybe get on buses to go to battalion headquarters for some sort of briefing.

But one evening, around 2300 hours, we were called
out on an unannounced alert. There had recently been some
ugliness by East Germany, and so we were sort of anxious, but
not really worried that it might get serious. Anyway, we started
playing catch-up and thinking about all the administrative
issues of departure—gas, beans, bullets.

This unannounced alert meant we would have to go out
into the black of night flying night-hawk (without any night
vision aids) and find the LZ (landing zone) in the dark. We did
it periodically, and someone in each platoon would normally
sneak out and plan the route and the parking plan details at
the FARP (Forward Arm and Refuel Point) in each holding
location. But this was unannounced. Even the vets who knew
the area had not been out to check the latest condition of the
LZs. It was just another factor in the stress.

Before departure we had to get our support crews loaded
up on the airfield and ready to move out with vehicles, tents,
gear, grub and gas. We then would meet each platoon at the
designated FARP site. All that went pretty well, but we were
not rested as we usually were. We were all tired and grouchy.
It was late, and we were already tired from a full day of duty
… not like the usual alert where we woke early for the mission
and went out rested. So it felt rather out of step from our usual
routine.

When our ground support was loaded for the road march, we all headed for the aircraft, parked on the airfield within 500 yards of our quarters. We waited on our little runway, and the airfield lights were burning. There were no operational problems, and there was no plan to low-boy the aircraft under maintenance, so we cranked and lined up ready to go. We maintained radio silence, but everything was well lit, and we all knew the drill.

Now, we had a couple of other combat units on post, ground units. And any time there was a serious alert, all of them could clear post rickitytickity. They could be out in the woods and under cover with little delay.

In addition to my attack company (C Company, 501st Attack Helicopter Battalion) there was an infantry battalion (1/6 Infantry) and an armor battalion (1/13 Armor). These folks had fool-proof procedures to get off post that were neat, orderly and quick. After all, if a tank drives off the road, they wave an apology and drive on. Helicopters require a bit more caution.

Anyway, we could completely clear post in record time if there was any hint of panic or real-world ugly around us. There just did not seem to be any of that, but the entire flavor of this alert was different. So we were still edgy.

The platoon leaders finished their brief and mounted up. We all knew we were leaving but were still unsure of our initial stop. There was no other flight traffic, and we were radio silent,

so we self-cleared and took off by platoons, flying stagger
left. I was chalk 2 in 2nd platoon, and we pulled pitch just after
midnight.

Suddenly, out of the radio silence, there came that quiet
voice that chills your blood, that prepares the group for
something they must deal with. That is what aviators do …
when something terrible or not fully understood pops up …
when you are trying to keep your cool and summon the grit to
face the problem.

"What the hell …"

That is all he said.

Below us, as we departed the active runway that night,
the airfield perimeter fence was illuminated clearly as a row
of tanks (M-60 A2s) rolled up to the gate at full speed.

I was thinking, *This is not the gate they usually take for
their departure.*

They did not even slow down. They drove right through
it. They tore out a quarter mile of fence and headed off into the
German countryside.

We were, each one of us, in one breathless moment, sure we
were off to war. Every aircraft commander was calculating the
same issues I was. We had not re-armed … we normally did that at
the range or in the field. We were topped off, and each of us had a

C-ration (combat meal). We knew we could expect a mission brief on an immediate move and a full reload when the FARP was set up. We needed a mission and a plan, and we needed it now.

Suddenly I could feel pain that shot from my navel to the small of my back. It was nerves, for my family, my world, my unit, my buddies. I did not think directly about any of these things. I just put my head down and pressed on. I was committed, I was ready, I was willing. Behind my seat I carried a little home-made survival kit; I suppose we all did. It had a shelter half, a tiny stove, a few fire pellets, an extra can opener, some water-proof matches, extra batteries for my flashlight, and a few stale snacks because I had not replaced them for several months. I carried an extra half-blanket and a sweater separate from my kit, in case I had time to get them all out of the aircraft after an unplanned landing. And I had filled only one of my two canteens because I was stupid.

I could not identify what I was feeling in my gut. I was sure it was just a bad porkchop.

I was wearing the Army-issue aviator flight survival vest with various cool stuff. I fished through my flight vest and took an antiacid I had squirreled away. It did no good.

We landed in a dark LZ, and we kept light discipline, so we sort of stumbled around to find the camp after parking. Someone whose bowels were more insistant than mine had to crap, so he simply did it in the very dark ... open parking area. It was embarrassing to see it out there next morning. It was a miracle no one stepped in it. Just one of the minor inconvneniences of combat.

There is more. Recently, we had transitioned from two-piece nomex flight suits to one-piece. They looked cool, like Air Force flight suits, and we all felt more macho. But the major disadvantage to them was ... wait for it ... if you had to relieve yourself, you had to be sure the top half of your flight suit was out of the impact area for the turd (the venerable "lost round") you were bound to deposit on the ground. From time to time, someone would come back into the tent with the tell-tale stink of ... you guessed it ... lost round. When someone had a lost round in the dark, it was very challenging for all in the tent.

But ... it was all for nothing.

Back at the airfield, a new tank platoon leader in the 1/13 Armor had lost his gate key. He was the guy who led the tank platoon to the wrong gate, and he ordered the breach of the airfield perimeter.

Actually, if he had found his key, he would have had to stop in front of his platoon, fumble with the lock using the wrong key, and still drive through it anyway. He would have been the unit buffoon. You just cannot lead a tank platoon if you are the buffoon. It is easier to be the leader even if you make mistakes, if you can make the tough decisions.

So doing that macho thing and ripping out a chunk of fence during an unannounced alert ... well, it worked out for him. It was the macho thing to do, fearless leadership that inspired his platoon. Except for the statement of charges presented to him, which I believe were dismissed by his battalion commander.

Even a battalion commander understands the merit of image.

I do not remember any pilot discussion of that moment until we returned from the alert. We all laughed about the idiot who tore out a quarter mile of fence. And true to the aviator creed ... not a dang one of us mentioned being scared.

But now you know the truth.

It was the scaredist I ever was.

The Annual Ordeal of the Christmas Tree

The annual ordeal of the Christmas tree happens every year. I write this in the month that is the season of the tree. This is the moment. It builds until it cannot be put off much longer. My family prepared for it as soon as the mom brought home the Thanksgiving Day turkey, and the children seemed to relish the anticipation which goes with the speculation. Every year, they asked more of the same questions. For example:

"Where will we put it?" (I wonder why Mom has cleared out the same living room corner with the anchor bolts in the wall again this year.) Or, "Gee, where will we get it?" This is a legitimate question, since the yearly finances determine how lavish we intend to be. Or, "How big will it be?" As though we might get a 20-footer just so we can get it home and cut it to fit. Or even chop it down so we can tie it to the car and get it home. "Will we all go out and cut it down again, or will we buy it on a lot? Or will Dad finally break down and buy that artificial tree he always swears he's going to buy *next* year?" You should know in our family, Dad is the cheapskate who always growls about the money. Mom is the hero who drags out the decorations and lines up the treats for our night setting it up.

Well, it is tradition. Do you remember that old song from *Fiddler On The Roof*? Well, this is the real stuff ... tradition, the sort your children remember forever. And the more the story changes, the more it stays the same.

In 1979 we flew home from our Army post in Germany to my in-laws' home in Holland, New York, for Christmas. The kids were all abuzz about the tree, which Grandpa Fancher always picks out at great pain. He has a rotating tree stand, so ya cannot simply hide a flat or open spot against the wall. And his eye for perfection included all of the process, from selection to mounting and trimming.

That year Uncle Jay (my wife's brother) had found the "perfect tree" while out deer hunting a few years previously. He swore it was so, and somehow, Dad Fancher relinquished his sacred duty to this assertion. Could Jay still find it?

"Why, shoooore." Uncle Jay drew up his belt and snorted. "We'll crank up the old pick-up and haul the kids over to the really rough terrain before we start out afoot. We'll have to walk a bit to find it, but it should be no problem."

This from the same guy who, as a kid, had taken me camping on a rainy weekend with a "waterproof tent." I am still not sure why we bothered putting it up.

So now, the bad omens started piling up like cordwood. From the moment the idea fell from his lips, it snowed. What we did not know was that this snow was to set a record for twelve hours of snow in Buffalo, a record that still stands. It was a quiet, heavy, wet snow, the kind that captures your voice when you talk, that makes it difficult to speak over a distance of more than 50 feet and be heard. The snow didn't even squeak, it was so wet. By the time we were ready to board the truck, you could see less than a quarter mile.

Uncle Jay forgot to mention his rusty old truck hadn't been started all winter, but he had a freshly charged battery ready. When he discovered the battery in the truck was flat, he hauled out his spare. The truck was an old Chevy flatbed with a 396 engine, and even with another fresh battery, it still had to be jumped to get it started.

We moved out with three little kids, my wife and I, Uncle Jay and Grandpa. Grandma, anticipating the need of her skills in a blizzard, decided to stay behind with Nicole (my youngest, age two) and Donny, age three, and have the hot chocolate at the ready. We were pretty excited when we crawled on board and had a really fun and bumpy ride for a couple of miles. Jay drove up as near as he could to the tree, but we then had to march over hill and dale for more than a mile to find it.

Well, by the time we stopped, the temperature had dropped like a stone. It was fun for a while, but as the snow piled higher and the cold sank in deeper, the fun became an effort. Soon we were packing the two youngest, and the fun became an effort, an effort that became drudgery. The kids were cold, the fun was gone, and Grandpa was puffing up and down those hills like the Little Engine That Could. We found a scrawny thing that Uncle Jay declared to be the perfect tree, and I was stunned. But we were too far into this, and so we all gathered around in a shivering circle, and even Grandpa, exhausted, pronounced it

"The Perfect Tree." We chopped it down without another word and started back.

We got that thing to the truck just about dark. We were cold and wet and tired, and just plain fed up when we got back. We didn't put it up for two days.

But do you know what happened? We hung our wet clothes over the living room furnace and shivered around the warm kitchen table, where the smells of a Christmas supper were a joy to all. We snuggled happily as the snow fell, the wind blew, and snow piled up, and the fire was toasty. Grandma, always the wise one, had the chocolate hot and the marshmallows and cookies ready in huge quantities for the family. We sat in the kitchen expounding happily on our adventure until dinner. Then we had ham, sweet potatoes, candied yams and pies… mashed potatoes and gravy, strawberry shortcakes … and love. Tons of it.

When we speak about that wonderful Christmas tree of 1979, well, we hardly remember the cold. What we are really talking about is the love of our great family in that warm, wonderful kitchen that night. Grandma was our hero, welcoming us back into our warm home. And the only food we remember is that wonderful hot chocolate and marshmallows.

Application for Promotion to Captain

When we returned from leave, I was very busy trying to improve my active-duty career. The Army rewards education, but they do, strangely enough, expect excellent performance on a professional level. So when Department of the Army Warrant Officer Branch published a program promoting W-2 or W-3 to captain, I jumped on it. And while I was still trying to build a warrant officer career, I started filing the avalanche of paperwork required by the promotion board for captain.

The program required the endorsement of my immediate commander and his commander. No problem ... I was hot on all the requirements. I met the time in grade, just now met the educational requirements, and I got my commander to write a great endorsement. His boss, the battalion commander and the brigade commander were laid on easily, and I thought my packet was going to be great. But as soon as I got it, I was especially disappointed with my battalion commander's comments.

Allowing me a bit of poetic license, he basically indicated that of all the warrant officers in the Army, I certainly was one. His actual comment was a slap-sided compliment in slang, and I asked my immediate commander about it. He tried to sooth my feathers and said it would be fine.

So I planned to become a captain, but in the meantime I was due for rotation to the States, and I had to apply all the rules for normal warrant officer assignment. Off I went to Fort Rucker, Alabama, for Warrant Officer Advanced Course and Safety School.

In the meantime, I learned I had made the initial cut and was on the list of the final hundred applicants. Only 50 would be selected from these for promotion.

My wife and family had left a couple of months before I did. When I went back to the home front to visit with her parents, we enjoyed a month of leave before going to Rucker.

WHEN FAT MEN FLEW

13

Fort Rucker, 1982-1983

I arrived at Fort Rucker for the Advance Course, but I was still expecting to make the grade of captain.

Captain's Promotion Board

Advanced course was fun, and it was easy. No long hours. I did not party the way of the average warrant officer, but I loved being with my family and having time at home.

In the meantime, the selection of the captains board was widely anticipated. Starting about four or five days before the published release date, men started getting quiet calls in the night from this colonel or that general, or some former commander, who in spite of confidentiality could not restrain their congratulations for the upcoming promotion.

But there were a number of us who heard nothing. Then the day of the release, and *still* we heard nothing. Then the days after ... and still nothing. None of the loud promotion announcements or newsletters that normally follow such a lofty accomplishment. Just that same stony silence that comes from a silent fart. Silent but deadly. Everybody laughed, but it was not funny.

Some of them took it better than I ... but I finally blew my stack and started calling around. You would have thought I was calling the city dog pound ... courteous, non-committed answers with no purpose. The personnel office knew nothing. G-2 couldn't tell us. The schoolhouse chain of command was adamant that they had no knowledge. I finally called the Department of the Army Warrant Officer branch, and I spoke clearly to some old warrant officer's secretary. She was incredulous that we had not seen the list ... and she promised to fix it.

I was sitting in class when someone came in and gave me a tattered little yellow slip of paper instructing me to go to an old abandoned barracks building on the edge of post, to a dusty room, in a darkly lit corner where no one ever goes. A GS-1 would be there. I did not believe government employees existed at that basement pay grade, but I was hopeful she was the clerk and not the janitor. She would return our packets.

"And, oh by the way ... please tell the other guys" (so I won't have to hunt them down, it seemed to say).

So after the day was over, the flag came down and, before dark, we all slinked down there ... got our packets ... and silently went back to the Army. We were all offended, not because we had failed but because there was a dark shadow of shame in it.

This was the single most important direction of my career.

Now, I know how lucky I was. Let's face it. I would have been a mediocre captain at best ... I mean, I might have done well with troops charging up a hill ... but the politics of peacetime commissioned service would have wrung me out. As it was, I barely managed to complete a warrant officer career without getting my butt handed to me in some one-armed politician's paper-hanging contest. I was a very good warrant officer without political talent. (Oh yeah, I was handsome and irresistible too ... according to my daughters.) Anyway, after a few more years of service, I learned that I was happy as a warrant. Happier than I had any right to be.

I was actually spared the really bad news, the news of the career I had planned in my future. Most of those guys who were selected, good as they were, and most of 'em were gooder than I—(*I know, I know… but gooder is the best word I can find.*) they got kicked out at the first and second selection boards of their commissioned career. I knew only one who was promoted to major.

It turns out that the life of old former warrant officers … what I mean is … old warrant officers who were suddenly captains … pretty much sucked. Not only did they suffer the indignity of non-selection at the end of their faithful careers, but they had to endure all the social and professional growing pains of soldiers who took this path to a commission. You see, there are a couple of normal paths to a commission.

One is West Point, a wonderful school attended by young men (and now, women) bent on a military career of leadership—some mentored by family or friends, some just bone headed enough to go.

Another is ROTC, a college program that leads to promotion to lieutenant when the student graduates.

Yet another is the enlisted commissioning program, in which an enlisted man with promise is allowed to go to the Officers Commissioning Course, or OCS.

Then along came the Warrant to Captain program.

FORT RUCKER, 1982-1983

With a few notable exceptions, the unspoken preference for career promotion is:

First, most (but not all) West Pointers are offered more significant career options and promotion favorable to their status. These are rewarded for their exceptional training and the devotion to duty required to accomplish a West Point degree. For example, of the three artillery battalions in the old 101st Airborne Division, one was for West Point leadership only; the other two were for the rest of those seeking artillery opportunity.

Second, the majority of Army commissioned officers are from the ROTC or other college programs. Many fine leaders are often able to show enough talent to achieve great success from this start.

Third, the OCS option is a wonderful opportunity for enlisted talent, but it is limited by two factors:

a) They are selected for OCS later in their career and only very exceptional leaders go far if they are old.

b) They have not been born and bred with the military career incentive of their fellows. Not many of them can show the talent of leadership and the burden of political correctness to go to the top.

Fourth, the Warrant to Captain program now comes into focus. I do not believe it was continued after the first two years of its offering. I never gave this process any thought when I made my career move toward a commission. Good as they may be, these warrant officers are behind in the competition for career trajectory. Though tempted by the potential opportunity, they start late in their career. They are already old. They are specialists in aviation and not able to branch out like normal career officers.

Advanced Course

Germany had been a very busy field assignment. Fort Rucker was an easy time, good for family and good for me. Advanced Course was ostensibly to teach a mid-grade warrant officer to be a better officer and refine some of his stock-in-trade skills. Warrant Officer Branch often attached an advanced school to this training, and in January 1982 I was slotted to attend the US Army Safety Center, right there at Fort Rucker.

While in the course I was given a research assignment, and I not only liked it, I did it well. Someone complimented me, and I became insufferable. Then I picked my topic for a writing assignment … on the '67 Arab Israeli War. It was a topic I loved; I did it well, and my head became swollen. This was my first real opportunity to research and write for some sort of credit.

Then I was able to lead a staff study on the OV-1 (Martin Baker) ejection seat, and it looked darn good. But when I tried to pass it uphill, some schmuck at the Safety Center weighed in and declared that I, a no-count warrant officer (a captain reject yet) ... had invented the statistics. The Safety Center was clear ... the paper was a fraud and the conclusions were delusional; they dismissed the study outright.

Fortunately, during my research, I had contacted CW4 (Mike) Novesel, the son of Medal of Honor winner Michael Novesel, who had gotten me those stats, and he verified that they were correct. I raised the dickens about it, but nothing happened. I was, on the surface, ignored as a fraudulent faker, and I moved on.

But it was not all wasted. The following year, that study ended up as the foundation of the evaluation of the OV-1 in Washington DC. Eventually the old OV-1 was retired, but not because of the ejection seat. It turned out that the Marten Baker ejection seat proved flawless within its own limits. It never failed except with pilot error (ejecting upside down at 200 feet, for example).

When the Advanced Course was complete, I had some time to kill before my Safety Course, so I asked to go to the Directorate of Combat Developments, DCD. I was sort of mocked, but I was offered an opportunity to write the first aviation Nuclear, Biological and Chemical Warfare (NBC) manual. I was given 90 days. It was a pain in the neck task, and they couldn't lose by letting me try.

I completed it in 60 days, including photos, and was asked to write an article for publication. I scrawled it out in crayon on toilet paper and carried it down to the Army Aviation Digest. Dick Tierney, the editor there for decades, picked it up, polished it off and published it. I then wrote another article which became Article of the Year 1984 ... and from that day on, every three months, I had an article published for the rest of my career. Dick took them all, and he sent me an award certificate or more with each one.

And I was very arrogant about it.

USASC

I finished Advanced Course and went to United States Army Aviation Safety Course, USASC. I loved it. I always had it in my head to be in accident investigation, but as my career went on, I never had the political contacts to pull to it off. I got to serve on various accidents (when the Accident Investigation Board pulled me in during their investigations at various line units), but it was nothing to brag about, and I was not a permanent accident investigator. Later I spent about a year as a snowbird there at the Safety Center, just running errands and even trying to write articles for them. But I suppose I just did not show the right stuff.

14

Fort Lewis, 1983-1986

Fort Lewis, Washington

The most exciting and successful part of my career came
along when I was assigned to Fort Lewis, Washington. After
the Safety Officers Course at Fort Rucker in 1982, I was
assigned to B Company, 214th Attack Helicopter Battalion as
the ASO (Aviation Safety Officer). We were one of those new
"company-sized battalions" that were developed to fill out the
Calvary Brigade, Air Attack (CBAA) organization.

Technically, this was the transformation of the standard
Attack Company of 21 Cobras and 12 OH-58 Scouts in three
platoons into a small Attack Battalion of 7 Cobras and 4 Scouts

divided between three tiny companies. There was a lot of experimenting with the firepower and tactics, but the unique place of these tactics, the money, and all the stuff we did made for some very arrogant aviators.

I wish I could remember all the guys I knew and loved there, but some of their comedy was priceless. I was sitting in a briefing when new Warrant Officer Cobra Pilot (WO1) Bowlin began ragging on about some far away conflict that was not being resolved to his liking. We were discussing the merits and effectiveness of various weapons when he stood up, spit in a trash can and growled, "Why, hell men, give me a platoon of Cobras, and we will cause more destruction and havoc than the world has ever known."

Now, pilots are not just arrogant ... they eat their young. There was some smirking, but the young pilot was not intimidated. Someone finally asked him if he truly believed he and his Cobra could do more damage than, say, a tactical nuke ... and I thought he was beat. But after only an instant's hesitation, he looked around at his fellows, nodding for moral support, and growled again, "Given enough time ... and ammunition."

I thought the place would fall down with laughter. And I think he was offended!

Anyway, the 214th AHB was only one of the units there, and I was a young CW3 trying to make my bones. My specialty was safety ... and I was the Company Aviation Safety Officer (ASO) for fewer than 30 men. You should know here that in the aviation community, a pilot comment on some topic requiring expert aviation commentary did not dare mention the title or topic of safety without snorting and spitting ... to show his disdain for those cowardly types who might, for example, use a parachute before they jump out of a plane. Anyway, the macho men of aviation were maintenance test pilots or instructor pilots. So aspiring to any safety job was bound to be a job challenged by the peer group.

Career Progression

I was looking for a slot as Battalion ASO. It was a normal career goal, a position which I judged to be more suitable to my personal career goals. I had heard the CAV (3/5 CAV, or 3rd Squadron, 5th Cavalry) next door needed a safety officer. And one of our senior IPs, an old warrant officer, nudged me and said he had heard via the grapevine that the 3/5 CAV Commander, LTC Bob Harry, wanted *me*.

Me ... and as I thought about it, I did not blame him a bit.

I should have known this lying, thieving old pimp (we warrant officers can slander each other as appropriate) was just trying to stir the mud. I should have realized that like most old warrant officers—and especially instructor pilots—if his lips were moving, he probably was lying. How would the CAV Commander have heard of me? What would he know of me? But I spun up like an old wind-up fire engine. That old warrant officer did not just hook me, he gaffed me into the boat. He knew it. He musta' told that story a hundred times, about the sucker he talked into going over to the CAV.

On To 3/5 CAV

Now, I realized the CAV was the wild and woolly aviation unit on post. Their former ASO was renowned for his short timer's attitude, and his safety library was full of Louis L'Amour novels. I realized the work would be tough and the effort required would be challenging. I did not care … it was a step up, and I was ready. My buddy CW4 Rex Swartz (another lying, thieving old warrant officer) was the brigade ASO. I was certain he would have no objections and would recommend me for the job.

But I was at a real disadvantage. My swollen head instantly popped full like a little balloon inflated by a CO_2 cartridge. (If you ever saw that balloon fish in the fish tank in "Finding Nemo," you get the idea) I was beside myself.

FORT LEWIS, 1983-1986

The CAV! Wow! I hated to leave my easy, old unit, but duty called. Maybe I could get one of those cool CAV hats … the Stetson … and be a real cavalryman.

Next day I called the CAV adjutant officer, a little oriental lieutenant, and made the appointment for an interview. I was clear that the commander wanted to see me. I showed up there squared away and expecting a welcoming committee.

Instead, I met LTC Bob Harry … and my first meeting was, let's say, not very encouraging. The adjutant met me and asked who I was. He obviously had forgotten how important I was. And what time was that appointment? And what in the world made me think LTC Harry wanted to see *me*.

The adjutant sat me down in the hall in a chair, which I learned was placed so Harry could torment his victims at his leisure.

When LTC Harry walked into his office, he passed me in the hall with a sneer and shut his door.

After an appropriate amount of time, he called me in and, following a few questions, demanded to know why I did not belong to the Officers Club. *(Are you kidding me? Officers club?)* He made it clear, since I did not belong to the Officers Club, I must not be a team player. And he stated that if I was not a team player, I was not the man for this job. That was pretty much it.

And he pointed to the door. I know Bob pretty well now, and I cannot remember his precise words, but I am certain he said something relating to *not* letting the door hit me in the butt as it closed.

And I stormed out.

I was furious. I felt violated, bent and bleeding. I was peeved, and I marched my butt over to my own battalion commander's office and planted it there until he let me in.

He was surprised to see me, and to his credit, he listened to me politely. I started talking and did not take a breath for 15 minutes.

I was offended. I was mad. I wouldn't work for that SOB if he were the last commander on this earth … who the heck did he think he was, anyway? Oh, did I mention it was the CAV Commander? That son of a bitch. Did I say I had interviewed for a job over there? *Interview*? Heck, it was a hanging … a lynching … Why, I love this unit. I was just trying to exercise some initiative to make my way up the warrant officer career ladder. Besides, I don't belong to the Officers Club because I don't drink, and I cannot be that stupid without being drunk … *like so many dang Cavalrymen* … and I think I took the liberty to spit in the trash when I said it.

Well, he not only listened, he told me he understood. He chuckled as he went on.

"Initiative," he assured me, "may not always be appreciated in the CAV, but it is always welcome in the 214th."

He had his eye on me, he said, and I would be high on his list of consideration in the unlikely event the battalion safety job came up. And I did not have to worry. I would *never* have to go to the CAV and put up with Harry. He would recommend me to any who might ask. And he would smooth it over with the brigade commander and his ASO. I still had a job to do in C Company, and I could get back to it today.

I limped home and reported all this to my sweet wife, who listened to rendition #2 of this entire story. I am certain it got bigger, more bitter and more aggravating. Heck ... *this version* is, I am certain, more embellished than I care to think about. But she told me that *she* too would recommend me to any who should ask ... and she told me ol' Harry was an idiot for passing me up ... and she was also glad I did not do the drunk and stupid thing at the O' club.

There is one more part to this story. My old scruffy pal in the CAV Brigade Headquarters, CW4 Rex Swartz ... he and I had known each other awhile, and I knew he would want to hear my story. He got rendition #3 of this story, bigger and more frustrating than the one my poor wife got.

And suddenly, he started whining. Loudly.

The CAV needs a safety guy. The CAV needs a safety guy who is not consumed with Louis L'Amour. The CAV needs someone who is not going to bow to Harry ... the CAV ... the CAV ... *blah blah blah*. I didn't want to hear about it. Too bad, Rex. It ain't happening ... it isn't gonna be m ... .

Well, I suppose *he* didn't want to hear it.

It turned out he had all the cards. Dang it all, anyway.

I went to the field that week with B Company, and the first night out I got a radio call as I was making a night approach into a field site.

"Kingsley, go around and RTB (return to base) Fort Lewis. You are going to the CAV in the morning."

Holy cow, I was mad!

I radioed my company commander. He tried to care.

I contacted my battalion commander. He said he would talk to the brigade commander, and he tried to care. I contacted Rex Swartz, that dirty dog. He tried not to laugh at me. And the next morning I reported to LTC Robert E Harry, the god of the CAV.

Now, I may take some humorous liberties with this narrative, but I swear I walked into Harry's office, and it was all he could do to look up.

"I don't want you," he said.

Crap. What are you supposed to do after that?

"I don't want to be here," I replied.

"Go to work," he said, and he did not even watch me go.

This inauspicious beginning could not possibly indicate the relationship Bob Harry and I would develop over the next eight years. Remember, Bob Harry was (and can still be) a pain in the neck. But he turned out to be a damn fine commander.

I went over to the safety and standards office and spun up like a Hoover vacuum. I found the safety officer's desk, and I cleaned it out. I threw out all the novels and all the out-of-date pubs.

I went to CW3 Dave Klindt, Instructor Pilot extraordinaire and got my CAV briefing. He and CW3 Lee Murphy were the primary IPs there, and *they casually informed me that if I had not been brutalized by Harry in the first interview and passed the test, I would not be here now.* They both chuckled and told me they were headed over to the club, if I wanted a beer. Murphy and I go way back, so he knew about my drinking. But Dave really insisted on buying me a beer.

For the next four months, I worked from 0400 to 1900 each day writing, organizing, inspecting and fixing the safety program.

As a side note for all you techies—I bought a new Commodore 64, a word processor called Easy Script, and an elementary data base (with 64 K of memory). I had to figure it out and learn how to use it. I eventually wore out three Commodore 64s and two Commodore 128s. I ended up writing 23 professional articles and two books on those things. I made up a data base and hand-jammed all the data I could get on my pilots into the 64K computer. And I used that terrible but dependable Commodore printer with the elevated "p" and "y" above the line.

But I was cutting edge when I did it.

There are other stories about the CAV I will go through, but my safety career was made there, in the field, doing hands-on training and inspections. We passed two surprise and one scheduled Aviation Resource Management Survey (ARMS) inspections in three years, conducted from the Department of the Army level (which had to be some kind of harassment record), and we earned exceptional marks on each. LTC Harry then did what he did so well, after all his antics to test and try his officers … he showered my career with professional awards and training opportunities, and he gave me superb ratings.

Lest you doubt it … Rex is still a dirty dog. And Harry is still a meanie jelly beanie … but they are good men, and they did what they had to do.

Air-to-air

During my tour at 3/5 CAV, an Army Guard unit in Utah developed a training manual on helicopter air-to-air combat.

Now, helicopter air-to-air combat was basically unheard of at that time ... much as it is universally ignored today. It was considered dangerous ... risky ... unessential. Helicopters performed three basic functions in combat, and *none* of them was in the venue of air-to-air combat.

1. *Ground Support* (AH-1/AH-64 attack helicopters in ground attack operations)

2. *Heavy Lift* (CH-47 cargo helicopters in lift/supply operations)

3. *Utility missions* (UH-1/UH-60 using medium lift helicopters in ground assault and medium lift operations)

4. *Scout missions* (OH-58) were a subset of utility aircraft missions

Did you see the note there about performing air-to-air combat? Funny thing about that. Not only was it considered non-essential, the proximity in which air-to-air aircraft were required to train was considered unsafe. The maneuvers were regarded as both marginally allowable and causing excessive wear and tear. Worse, due to the flight limitations of our Bell fleet, there was real fear

307

that an aircraft could get into a "zero-G" (zero gravity) maneuver and be unrecoverable. Our teetering main rotor hub-type aircraft were unable to accomplish even the most basic zero-G maneuver. So, we would have to learn to conduct aerial combat without zero-G maneuvers.

Several instructor pilots at Fort Lewis, among whom were CAV IPs CW3 David Klindt and CW3 Lee Murphy, caught fire on this issue. I am very sorry I may not remember all the players, but I know these two. A small group of them became qualified to teach it, and they brought it home to I Corps, Fort Lewis. It was the experimental aviation combat technique of the day.

That was more than 30 years ago (yesterday to me). I find it rather hard to refer to men I knew as mere mortals then and today give them full credit, calling them out of obscurity and to full hero status as men of foresight and initiative. But these two guys took the concept and ran it up the flagpole. President Ronald Reagan was the one who released the military to experiment with new weapons and other experimental equipment concepts. Klindt and Murphy found the Reagan Army at Fort Lewis receptive to their ideas. No one in the Army except line pilots were even considering meeting Hinds and Hounds (Russian first line helicopters) on the battlefield. This group of instructors convinced the brigade commander how important it was. Then the concept ran up the chain of command to I Corps. They were allowed to train only a few of us (maybe 20) in these techniques.

The basic principles of air-to-air remain constant once you establish the airframes involved. Each aircraft has limitations, and each has advantages. The Bell products were hindered by their teetering hub main rotors. Zero gravity maneuvers would cause the main rotor blade to oddly seek lift, and thereby sweep the cockpit or knock off the tail boom or suffer mast bumping and separation. The Hughes (AH-64) and Sikorsky (UH-60) had elastomeric bearings (basically, rigid rotor systems) that did not easily cause catastrophic damage to the aircraft, which allowed them to do zero-G maneuvers (although they were then and are now absolutely, forever and in all other ways *forbidden* to do zero-G maneuvers).

We studied the comparative characteristics of the aircraft in detail, but we pretty much understood the principles already. The Cobra was faster than the Huey or '58, but the Cobra could not turn inside either the Huey or the '58. (We never expect to have air-to-air combat with another Bell product, but in our training, that is what we used.) The Soviet Hind attack helicopter was faster than all the others, but it was a lumbering pig, and even lipstick could not make it fly any better. The UH-1 and OH-58 were most maneuverable, but they had no armament. The AH-1 could not outrun the Hind but could easily outmaneuver it, and if the AH-1 got in close enough, it could chew the Hind to pieces with either gun the attack helicopters used. The 7.62mm 6-barrel Gatling, or the 20mm 3-barrel Gatling were the Cobra guns, and we had no AH-64s. Of course, the Hind had a bite of its own. If it could make a straight run on you, all you could do was jink to avoid him. (Jink is an Air Force term describing an avoidance maneuver that was an attempt to break the plane of the incoming attack and make him *miss*.)

It is significant to note here that all doctrinal air-to-air information available at the time was related to fixed wing aircraft, and not rotary wing aircraft. The experience of propeller-driven air-to-air (fixed-wing) combat was extensive and well written. The public record of WWII German fighter pilots and that of some of the more classified briefings on the topic uniformly stated the same thing as the unclassified commentaries. In effect, in any air-to-air engagement, the wisest things to do are, "Get in close … get in behind … make the first pass count … use the weather, the sun, the terrain and the strengths of your aircraft and the weakness of *his* aircraft to your advantage."

We did a lot of studying. Our first air-to-air class was weathered in for an extra week, so our discussions were wide ranging. We were keenly aware that none of our helicopter armament was designed for air-to-air engagement, but we had very few of the modern electronics like GPS or radar guidance on our aircraft. So we improvised. Against fast-movers, we used a multi-helicopter engagement philosophy. All of us turned on the bogie and provided as much excitement as we could for the incoming bad guy. We used Air Force common terminology in our radio calls to direct the battle. We would all come on line facing the bogie and make unanimous actions against the bad guy in the engagement. The Air Force terminology was different, precise and specific to helicopter air-to-air, so there was no confusion between the ground mission and the onset of an air-to-air moment. Against fast movers, we were primarily defensive. Against helicopter gunships, we relied mostly on escaping unnoticed if we could. Otherwise we did what came naturally. An unarmed, very maneuverable helicopter (OH-58) would try to stay in close and hope for assistance or wait for the Hind to break away for a better pass, and then the victim would try to escape before the Hind came around. A Cobra would try to stay in close and destroy the Hind. We expected that the Hind would probably try to make only a direct pass; his firepower was deadly, but he could not maneuver in close.

After we were trained, we were expecting air-to-air combat to be required in Aircrew Training Manual (ATM) tasks, but air-to-air training was placed in a dusty corner on a dark shelf in a room where no one ever goes. That is probably the same dark room and same GS-1 clerk where I got my rejection to the captain promotion. It is still there.

We all know the Apache and the Cobra attack aircraft were specifically ground support weapons. We were just trying to add an optional tool for the advent of the real battlefield.

Ground support required a burst of fire at a ground target, observation of the impact zone, and then movement of the impact zone onto the target. Engaging an aerial platform from another moving platform was more difficult. In reality, the only potential opponent with capability to field a helicopter gunship fleet at the time was the Soviet Union. As the potential of this combat diminished with the decline of the Soviet Union, so did the interest in the methodology. Anyway, the air-to-air training is still on the shelf, as far as I know. But it is not trained, and it is not used in any capacity that I am aware of.

POL Platoon

LTC Harry pretty much handed me the Petroleum Oils and Lubricants (POL) platoon, and I did some odd things that turned out wonderfully. We volunteered to run the hot gas operations on the airfield, and by so doing we had fully functioning equipment and experienced operators at all times. I not only inspected them often myself, but I encouraged old Rex

Swartz and every other ASO on post to find fault with them. I was an aspiring writer, and I wrote an award for every single exceptional inspection, every effective action or any sign of life from my men. And they were eternally grateful.

Once having peeved the HHT commander during an exercise, I arrived in the field with my gear conveniently unavailable due to his transporting it to a different campsite.

I flew into the POL site, and the POL platoon not only fed me but set up a tent, carried me wherever I needed to be and welcomed me at each site. This, when they were expecting an inspection and more training.

Maybe I can expand this a bit. The Army is renowned for taking the less-than-average soldier and putting him in POL operations. It was no secret, and it was accepted that if you found a good NCO (non-commissioned officer) in your section, you would be well served to rate him highly, get him promoted and keep your secret to yourself.

I had an old, crusty staff sergeant working the section who not only believed in training hard; he believed in rewarding his men. My efforts to ensure the sharing of glory and my writing skills made him my slave. He trained hard and worked hard, and he was pleased to take full credit for every award recommendation that went uphill from the platoon.

One day he came to me nearly in tears, panicked and stressed out. He had been involved in a training operation when the HHT commander came along and interfered in his operation.

Now, the HHT (Headquarters and Headquarters Troop) commander may have been careless, foolish, mean or worse, but he is *authorized*. He is, in fact, authorized to be a darn fool if he wants. This NCO understood this, but in a prideful and foolish moment he had talked back and was now fully expecting a courts martial. He had four months to his retirement. His entire life was in the balance, and he was at my door pleading for help.

Well, I yelled at him awhile. Then I yelled at him some more, and I 'splained how stupid he was for such an impropriety.

I walked over to see the squadron commander. *He* chewed on *me* awhile and yelled at me for interfering, and he 'splained how stupid the sergeant was for such impropriety. But we discussed what the POL platoon owed his leadership, and we discussed his upcoming retirement. I reminded LTC Harry that this NCO, a man fundamentally unrecognized with advancement or major awards during his 20-year career, had made this platoon what it was. In one year, he had taken this platoon from nothing (green troops, no other NCOs, bad equipment) and created a great operation with two competent, up-and-coming NCOs.

LTC Harry was, if nothing else, a man who recognized and rewarded initiative. He did not tolerate insubordination or anything that would jeopardize the mission. If I remember right, Harry called this NCO into his office and tortured him. He did not courts martial him but assigned him extra duty, assigned him duties *not* in proximity to the HHT commander, and reminded him that any other issues would invoke a complete recall of sins and severe punishment.

That grateful NCO retired on schedule.

Flight Evaluation Board

After I was established in the CAV, the HHT commander was selected to conduct a *Flight Evaluation Board* (FEB). He asked me to be the secretary for the board. That meant I would be privy to all things going on, and I would be tasked with some things, but would be silent. The HHT commander was the sort of man who was a "take-charge" kind of guy and presumed that I would be seen and not heard.

The FEB is a board convened to decide whether an aviator should keep or surrender his wings. An aviator is usually found in violation of some rule or currency requirement, and if his disciplinary action does not address his flight status, FEB does. An FEB is a terrible thing on your record, but it is considered only administrative, not punitive.

The secretary to the board is a non-voting member, so he keeps records, submits board findings, researches things for the board president and conducts the board meetings over which the board president presides.

In this case, a young lieutenant had not met his flight requirements (had not flown the required hours or tasks during the allotted time frame) and had not gotten the mission time (some types of missions have requisite amounts of time to be flown during each half-year), and he had not completed his check ride on time.

The board president, who was a major as well as the HHT commander, was really breezy about this. He was sure it was open and shut, one of those "after his fair trial, we're gonna hang 'em" kind of things. I did not feel very comfortable about it. It was just too pat. My name might not go on the blame line, but the board would be what I made it.

As a senior CW3 (Chief Warrant Officer Three), I had some unusual background in this case. I had some stuff to gather as the secretary of the board (such as unit records, aviator records, personal data on all concerned and paperwork to document the board).

I had some of the back story on this action. I had known this kid, who was in the old 214th, though not in C Company. I knew all the players, including commanders, instructor pilots, the SIP (Standardization Instructor Pilot) and all individuals of interest to the board.

So I wandered over to the unit and before I proclaimed my place in the pecking order (i.e., secretary to the FEB), I started chatting up the issues. It was no secret, I discovered. The kid had come to the unit, been trained in the AH-1 Cobra (gunship) and then started proceedings to declare himself a conscientious objector (CO). There was a lot of anger in the unit about it.

In passing, I asked about several other lieutenants in the unit, both of whom had also been late in their check rides and flight time. This is not uncommon, because commissioned officers are often busy in their careers and sometimes are late in accomplishing their requirements or even late in obtaining waivers to the requirements.

In these cases, both lieutenants had applied for and been granted waivers, and they had completed their requirements during the waiver period. They had applied for and received these waivers because their unit instructor pilots had ensured that it happened. What about this kid? Well, neither he nor his chain of command had submitted for a waiver. Thus an FEB was being convened.

Further checking revealed that our victim ... I mean our young lieutenant ... was still in his waiver period. He could still be trained; he could still qualify and pass his ride. But his

SIP (the big-dog Standardization Instructor Pilot) was being a turd. No waiver was offered.

My business was not only to run the FEB but also to protect the good name of 9th CBAA. So I made up an MFR (Memorandum for Record), a handy little legal observation for which I was famous in the CAV and met with the board president, who was anxious to get done and move on. He asked how I was coming along, and I was coy. You can tell a major, but you cannot tell him much. So he needs to be interested.

I told him, "Fine."

"And?"

Remember here, the board president has to feel the inspiration to pursue his board, not be directed by a lowly warrant officer.

"Well, sir, it is fine, and I have gathered most of the paperwork already, but *we* need to make up our minds on just how bad we want this kid."

I used the word "we" so as to not infer he might be pointed out for the responsibility of his board. But he instinctively knew this did not bode well.

"Mr. Kingsley, what does *that* mean, exactly?" He was trying to be intimidating.

FORT LEWIS, 1983-1986

"Well, sir ... the kid was late, no excuses. But there were two other lieutenants also late. They got waivers and completed their minimums without issue. Worse still ... the kid is still in his waiverable period ... and there has been no effort to get him finished."

"Mr. Kingsley ... you are telling me—"

"Sir, if you go with this, you are going to be real embarrassed, because he is going to kick your butt in public. The kid has, as you know, become a CO, and there *are* a lot of hard feelings over it. This is, I think, the real cause for the complete lack of support he has had in getting this done."

"Damn it, Kingsley. You get back over there and tell 'em to get it right!"

"Sir ... I am not going to do that. First, I know that whatever I do for you, or whatever I say about this, you are going to check to see if I am on the mark. And then you will step on my actions for whatever you declare is wrong.

"Second, the board secretary (*me*) does not make pronouncements or give direction to the board. *You* do. But if I were 9th CBAA, I would make this fixed. The kid can beat this based on harassment, and this is prime harassment. *Religious* harassment to boot."

The board never convened.

The kid eventually got out of the Army.

Murder in the CAV

Any career soldier will tell you that are some bizarre things that occur in the management of men at arms. But this is the strangest thing I ever saw.

The 3/5 CAV was a lightweight, fast moving, air transportable organization designed to be the eyes of the brigade. Our unit was designed to find and identify the enemy in the air and on the ground, probe the forward edge of the battle, and report the situation in real time to the commander of the brigade.

The permanent facilities of 3/5 CAV were scattered along the sides of a broad square on Fort Lewis, Washington. Administratively, I was assigned to HHT (Headquarters and Headquarters Troop), but I worked directly for the CAV commander. I was responsible for all safety issues and all the stuff he could pile on without killing me. These were considered my "extra duties," because my primary duty was to be a Cobra (gunship) pilot. Actually, as the ASO, I was assigned to fly the OH-58 (Scout) aircraft so I could more easily apply it to my work.

Now, my office in the CAV was 300 yards away from the HHT office. It was a quiet office, fairly close to the airfield but without much street noise. One day I noticed sirens, whistles and a lot of commotion somewhere downstream from my location, so much noise, in fact, that it interfered with my work.

I set out to see what the commotion was and soon found myself in the dayroom of HHT, facing a very flustered 1SG (First Sergeant, or E-8—the senior NCO of the troop).

"For cryin' out loud … Mr. K … get outta' here, and I will fill you in later!"

No need to repeat the advice. When Top spoke, we all paid attention. So, disappointed but curious, I headed back to my office and carried on while the world returned to normal.

About an hour later, *more* sirens, flashing lights and cops invaded our little CAV area, but without the rush of soldiers you should expect from such an apparent emergency. My interest was really piqued now, and I hoofed it all the way back to the CAV for a repeat lecture.

"Mr. K … I told you … I will call you later." As any soldier will tell you, when the Top tells you to pack sand, you just get out your little sand packer and go for the gusto. I left.

Around close of business I went back down to the HHT and wandered around. Top saw me and flagged me into his office. He closed the door, the first sign this was not gonna be easy. He sat down wearily, and as the inventor of perpetual motion, I knew he was pulling a big train and wanted to talk. I was not part of his chain of command, just a warrant officer/ friend. He seemed comfortable telling me. I pulled up a chair and listened..

"Sir, yer not gonna believe this."

I thought he was going to bait me with some magical story, but he was clearly venting.

"After morning count, Private (So and so) stopped in, white as a ghost. He told me he had to see me *now ... alone ...* and with the *commander*. I calmed him down and learned that his pal PFC (Such and such) had been bragging that he had killed a couple of girls. He had hidden them out in the training area forest. He had taken Private (So and so) out and showed him the bodies.

I was stunned. My mouth opened, but I did not know what to say. Anyway, he had that "I ain't done yet" look on his face, so I let my questions pass.

"Well, we were stupefied. We grilled him some and called the CID (Criminal Investigation Division) and the MPs. They got here and hauled PFC (Such and such) away."

I was still mystified. The second commotion was making no sense to me.

"They came back an hour later and arrested Sergeant *Snuffy*. "

I burst out of my pondering like a shot. "The hell you say—"

"Yep. Seems like the crazy kid (PFC Such and such) was lying. I cannot imagine what he was thinking. Sergeant *Snuffy* did it, and he showed the crazy kid the bodies during some brag time, and the idiot thought it was so cool *he* tried to brag about this to his friend, Private (So and so)."

Now I was stunned. This wasn't just any moron. This was SGT *Snuffy*, my maintenance chief. He had maintained the OH-58 that had my engine failure at Yakama Firing Center … He had a wife and two kids. He was an exemplary, if not an overly intelligent soldier. I was proud to serve with him. This had to be a set up. This was a lie; fraud on a grand scale.

I tried to visit him in the brig, but I couldn't get in because I had no legally recognized reason. He was under full suicide watch, nearly naked in a cell watched by big ugly guys who I could imagine were scum. They had to be. My comrade, a man I trusted with my aircraft and my life, was being held in some sort of legal mumbo jumbo on fraudulent charges.

Weren't they?

I learned more over the year during which his trial took place. Seems as though he did it. He had been visiting ladies of the night, and one of them did not measure up, so he apparently choked her to death. Well, it happened a second time, but he picked a tough one. She would pass out, he would stop, she would come to, and he would start over.

He was convicted of murder. I am not sure what degree. Two life terms. No parole.

Well, my involvement did not end there. Over that year,
I toughened up some, and my disappointment deepened. He
went off to Leavenworth with his dishonorable discharge to
spend the best years of his life making little ones out of big
ones, and I went on with my career. But I wrote to him.

Three years later, I visited him in Leavenworth. I
had never visited a prison, and it was an eye-opening
experience. I managed to get myself on his list of authorized
visitors, and I showed up on my appointed day. I had no idea
that the jail opened at 0900, and I showed up at 0830 in suit
and tie, prepared to wait my turn and not be late. I parked
down the street and walked to the jail.

My naive and foolish eye noted a covey of beautiful,
manicured, painted and scented women waiting about a block
away at the corner. It did not occur to me that I might have
any business with them, or that they might be going my way.
I paid them no mind. I pressed on, the soldier doing duty to a
comrade, whatever his issues.

I entered the building and was greeted by the desk sergeant
sitting at his official desk, wanting to know who I was and what
I wanted.

I pulled out my handy dandy active-duty Army Identity Card,
the one with the big "Chief Warrant Officer Four" stamped on the
face, and I stood up straight just for effect.

He shrugged. "Well, take a number and have a seat. We don't open until 9:00 A.M., and usually don't allow anyone into the building until 08:50 A.M." I signed into Snuffy's book. I noticed that in the five years since his conviction, he had received two visitors. I was the second. Five years later that book would contain three visitors. I was two of them.

I took a number and sat down at the far end of the bench, a rather long bench, which was conveniently near the coat room. I was minding my own business when I heard a shriek. It was one of those emotional, chilling, cold, mournful-angry guttural things that makes your hair stand on end and your diminutive manhood shrink up in horrible anticipation of sudden, instant and irrevocable death.

It was a Filipina, a tiny beauty most recently associated with that crowd of women I had passed in the street, holding up her card with her number "2" on it. She stared hard at the sergeant. She shrieked.

"What the _____ is going on? I was first! Who has it? Who has number 1?"

I instantly looked at my number ... the dreaded *number "1"*. I palmed it and tried to be invisible.

She was loud ... she was bold ... she was rude ... she was mean as a snake, and I instinctively hunkered down to be as small as possible. Maybe she would miss me so far down the bench, blending with the coats in the cloak room.

The sergeant was on his feet trying to calm her down, and she would have none of it. I was thankful she could not see me because she was in his face, leaning forward on his desk, demanding that "stupid private" (the sergeant) give her the number "1" pass, and he had better shut up.

If you ever see the movie *It Could Happen To You*, think of this angry woman as the twin sister of the wife of the cop, and you will get the picture.

But the sergeant was unimpressed. He had apparently dealt with her before. He calmly asked her to quiet down, take a seat and she would get her turn. But he made it clear she would be removed if she did not quiet down.

She spun up quicker'n a children's fire engine. She started yelling at him some more and demanded to see the officer of the day. She was not gonna put up with this … and my cowardice notwithstanding, she was tossed out on her ear two minutes later.

I still sat back, shrinking from my imagined wrath of the *next* howling spouse when a delightful, pretty little gal wandered back to sit down with the card number 2. Obviously a veteran of this show, she laughed at my apprehension.

"Don't worry. She does that periodically ... but she won't be back today."

Reassured, I chatted a bit and took in the perfume, the excitement and the focus of all these women.

When I was called, I went into a room where (former SGT) Snuffy sat alone. He had aged and gained a lot of weight. He had the dreaded "Ode de Locker Room" smell about him, but he was glad to see me. Every other man but Snuffy was allowed one kiss and was wrapped up in a moment of ecstasy with his visitor. I may have been a poor substitute, but Snuffy was still happy I came.

His world was gone. He was divorced. His wife had remarried. He was trying hard to have his sentence changed from two counts of "life" to any number of years. You cannot get credit for "good time" unless you have a sentence of some number of years. He told me no one had ever served any sentence of more than 25 years there, and he was hopeful he would be no exception.

Did he commit the murders? Yep. Why? Well, this is the way it went. The first prostitute simply did not perform according to his expectations. The second one ... well ... she just wouldn't stay dead, so he had to try to choke her several times. This record of notes seems to be missing some commentary ... It has been, after all, 22 years since that visit.

He first went to jail around 1985. He is still there. He went to Leavenworth and apparently got in a fight and was transferred to a high security prison in Oregon. I have only just started writing to him again.

Christmas in the CAV

Once upon a time, in another world my children remember much more clearly than I, the CAV consumed my life. It was a hard organization, partially because of my duty, and partially because the CAV has a thankless mission that requires a lot from its soldiers.

We had a black chaplain, Captain Armstead. He was one of the finest chaplains I ever knew. The CAV chaplain was not of my denomination, but he was capable of calling down angels whenever they were needed. He was devoted. And we all loved the guy.

Christmas came right on time, and we had been through a hectic year. Home interest rates that year went up to 21%, and money was tight (as always), especially for the junior enlisted folks.

The CAV always tried to take care of its own in everything, work or play. There is an old guy hanging around Ozark, Alabama, these days, Bob Harry, who commanded the

CAV in those days, and he was a wild man. He drove the men to distraction with his constant efforts to train, test, prove ... and train the men some more. No training lesson was complete until all the officers heard about it, discussed it, considered the options, and critiqued the decision of the individual who had screwed up. Very quickly, individual pride became lost to the need of the organization. I saw him relieve an NCO once for not getting men at a distant post hot chow, and I saw him chastise a captain or two for not caring well enough for their men.

There they were. The CAV in a tough year, the chaplain in a tough organization, the commander and Christmas. All together at one time and place. The commander heard the chaplain wanted to get up a list of names of folks in need, and he encouraged the officers to contribute to the Thanksgiving baskets. All the First Sergeants began collecting canned goods, and the wives began to bake ...Thanksgiving was a smash!

Then Christmas. The mood all over the CAV was festive, because we were in garrison for the whole holiday season. The giving was in full swing at every level. I became caught up in this effort, and when the chaplain asked, I offered to play Santa. My visit was to happen two days before Christmas, and I was given a list of addresses and a time to be at each home.

My little son, age 9, was absolutely furious that I should be dressed up like Santa and wouldn't be doing it for our family.

So I sat him down and explained that I was going out to help families in need by dropping off some food for Christmas and at least a toy for each child. He was speechless. He became instantly ashamed for his selfishness and begged me to let him go along and help. I got permission to put a cap on him and take him as Santa's elf.

We went to five homes. We got lost in every neighborhood, most of them very poor neighborhoods, and had to walk around to find each apartment. Everywhere we went, children ran around yelling to Mom and friends that Santa was visiting, and spreading the word. In one place, we had to walk to several apartment buildings, and the little kids started following us around excitedly in a big crowd!

My son was dumbstruck by the things we saw. Santa represented more than toys to these kids. He was the hope of good and better things to come, the universal bond they shared with all other little kids, rich or poor.

Our last home was in the best neighborhood, and my son was really upset by this time. As we went to each family, he kept asking me if this was all we had for them, if that was really where they lived, and why they didn't have this or that item he considered essential to life as he knew it.

But the last place was really difficult for him.

We walked in and found nothing there except a tree and two chairs. No lights on the tree, with only a few decorations, and a couple of dirty plates with forks on the living room floor. They had a baby and a little boy. The place was clean, but there wasn't much there.

The wife was embarrassed; Dad had not told her we were coming. The little boy thought he was in heaven; the father nearly cried when he saw the basket and toys. I did my "Ho, Ho, Ho" thing and left quickly after playing with the little boy.

My son rode home in silence, crying. He ran in and hugged his brothers and sisters, then his mom, and he took her by the hand to tell her of his evening. Reverently, he described each family, each event of the evening.

My son learned something I hope all children can learn at some time. He learned there is a side to humanity you cannot appreciate until you've played Santa Claus to a sweet child whose father can't rub two nickels together, but out of gratitude would make you wealthy, were it in his power.

Is this not part of the scriptural "treasures stored up in heaven"?

Our Friend Danny

Danny was a friend of my oldest son, Jeff, when he was about seven. We were living in Yelm, Washington, a little town near Seattle, and they went to second grade together. They were casual friends. We would hear about Danny once in a while, like all Jeff's little buddies. You know how it is with little kids. But one day that all changed.

Jeff got off the bus one afternoon, crying his heart out. Danny had rabies, he said, and he was going to lose all his hair and die. My sweet wife was overwhelmed by his little breaking heart. She immediately got on the phone and tried to get more on the story.

You have to know a bit about this kid. Danny was pretty savvy for a kid. He always seemed happy to be at our house, and he and Jeff seemed to be good together. His parents were divorced, but aside from trying to balance his affections between them, he seemed to do all the regular kid things. The two boys caught worms, fished together, hunted crawdads together, and did other things boys do. It just seemed as though it would never end.

It took a while to locate someone who knew, but the short of it was that Danny had leukemia. It was acute, and in the best case he was going to be sick a long time. We were told he had been transferred to the Children's Hospital in Seattle and was undergoing chemotherapy.

Jeff took this pretty hard, but it meant there was hope, and our whole family rallied around him. We decided to go into

Seattle to see Danny, and Danny's Dad okayed the idea. Jeff now made plans.

This wasn't going to be just any visit, because this was his pal, and his pal was in trouble. Jeff is unbelievably loyal, and he felt he just had to do something special. He felt if he could make something, it would be so much more personal. So he got a big rock and a bucket of yellow paint and disappeared.

The rock was about half the size of a bowling ball, fairly smooth and shaped like a headless box turtle. And this wasn't ordinary paint. Jeff had found it in a pile of trash, and it turned out to be curb paint. You know the kind I'm talking about. It is the stuff that goes on ¼-inch thick and chips off like armor plate. It was bright yellow, epoxy enamel, and it stuck to everything within 10 feet of its application. My pack-rat son had laid claim to it as a sacred treasure. Now it was to be part of his special gift to Danny.

Jeff spent four days painting that rock. Unknown to me, each day he would try to wash out his brush with water. (Dad always washed *his* brushes that way.) Jeff had to throw each brush away next day because it was unusable, but he didn't say anything, and he wouldn't ask for help. And there was a little bit of yellow paint on his clothes each day, which we didn't understand till later.

As we prepared to depart that Saturday morning, Jeff came out with his rock. It was beautiful—as beautiful as a perfectly smooth, bright yellow rock can be. He was very happy that we liked it, because that meant Dan would.

We carried Jeff and the rock into the hospital, and we wandered around trying to locate Danny. We had to go through a children's ward to find him, and we saw some pretty sick kids there. I suppose I should have been steeled to this reality, but daddy hearts are pretty tender stuff, and I kept thanking God my kids were healthy.

My son was also stricken by the sight of the sick children. He took it well but paid close attention to everyone we saw there. And he was all the more bewildered when we found Danny.

We were surprised to see Danny happy, and in a bed with several thousand dollars' worth of the latest toys. He had his own telephone and could call somewhere in the hospital to have any TV program he desired (if they had it) to run on his TV. He had an IV in one arm, but it didn't seem to bother him, and he seemed unchanged on the surface. It was obviously one of his good days.

Jeff was almost embarrassed to give him the rock, but Danny was glad to have it, and he placed it among his favorite toys. They watched a little TV and then played with the toys. When Dan got tired, we left.

Jeff was pretty quiet on the way home and didn't say much until we were outside Seattle. He made the comment that this must be cool stuff, being sick this way. I reminded him of all the other sick children and asked him what he thought of them. He answered that they were real sick, and he was glad not to be one of them. I then explained that Dan was more seriously ill than all of them. I don't think Jeff believed me at first, but he said nothing. He only looked confused.

After that we heard about Dan only when things changed. Jeff would call Danny's dad at least a couple of times a week to get the current news.

Dan finally came back to school. He had lost all his hair and lost some weight. Then his blood count went up, and he started gaining weight. Danny was wearing a cap to school when someone stole it and made fun of him. Jeff slugged the guy and got sent home from school. Then Danny got worse. He lost weight and his hair looked awful. When Danny went back to the hospital, Jeff was really worried about him.

After Danny went back to the hospital, no one was talking. We knew it was bad, but Jeff kept calling and hoping. When Danny died, a teacher called him aside and told him almost matter-of-factly; it broke something inside. He cried; he hid in

335

the bathroom for a while. He was really quiet about it for a long time. Jeff just stuffed it into his little heart and never let it out.

We went to the funeral. Jeff was unhappy about it. Danny was no angel, just a good kid, and Jeff did not know the kid they talked about. But Jeff packed all these things up in his heart, too, and he is a better young man for it. Throughout his childhood he would still come to tears over Danny, but there was a real determination to be a strength for those in need around him.

His dad brought Danny's bike over and gave it to Jeff. He retired his own bike and rode Danny's until the wheels fell off. And Danny is still an honored memory in our family.

The tough breaks are the ones that make us strongest. Jeff gained a great ability to share empathy with others less fortunate than himself.

But if you wanted to see my son fight, all you had to do was rip the hat off a bald-headed kid.

Safety at Yakima

We did a lot of training in Yakima, a firing range with a lot of desert and maneuver area around it in Yakima, Washington. And the miracle of the United States Army is that not more people are killed or injured in our training.

These stories may be from memory but are basically true. Some are just stupid but true. If I remember this correctly, these three incidents all happened in October 1984.

The Hole in the Ground

We had an upcoming cross-country trip planned from Fort Lewis and across a lot of desert to Yakima. Just on a fluke I had taken an aircraft to fly the route to be taken by our ground troop, A Troop, and I happened upon a large hole in the ground. It was not precisely on their route, but I knew it would be shining like a beacon in the night if it could be explored and ... well ... whatever soldiers could do for excitement.

I flew home and prepared a briefing to all the troop commanders, but to A Troop in particular. It was not just a hole in the ground. It was a collapsed roof in an underground railroad tunnel that was so old the tracks were not even marked on the maps now. All the troops had ground elements going in night- and day-moves along the route, but only A Troop would be going in mass ... and I wanted every swinging Richard to know this was not a place to play. No one would be allowed to climb into the hole. There were no exceptions. The CAV commander nodded his solemn approval, as did all the other talking heads, and off we went.

The second day out I intercepted a call for Flat Iron, our medevac operation, to carry out a badly injured soldier from Yakima. Yes, *that* Yakima … and *that* hole in the ground … and I was dizzy with indignation and aggravation.

So we all had a meeting with the CAV commander, LTC Bob Harry, and the A Troop commander, whose name slips my mind just now, and I began to huff and puff and blow the house down.

I finally asked what the hell they were thinking, and the A Troop commander, who certainly outranked me and whose sterling performance certainly was not imperiled by this stupidity, looked at me with a helpless, innocent stare. It was as though his brain was a quart low and his eyes were blue only due to a shortage of motor oil.

"But Mr. Kingsley, they did not climb into that hole."

At first I thought I had heard something wrong, or perhaps I was having some sort of hallucination. He seemed smug about it. He was bold enough to look at the Cav commander, and they both assumed the look I refer to as "invincible ignorance." It is the way a soldier, if he has not murdered someone within eyeshot of his mother and can get away with any stupid excuse in history by simply denying its existence. These are the same men who ask, "If a tree falls in the forest and no one hears it, did it make any noise?"

So I asked him just what that meant. And I could tell by the distant look in LTC Harry's eyes that since the soldier did not die, there was no reason for me to get my panties in a wad.

This is what the A Troop commander said. "Mr. Kingsley, a jeep reconning the area happened upon a railroad track. It followed the track into a tunnel and drove half a mile or so until it came to the collapsed roof of the tunnel. That is all."

What?

"Yeh. The two back seaters got out and decided they could climb to the top of the hole. That is all. But *when one got to the top, the other was not with him.*"

What? I stared with wonder at the Cav commander, who just asked me if I had any other questions for his prize captain.

"Sir, are you kidding me? You let them climb out of the hole?"

"Well, chief," the captain said, *"They did not climb into it, after all.*"

I could see in my mind's eye that silly barn owl look … big eyes … crazy nodding head … an occasional unseeing blink of complete oblivion.

Okay. You get it.

Crash of the Chinook

On another day, the courage of A Troop really shone in a very dangerous moment.

A Chinook helicopter is the heavy lift, twin 3-bladed troop aircraft that is still in service today. This aircraft is large and noisy, and the efficiency of the pilot depends in part on the effective observations of his crew. In this case, the aircraft was ramp down, unloading troops onto a small hill-top. The front of the aircraft hovered over the side of the hill, the aft over the hill-top, low over the ground, and the crew chief monitored both the altitude and the process of disembarking by the troops.

The aircraft has a great many hydraulic lines that are under very high pressure, filled with flammable hydraulic fluid. A line may break for a variety of reasons, perhaps a trauma such as an accident, or a pinhole leak caused by rubbing the line against something. The pressure is so high that once a breach occurs in the line, the fluid can quickly leak out in a thin vapor and become a terrible fire hazard.

In this case, the aft of the aircraft dipped, the main rotor blade on the aft transmission struck the ground, and the aircraft came apart as it flipped over. Crew and men were trapped within, and the aircraft started burning. Alpha Troop was just below the crest of the hill and responded immediately. To a man, every jeep drove immediately to the aircraft, and every jeep fire extinguisher was used while every co-driver (spare man) went into the wreck and pulled out every survivor.

Well, it is true the aircraft was never the same.

But we did not lose a man. We did not lose a jeep. We did not lose any aircrew or passengers, although some were pretty well beat up. A Troop rescued and bandaged every injury until Medivac could arrive.

I was really proud of my boys that day. All is forgiven when the best outcome is accomplished.

Night Move

Our tactical troop (A Troop) made a lot of night moves, and they were dangerous. These were exacerbated by the instruction to have light discipline enforced. Our headlights were all covered by plastic with a small slit in them (for a tiny bit of light), and the very dangerous trails along ridges and valleys were an invitation to accidents.

On this particular night, a soldier was in his jeep in his sleeping bag, propped up and stretched out between the two front seats, wearing his helmet and supposedly standing his watch in-place. It was a common practice, but it was not a wise one. The cavalryman fell asleep in his warm sleeping bag.

He had parked the jeep downhill, along a steep ravine, with (a loaded) jeep trailer behind. Somehow he kicked the transmission out of gear and released the hand brake next to the driver's seat. When it let go, it took off downhill into the ravine.

The soldier tried to escape by rolling out of his jeep, still in his sleeping bag. His helmet strap caught on the frame of the jeep top. He could not release his helmet or his sleeping bag. And he was dragged by the neck into the ravine with the jeep and trailer. He was not killed, and his story became grist for another pre-mission safety briefing that may still be given to cavalrymen everywhere.

Another passenger was hurt but not as badly as the driver, who spent a couple of days in the hospital and two months on special duty.

You got to admit it. Those A Troop guys were tough.

Testing the Chain of Command

One of the things I learned from LTC Harry was his constant attention to detail. His efforts to train included measuring his success in communication to the lowest level of the command. He was demanding but fair. He was always on the hunt to be sure his guidance was clear throughout the chain of command, top to bottom.

In addition, he wanted all lessons learned by detailed debriefing of every mission. In this effort, leadership was to be advanced, and every improvement to be understood. You could hardly be relieved by him unless you disobeyed orders or lied to him. Anything short of murder could be forgiven, even if it required some sort of discipline. His loyalty was never a question, and he demanded the same in return.

I happened to be aware of a regular part of his marching orders to the ground troops, which always included guidance for road stops. In each stop, all hoods were to be raised, all hand brakes locked, a driver in each seat at all times, and no smoking fires lit at night for any reason.

Although most of it was simple logic, it was explained that hoods-up would help cover the windscreen and reduce the glint of sunshine that might be spotted by distant aircraft or ground observers.

I never gave this a thought, since I must not be that bright. But I happened to be flying the commander around when he saw a ground platoon pulled over with none of the hoods up. We landed, and he demanded to know why the hoods were down. The young platoon sergeant was very surprised.

But hoods-up had nothing to do with it. The man who caught the tapioca for this foul up was the A Troop commander. This guidance had not been received up and down the chain, and his new-found respect for chain-of-command awareness made him a better leader.

Engine Failure at Night... 19 Oct 1984

So, there I was … plugging away at my career in the CAV … still kind of a new guy … and a *safety* guy after all.

Before coming to Fort Lewis, when I served in an attack helicopter unit in Germany, an IP there, a friend, took me out. While we were flying along, he rolled off the throttle to simulate an engine failure. Normally we only do this over a runway, or we recover mid-air, but there was an approved sod area next to the runway in front of us, and I landed on it. I still scared the crap out of him. He yelled at me about some of my technique, but he did not slap me. After all, we *had* landed upright and without injury. So he warned me to be more … careful. I paid attention.

When I arrived in the CAV, I was, in the lingo of the day, a "Cat B Aviator," in other words, I was real busy doing cosmic stuff for the Army, so the Army did not let me fly as much. That saved them a little money, but it reduced my proficiency even more. I think in those days I was required to fly 25 flight hours per half (per six months). After my experience in Germany, I was concerned about my ability to handle the dreaded engine failure. I mentioned my dangerous experience to a CAV Scout IP, one I trusted to beat me when I needed beating and train me when I needed training. He took me out, and after a single autorotation, he agreed. I needed some refresher training. I did not need a lot. I was, after all, fully qualified, and I had recently taken a check ride with this guy, the most respected in the unit. I needed some polishing of my technique, and he gave it to me. I cannot think of his name, but he was good. And I was a good pupil.

The 3/5 CAV had a field exercise coming up at Yakima Firing Center, across the mountains from the Olympia area and Fort Lewis, Washington. I was determined to catch up on my flight time to meet my "minimums," and I was not letting any moss grow under my feet.

The rest of this story was published in Army Aviation Digest for the benefit of the Army, but it was not published like this, I can assure you.

The Yakima exercise went well enough. There had been very few training incidents, and I had just completed about 25 hours flying in the same aircraft. That made me fairly proficient for a change. I was expecting to get an extra few hours on the books when I was given an ash and trash mission late one afternoon. At the end of the mission, I had a terrible disagreement with my … well, my administrative commander. I worked for the squadron commander, but for administrative purposes I was assigned to HHT just like all the other officers working at Squadron. I was flying the HHT commander that day, and I was the Pilot in Command (PIC). He made a decision I did not like, so I took control of the aircraft. I was polite and professional, and within my rights to do so. He was … displeased. Really displeased. He started yelling at me, so I landed the aircraft near his tent. When I asked him to get out, he informed me (in a very loud voice) of the complete lack of merit in my ancestors, of the fruitless condition of my soon to be lifeless career, and of his intention to focus now and forever on its complete and utter demise.

Whew.

It is funny now. But not then. I took those affectionate words to heart. I was sure my tattered career would not make it up the flagpole with such venom spewing from the mouth of the HHT commander. So I flew immediately a quarter mile down the line to see my squadron commander, LTC Grimsbo. I found him in his tent, explained my situation briefly, and advised him that my world was collapsing. I needed his protection. I had never asked for any assistance from him or any commander before. I was not doing well in the political arena, and I felt helpless.

He started laughing. It was just a misunderstanding, he said. He assured me the HHT commander had a lot on his mind and that he was leaving; he simply did not have enough spare time left in the CAV to destroy me. The squadron commander would take care of it, so I should stop worrying. I would, he assured me, never have to fly with the HHT commander again.

I was grateful I had his confidence. I was reassured. I was invigorated.

Next morning I was scheduled to arrive at the aircraft (at the field site) at zero dark thirty (cool CAV talk for "real early in the flippin' cold, black morning"). I prepared to run it up so it would be warm for the staff member I was flying around. It was not as cold as expected, so I tied my arctic parka in the back seat and got ready. But it was still very dark. After checking the fuel and oil, I ran the aircraft up and waited.

Out of the darkness, as though my worst nightmare could be realized on this gloomy morning, came he. Could it actually be so?

Yes, I looked a second time, and it *was* he. He was going to be my copilot. That cold prickly shiver washed over my heart like dirty road slush. In the classic way of arrogant aviators, we were both professionals, and we both acted like professional asses. In stony silence, we both pretended the other guy was not there. We each did our job. He stared at me, but said nothing. I tried not to scowl at him, but said nothing. I sat in the running aircraft. He tied his parka in the back seat and got himself belted into the aircraft, sitting right beside me. In fact, the aircraft is so small the pilot and copilot can hardly keep from bumping arms over the console above the collective. When he was locked in, I ran my own checklist and pulled a HIT (health indicator test) check to ensure the engine was running well. It was. All was done in complete silence. He watched. As I hovered to take off, he called off (speaking to the TOC, the Tactical Operations Center and telling them we were departing).

I pulled off the hill and into the darkness intending to break right, follow the ridge line around the impact area and land at the Brigade TOC. As I nosed it over, I saw the torque meter flickering plus or minus 20%. There was no vibration or hesitation, but I instinctively knew it could turn out bad. That gauge is a direct wet line. It simply does not fail unless the needle falls off. It was reading precisely what the engine was doing. I had changed my take off path and was banking left to return and land when the torque meter slammed to zero. And I mean *zero*.

I felt my chest tighten. I swore. I yelled, *"Engine failure!"* I forgot to use the intercom, but the copilot heard me just fine.

He came off the radios as though his hair were on fire. He said something like, *"What the hell are you doing?"* And then he swore. And he yelled, *"Engine failure!"* He, too, forgot to use the intercom. I heard him just fine.

I think you could say we were both pretty excited. And we still were not talking much.

FORT LEWIS, 1983-1986

Now I was instantly faced with that terrifying moment when the collective *must* be lowered in order to preserve the main rotor RPM so I could cushion the landing, but the fear of descending into a black hole ... well, it simply cannot be described. And the conflict of the desperate choices is mind-numbing.

Anyway, I lowered the collective and banked left into that dark valley. My primary thought was that I did not want to clip the ridge prior to impact. I got into the long axis of the valley (what I could make out of it, which was just a long patch of blackness), paralleling the slope of the mountainside. We were both suffering from an adrenalin buzz. It is a miracle we could think. We were too scared to talk on the radio, so we continued to yell at each other.

Suddenly I felt the throttle moving on the collective, and I was mortified. I forced it open and felt it moving again. What was this, a ghost? *No*! It was my illustrious copilot! He was testing the throttle on the other collective. (There are two of each control in the aircraft so either the pilot or the copilot can control it.) He was testing to see if it was still on, to check and see if I hadn't turned it off somehow. I was furious. I could not believe it. I asked him what he thought he was doing. He asked me if I had rolled it off. We were both mad ... terrified might be a better word ... but at the same time we knew these were critical, honest questions. He had to ask. I had to hate him for it.

About this time I got off my emergency call, "Mayday, mayday, mayday, 357-is-engine-out."

In my mind's eye, it was spoken like Chuck Yeager, "Mayday … mayday … mayday … Aircraft 357 is engine out … landing west bound vicinity Badger Gap."

But when I did it, it was all run together just like that. I was sure it was John Wayne personified. And in that terrified moment I was proud of it. I mean, if yer gonna die, you might as well do it with a smile on your lips and all of your maydays out. And I choked on my location. But the damn flight operations clerk who was monitoring the radio said it sounded like three cats in a room full of rocking chairs. He could not understand a single word.

Dang him anyway. The CAV guys never let me forget it.

Pardon me for this little detour for the benefit of young pilots. In the back of my head were old valuable lessons stored for such a moment, the kind that every pilot turns to when the operational tapioca hits the fan. And I want to review them now.

First, *Autorotation Defined and Clearly Understood* — This was the maneuver (required) to allow controlled flight in a single engine helicopter (at least they were single engine in those days) that allowed the helicopter to descend and terminate flight with gentle contact on the ground without injury, or worse, resulting in little or no damage to the helicopter. It is accomplished by reduction of the collective pitch, controlled deceleration of the aircraft, and an efficient trade-off of airspeed for lift, to arrive on the ground in the aforementioned condition. This maneuver may become complicated by bad weather, darkness, mechanical failure, wires or other obstacles, and, if it must be mentioned, pilot error.

Unfortunately, the most common fault sited by most accident investigation boards is pilot error. In the back of my head, I was looking for some way to blame someone.

Next, *Experience*. When working at the Army Safety Center, I had done some research that discussed the likelihood of survival in a helicopter accident. Paraphrasing, if you impact the ground slower than 60 KIAS (knots indicated airspeed), you should survive. And above 60 KIAS, you might not. Then there were always exceptions.

Just to drive in the point, 3/5 CAV had just experienced the severing of a UH-I main rotor system at zero knots, 100 feet, in a terrible wire strike. What to my wondering eyes did appear but all eleven passengers alive (barely) and battered. Badly battered. That event, and the survival with zero forward airspeed, had burned itself into my memory.

Vertical, Zero Ground-Run, Successful autorotation. There was another final and very unlikely bit of knowledge included in my reference-experience. This was my understanding of the legendary vertical, zero ground run, successful autorotation.

In the OH-58, a successful autorotation is usually done starting at the optimal airspeed, in this case between 60 and 80 KIAS or 70-90 MPH. It requires some acquired skills and good timing.

I had known a pilot sent to a civilian helicopter school to learn zero-airspeed, 200-foot vertical autorotations in forestry operations. The Army did not even consider this maneuver a practical aviation task. This was very unusual training, since Army training refers to zero airspeed above 50 feet AGL (above ground level) envelope as the "dead zone." The Army considers unpowered flight to the ground in this situation as being nearly unrecoverable. They do not teach it because you are expected to suffer catastrophic consequences resembling death. (*There being no time to first lower the collective to preserve main rotor RPM, then to establish the landing point as that you see directly between your torque pedals ... then to build up enough forward airspeed for the tradeoff of speed for lift to cushion the landing, or the reaction time to prepare for the very rapid descent to the ground*).

And ... as an aside, normal Army autorotation training during flight is restricted to successful mid-air recovery of power and flight, or termination on a runway. This allows IP evaluation of the pilot response to an unannounced engine failure without the added complication of typical landing hazards.

So I had listened carefully to the story of the pilot who went into forestry training, because I had been fascinated by the potential of such an emergency, and I was filled with the dread that it might happen to me.

Anyway, my buddy talked about his two weeks of training in great detail, emphasizing the precise training required. This consisted of careful hands-on tutoring by an experienced instructor pilot, in ever-increasing levels of difficulty.

His training was conducted over several days. First he was asked to do normal hovering rotations until the IP was comfortable with his skills. It was a normal task but it was a critiqued, one autorotation at a time. Each iteration of hovering autorotation was critiqued, and then followed by the gradual increasing of height, making greater difficulty for each autorotation. The first autorotation would be at three feet, then another. Then at five feet; then after several perfect landings, he would be allowed to increase his height with each perfect touchdown. Eight feet, ten feet, until he was doing them from 50 feet. From there, it was 200 feet.

This was the simple crux of it. All autorotations at zero airspeed above 50 feet were basically the same ... that is, beginning at 40 to 50 feet, you had to use one long, continuous smooth application of collective until you touched down, preferably with gentle perfection.

He emphasized that if you screw it up, and the main rotor RPM is too slow on "landing," you can knock off the tail boom, or worse, sweep out the cockpit with the main rotor blade.

He had been careful to avoid discussing the limited options of sharing the cockpit with a main rotor blade. But he acknowledged that if you landed with too much rotor RPM, it probably meant you did not use enough of that rotor inertia to soften the landing. With that said, it would be tough to accomplish such a landing with all the big pieces still working.

There is another valuable (?) old adage amongst pilots that goes like this, "If you are in an engine failure at night ... and you turn on your landing light ... and you don't like what you see ... *turn it off.*"

Hell, until that night, I always thought that was a joke!

So at this moment, we wer*e sinking* like a stone, and now I could not find the stinking landing light, which was right above the throttle and under my left hand.

Well, I was busy. I yelled for the copilot to turn on the landing light, which he did. Our eyes were big as saucers trying to identify any tiny bit of recognizable terrain to guide us to landing. We were immediately blinded by the white light shining on the silica dust inside the chin bubble. I turned it off instantly, but it was too late. That two or three seconds of sheer blindness in a descending aircraft is horrifying, but we still could not see the ground. I told the copilot to adjust the light and try again. It blinded us again, and this time *he* shut it off. And he left it off.

Somewhere in this sequence I began to see the terrain (specifically, desert brush going by) and guessed I was about flare altitude. It was really hard to judge, especially with that damned red *engine out* light there in the middle of the windscreen. It occurs to me that you *just had to be there* to appreciate what I am saying.

A helicopter has the relative glide slope of a flying brick. Maybe a bit better than that. But we were too far along to do anything else in our choice of landing areas. We were going to land where our glide slope intersected the ground. I really wanted to be sure to stop the forward motion no matter what else I did ... so I hauled it back into a steep flair. It scared the copilot, who sort of caught the cyclic in his lap and yelled that it was too high, but I held it in. Stopping the aircraft forward motion ... that was good. Starting our descent too high ... that did not matter. Not yet anyway. So long as we landed vertically, we would probably survive, and I didn't owe this tin can a darn thing. If we walked away, it was a win.

By the time I could identify the brush, I still could not tell exactly how high we were. But we had developed a rapid vertical rate of descent. *Now* that rate of descent mattered a lot. I leveled the aircraft and snatched an initial pitch-pull. It seemed only to slow the descent, not stop it as I planned. I kept pulling, and in one continuous tug, got it all. I hit the stop and was giving it one last wringing effort while I caught my breath and braced. The aircraft hit hard, twice, and we both grunted like football players in a mid-field tackle.

Now, nothing but silence. My ears were ringing, and it was eerie. I was fried. I was dazed. The aircraft was on the ground, but I still held the collective up. I had a steel grip on the cyclic, and I wasn't breathing. The copilot gently pushed down the collective, and he began to talk. I wondered what the heck was wrong. A moment ago he and I had been screeching at each other; now he was Joe Cool on the radio. I was mad … I was scared to death … I wondered how the world could be so peaceful when *this* was going on.

My copilot turned to me and said, "Dan, thank God you were flying." I thought he was kidding, and it made me mad. The noise of his voice and the ringing in my ears simply seemed to scratch my soul like fingernails on a chalk board.

So I climbed out of the aircraft and did what I could. I entered a terrible comment in the log book, but I mentioned that the engine temperature seemed pretty high for a dead engine. I checked … it was not on fire. I took the valuable things out of the aircraft … my MREs (Meal, Ready to Eat) and my -10 (dash 10, the operators manual), which was very hard to replace, and I walked to a nearby tent. I entered without knocking. I sat down at the stove and stared for a moment. I heated my meal, but I spoke little, and the captain there got most of his answers from my copilot. I was so fried I had left my pistol, my gas mask, the aircraft key, my CEOI (crypto codes book) and all else of military significance in the unguarded aircraft. After eating, I retrieved them all and walked uphill to my flight operations and then to my own tent. That is where my day really began.

The sun came up. It turned very hot, and I sat in that tent all day, alone. Emotionally as well as physically, I felt abandoned, outcast. I was sweaty, dirty and without a clue. The major, my copilot, had been picked up and driven away. I was truly alone.

Had I made a mistake? What had I done wrong? Had I remembered my fuel sample? Oh yes, I had. And where was the crew chief? All this time he was down faithfully working on the aircraft. Periodically I would wander over to the edge of the hill and look down at him. From where I stood, all the big pieces seemed to be there, but I did not know what he was doing.

What else? I know we hit hard, but it was *night*. What could they expect? Too bad ... probably broke something. The major probably had something awful to say about me. My tattered career was now officially in the hot grease. Not even the squadron commander can tolerate crashing an airplane.

Suddenly I was awakened by the aircraft starting. I ran over to the edge of the hill again to look down at it awhile. It continued to run. Now they would see. The dang thing just did not work.

After about an hour, it simply flew away. I didn't even look up. I was crushed. Maybe I *had* shut it off. Maybe I had screwed it up somehow.

Around 1800, just as the day was cooling, a grungy sergeant in a dirty jeep drove up, and he was eloquent. "Get in. The commander wants you."

Great. I was going to a hanging. This is especially good stuff for a safety officer. So much for CW4 Rex Swartz and his effort in CAV safety.

It took us an hour to get to the meeting. My heart sank as I realized the entire squadron was there, and I was the last one getting in. Not only was it gonna be ugly, but I, an aviator extraordinaire, was being dragged to the meeting in a jeep. Okay ... I get it. Well, I was a former Marine ... that had to count for something. Anyway ... I loved jeeps.

FORT LEWIS, 1983-1986

I had a friend there, one of our two maintenance officers, CW2 Vint Fantin. He nearly ran up to greet me with his hand out.

"Way to go Kingsley!" I knew he was harassing me. Aviators traditionally eat their young when they screw up. He tried to grab my hand and I was ready to hit him. I was in no mood to be skinned tonight. And suddenly, he got it.

"Dan! Take it easy. Yer gettin' a Broken Wing. Yer a hero!"

I realized he wasn't kidding, and I turned around so he could not see me. The relief was nearly paralyzing. I was trying not to cry when I turned around and asked him what the hell he was talking about. He spun up like a top. He was the one who had gone to retrieve the aircraft. He had read the log about the TOT (Turbine Outlet Temperature) being high, and he thought maybe it hadn't died. He ran it up … it started fine, but as he was running it up, his crew chief was playing with the lines in the engine compartment. When he handled the bleed air lines (which actually power the fuel control), the engine suddenly went to flight idle, less than the normal idling speed. There was no damage to the aircraft, and my illustrious pal, the major, had nothing but praise for my skills.

So, on that day, I learned it is not a far trip from being the zero to being the hero. All the aviators in the squadron came by and did the pilot-homage thing and shook my hand. And I felt like a fraud. But the air smelled sweeter. The food tasted better. And life ... well, life was suddenly grand.

Next day, I was the hero. C Troop invited me to fly in their formation, and I accepted a ride with one of their IPs. I had a picture taken with them ... even though I was not part of their troop. And I saved a picture taken of me with the major (my copilot in the escapade). Man, I was pretty rough looking in that.

When I got home from that exercise, my wife came up and slugged me on the arm. My friend Elmer McNutt had called her from Yakima and started his conversation with, "Now don't worry ... Dan is not dead." But she was glad to see me.

Well, two months or so later, I received that Broken Wing. I stood up in front of 500 men and *they* did the pilot homage thing. And I actually heard an enlisted man say something about how he wasn't gonna fly with anyone but Mr. Kingsley.

The Aviator Secret

Now I will reveal to you that there is a little private secret among Army aviators.

A Broken Wing is not an Army medal. It is awarded by the US Army Safety Center with a certificate that says yer a heck of a man. But that tiny trinket is recognized by all

Army aviators because it implies great skill performed under life-threatening pressure. It is an unofficial award for safely bringing an aircraft and crew home in spite of the odds. And all Army aviators know it well.

The chain of command quietly allows you to pin that tiny medal to the back of your cap in spite of a strict rule against unauthorized additions to your uniform. It is a nearly invisible, barely noticeable token of the monster aviator ego. But every soldier with wings on his chest can tell you who, around his unit, has one. If anyone does have one. And you cannot even buy one, as I discovered when mine was stolen. Only the Safety Center has one, and they allowed me a replacement.

Now I know better than to fall for that old ego stuff. Life is just sweeter. Air tastes better. I am just a man, and I do what I can. I am not a hero but a lucky imposter. And I know now that whatever I do, if I can feel good about myself, it is enough.

Now, I have been retired 30 years, and I still wear the damn pin on the back of my cap.

I just can't help it.

CAV Change of Command

In 1984, a lot happened. I will try to manage the chronology, but it may be a little out of line.

Bob Harry completed his command, and because he could not be retired just now, he rotated back to Fort Rucker as exec for DGFS, Directorate of Gunnery and Flight Training. He was replaced by LTC Grimsbo.

Now some of this is pure recall, but it is the best I can remember. You figure it out. It is a great story anyway.

I had my engine failure in October, and Colonel (soon to be Brigadier General) Dave Robinson was the 9th CBAA commander. He gave me the Broken Wing. In a private conversation we had, I had whimpered some of my aspirations to return to Rucker. For whatever reason, he took my name in tow when he left town.

Bob Harry was on the outs politically, and we all knew it. Officers do not rise very far if they cannot play the political game. Bob was an expert manipulator and an outstanding squadron commander, but he was not a politician. With all that said, it was believed he would not be picked up for promotion to colonel, and he was not sure what the Army would offer him. When he completed his command, he was sent off to a dusty corner of Fort Rucker, supposedly to cash in on his retirement.

But we all knew he would be rooting around looking for some kind of mischief.

Bob was widely known as a magnificent trainer, whatever else you thought of him. Not a trainer who kept little stars on a list of soldiers, but real combat decision making with a penchant for leadership skills. And I believe General Parker at Fort Rucker got that word.

The World Helicopter Championship was a high-risk event. The Army had to do it perfectly or not at all. So, frankly, here was an expendable lieutenant colonel who loved to train under stress. The World Helicopter Championship had been won on a fluke in 1981 by CW2 George Chrest, who had gone to compete in Poland with a small crew. This did not diminish his accomplishment. His victory was scrutinized and tortured as both of John Iseminger's wins would be, but this set up the Army for a polishing of its image around the world.

This was a hard decade for image, and the Army could hardly turn away from sending a team. If we lost, they could throw Harry under the bus, and he could retire quietly. If they won, he would go out on top. The challenge to the Army seemed very tough both in terms of the competition and in terms of the required logistics.

In early 1985 it was noised about that the Army would finally create the United States Precision Helicopter Team. The

WHC (World Helicopter Championship) would be held again, sponsored by the FAI (the French organization that monitors world records in aviation) in England. This was not well known around the Army, but it was not a secret. I got a sneaky call from Bob asking if I would like to be the ASO (Aviation Safety Officer) on the 1985 team, but I told him I had already been notified I was going to Germany when my tour was up. The truth was I had always wanted to go back to DCD (Directorate of Combat Developments at Fort Rucker) and make a mark there. So I put in another dream sheet knowing it would be rejected.

I got called down to the brigade S-1 (the Brigade Admin officer, who presumes authority to embarrass and humiliate persons who are out of line but not breaking the law around the brigade). He chewed my butt for daring to ask such a thing. I had shaken hands on a German assignment, he said, and I needed to keep my word. Then the exec (LTC Bill Reeder) called me in. He listened for five minutes and told me to do what works; they could always turn me down.

The Readers Digest Version

Okay … the 1985 USPHT never happened, and I thought it was cancelled. In the mean time I was awarded my broken wing. Dave Robinson picked up his star and moved on. I lost track of him. Unknown to me, Bob Harry (at Fort Rucker) was appointed to be the next (1986) USPHT Commander, and I got my orders to Germany.

I think sometime in August 1985, while keeping my silence in my secret office (read on), I got a call that a general was on the phone for me. General Robinson answered and told me to get ready to come to Rucker. I was going to be a Cobra IP. I discussed that topic a bit, since all the IP in me had been scared out in October (with my engine failure). He said Rucker would have to work it out. And they would be considering me for the USPHT safety slot, and by the way, good luck.

For a while, nothing happened. Without orders, there was not much to do. Anyway, LTC Grimsbo had a heart attack, and he was replaced by a new CAV commander, who was a hard charger.

I prepared a detailed in-brief for him and sat down to talk. He simply asked for the papers and told me I was not needed here. He appointed me the ALSE (Aviation Life Support Equipment) specialist. He had his own safety officer, who would be along in a few days. I had three months left before that happened, and I should report to him once a month. And I left.

I tried to be offended, but I was a liability to him—a short-timer with all the connections and no long-term accountability. But I felt … violated.

The HHT first sergeant was awesome. He had a secret (unused) office and set up an area for me to work in. I did my due diligence in the ALSE business each month and wrote professional articles in my spare time. I made my rounds in the brigade and did not spend a minute overtime around the area. The new 3/5 CAV commander did not so much as wave goodbye, and I left without any other professional issues.

November 1985 was a stormy season. I became tangled in clearing my housing and packing my family. We finally left after a very stressful effort, in which many friends helped us pack. We drove home on leave and rolled into Fort Rucker in January 1986.

15

Fort Rucker: 1986 - 1989

USPHT 1986

On 03 Jan 86, I arrived at Fort Rucker after my PCS (Permanent Change of Station) from Fort Lewis, Washington, with my family. I called LTC Robert E. Harry, USPHT Commander. He had a support staff already preparing to create the US Army Precision Helicopter Team. They had been working on it since November.

I was supposed to be their new safety SME (Subject Matter Expert), in other words, just an additional safety instructor.

Harry was glad to see me, but we saddled up right away. We worked hard, and we did what we had to do. I realized it would be tough and that I would become his errand boy.

My wife was expecting our sixth child. We had some adjusting to do to manage it all, but she was swell.

I was immediately swept up into the USPHT.

I jumped in as gopher for LTC Harry, who simply gave me points of contact and assignments to coordinate. He was hiring staff every day, and we ran hard just to catch up.

We got off to a rough start.

UNITED STATES
PRECISION

HELICOPTER
TEAM

JOURNAL

Cover for the 1986 USPHT JOURNAL

*This following excerpt is a very brief review of the 1986
USPHT Journal*

28 Jan 86

The space shuttle blew up today. The whole world, and especially all airmen, mourn their loss. I was filing a flight plan when someone yelled it was on the TV. I saw the newsman as he appeared to be sort of confused over what had happened. He

could not see the monitor, a fact that became obvious as they played it back, and he talked of possible survivors. I watched the shuttle evaporate during the re-play and cursed the feeble nature of men, whose only genuine lasting quality is their fearless pursuit of lofty goals in the face of incredible odds. God bless them. I would hope that somehow the esteem we feel

370

for that crew would make a difference in the merit with which their lives on this earth are judged.

Mon 10 Feb 86

We were all rookies. There were no veterans on this team, so we had to learn all the administrative stuff on the run. The run up to the first week of training consisted of allotting aircraft parking and training areas to the gathering teams from around Fort Rucker. The first week was wild, and we learned a lot more about running the events safely, including administration of rules, controlling separate events, preparing maps and setting panels, judging and coordination with new competitors. We had some bad weather, but no major incidents.

Feb '86

We ran with the Fort Rucker competition, mostly to practice running the competition. We met our judges and all the major US players who would run the administration with the FAI.

Then we ran the US competition, which was our first really serious competition.

Mon 10 Mar 86

WO1 Gary Reynolds was killed in a UH-60 accident this evening. He was a 38-year-old warrant officer who was easily superior to any other new warrant I ever knew. He was respected and liked by all who knew and worked with him. We on the staff are stunned, since he was a pillar in the planning and execution of the first two months of the staff's existence. We are keenly aware of our loss.

1986 On the USPHT SLOLAM COURSE

WO1 Reynalds   WO1 Morrison

Throughout April and May the team briefed and flew missions morning and night. Mistakes and lessons shared were done with ribbing, and it was brutal. But all the teams worked to help each other. We ended up with many incidents that were funny only in the context of our intensity.

FORT RUCKER: 1986 - 1989

The commander created the Broken Bucket Award for the most difficult but survivable blunder of the day. That would include training cell goofs, such as sending out crew(s) with the wrong map or failing to properly mark the map. There was no mercy.

The commander did a lot of stuff that drove the teams crazy. Once, when the winds were too bad to fly, the team took written tests on the 5K zone around Castle Ashby, England, and one on the international rules. LTC Harry preached that knowledge—all knowledge concerning the team, the rules, the aircraft, and the current team events—all of it leads to team success and individual crew victory. So our testing never stopped.

As an old warrant officer and a real believer in mentoring, I became the class sponsor for Gold Flight, a warrant officer flight class here. I suppose they cut those orders because I had nothing else to do. I went to a phase party in April. (Am I that old? *Really?*)

Fri 18 Apr 86

This morning's brief was sort of funny. A police captain called the S-3 (training officer) yesterday and asked if we had any aircraft working in the vicinity of Marianna, which we did. The S-3 assured him, without waiting for more information, that we had gotten the right to land in all the panel areas. The policeman answered that this was a different sort of problem. Seems that one of the drop panels was around 200 meters from a house that was staked out by cops, who suspected the house to be a center of drug trafficking! Imagine what a cop would think of eight aircraft dropping packages at that panel!

Thu 24 Apr 86

Tonight there was a major argument among the pilots. The course time was done without figuring in the time required for the pickup and drop points, and the inbound leg was only 13 kilometers long. There was no way anyone could make it up if they didn't plan to be fast all the way around. Two of the crews were complaining about it (they complain even when something is legitimate), when Pappy Proctor jumped up and told them all to quit crying and start living up to standards. One of the crew members jumped up and told him if he had ever read the rules, he would know the inbound course had to be 30 kilometers long.

We showed our real integrity by sharing some dreadfully tough bruises.

LTC Harry had a different take on this, even though it was a staff error. "An error is just part of the training. The

WHC Host will make mistakes … we will have to be better than they."

28 April to 02 May 86—Team Leave

Wed 07 May 86

Today we had our first real incident. OH-50 #72-21182 hit a buzzard with Seale and Pascalar aboard. Didn't do much damage, but there was blood and guts everywhere.

Tue 15 May 86

Today the tension came to the top. One of the pilots stood up and hollered during the brief. All the men feel the pressure, and each shows it in his own way. I am certain what doesn't show here shows at home, though I have no way to prove it. Even the wives are intense when they get together.

One of these guys is as moody as a pregnant cow. Another couple of them are whining about everything that doesn't go their way. All of them bitch about the commander. "He isn't doing things right, isn't in touch with the team, isn't capable of making these decisions. He loves *that* guy but hates *me* … he doesn't understand me … he has too much PT, too often, too hard …" and on it goes.

Fri 16 May 86

After the practice, we shot the official team photos. We got one of all the team and staff, but some of the staff couldn't stand around another 30 seconds to be in one of the staff alone. I suppose it is another indicator of the stress on the staff.

Sat 17 May86—Fort Rucker Air Show. Went well

Tue 20 May 86

Jimmy Greene came out of the latrine today shaking his head, mumbling, "You know a man is tired when he throws his trash in the urinal and pees in the trash can."

Fri 23 May 86

My sweet wife gave birth to our sixth child today, Michael Paul Kingsley, 8 pounds at 2127 hours.

Mon 26 May 86—Memorial Day

Tue 27 May 86

Noel Seal, hearing I intended to move to Newton, Alabama, commented, "Well, Newton isn't the end of the world, but you can see it from there."

Fri 30 May 86

Stopped by to see my old friend Dick Tierney, editor of Army Aviation Digest, about writing the USPHT article for the magazine. He will publish all I send him.

Sat 07 Jun 86—Departed for the World Helicopter Championships.

1986 TEAM PHOTO

Top LR: CW3 Maddox, CW4 Loftice
CW2 Seale, CW3 King
Kneeling L-R: CW3 Fancher, CW2
Wright, CW2 Pascalar, CW3 Kent

1986 USPHT

Top L-R: CW3 Iseminger, CW2 Egbert
CW3 Jewkes, CW3 Church
Kneeling L-R: CW3 Greene, CW3
Hendricks, CW2 Reed, WO1 Harless

Back L-R   CW4 Adkison, Cpt "Doc" Martin, Cpt Walters, CW4 Pappy Proctor
Middle L-R   Sgt Manuel, PFC Connell, SSG Harris, CW3 Dan Kingsley
Front L-R   Civ Ms Berkypile, Commander LTC Bob Harry, CW3 Walters, CW2
McConnell

President Ronald Reagan meets with members of the United States Precision Helicopter Team, World Champions, 10 July 1986, Dothan, Alabama

1986 World Championship Team
John Iseminger and Jimmy Green

The politics of the WHC were incredible, but Bob Harry navigated our way through it. In the end, Iseminger and Green, Crew 77, won the contest.

For their outstanding effort, Loftice/Wright received a certificate from the FAI for their participation. Maddox/Fancher received a certificate for the highest score in the Slalom Event (192 points).

Iseminger/Green received the Gold Medal for being in first place overall, and a certificate for having the highest scores in Event 2, Precision Hover Course (200 points, a perfect score) and first place in Event 1, Timed Arrival & Rescue (199 points).

Kent/King, Egbert/Hendricks, and Iseminger/Green were all given certificates for being the #1 WHC Team. This honor was given to the three highest scoring crews of the winning team.

Tue 01 Jul 86

Arrived at Dover Air Force Base, then next morning into Dothan, arriving around 0830 hours local. When the speeches were over, my sweet wife came over and gave me the kiss of my life!

Thu 10 Jul 86

One last thing before I close this out. This operation isn't winding down now; it is crashing in. We met the President of the United States today (Ronald Reagan), the biggest thrill of my tenure. And that was that.

Then we all went back to work.

1988 Fort Rucker Air-to-Air Article

While I was the safety subject matter expert for DGFS, I continued to look for topics of major interest to the Army aviation community to write about. Having been among the very few trained in air-to-air combat training, it seemed a worthy subject. In DGFS, I met CW4 Cliff Whitten, an old Cobra instructor pilot who was really interested in air-to-air.

The AH-64 and the AH-1 fleets still had no automatic or radar target acquisition capability, and attack crews still had no air-to-air training.

Cliff had thought about the practicality of making aerial engagements on aerial targets, and I started running the issues with him. He found a World War II Bomber Gunner's Handbook, and he had developed the principles of engagement from those rules. We found all the firing tables for our modern weapons systems, and we used the figures in estimating weapon ranges and ammunition times of flight to the target. By default, we had to estimate the lead on a target based on all the variables—size, distance and rate of closure (basically, airspeed). We developed tables of engagement using doctrinal sizes of enemy aircraft at (I think) six angles of approach, using the doctrinal airspeed they would be expected to fly. We then included drawings that placed the appropriate size silhouettes of enemy aircraft (at a particular distance and angle) against the mil lines in pictures of our heads-up-displays of the Cobra and the Apache.

This took a lot of time … all of it on our own. Cliff had already peeved some folks trying to get this going, and our DGFS commander was outraged when the article was published in Aviation Digest without his permission.

Don't hold this against me. This article was run up and down the chain of command and was missed by his own carelessness. But when we actually got a call from the USMC, the tapioca hit the fan. They offered to fire, without any cost, the tables we had developed in all modes, if we could get the approval of our commander. Cliff and I were pretty excited about this, and we considered this as a real contribution to the mission.

I honestly do not remember the name of that colonel, but he and I had a history. He had chewed my butt a couple of times for wasting time on this and for other issues, primarily my refusal to be an instructor pilot. Now he was furious that he was expected to be responsible for that signature, with another service yet, for something he refused to support. Yeah, Cliff got his butt gnawed on, too. So, the colonel rejected the offer and ordered us to stop this work.

Well, when you are a CW4, they can bend your dog tags or step on your squash bug (warrant officer insignia) but they can't bust you unless you deliberately break a written rule. My political brand, that is, my label as someone who would not conform, followed me around the rest of my career. I thought it was unfounded and unfair, since it cost the Army nothing and gave the attack community a standard by which to respond to the threat. I am still not sure just how important this article was, although every time I tell it, it just has to be bigger and better. Fortunately for us, helicopter air-to-air combat was never tried in the field, and it never became a major battlefield player.

At least not until now.

The Friend We Cherish

Some years ago, when I was new in the CAV, I met a jerk. Andy. He was sort of a clown, wore a big obnoxious watch that went well with his personality, and I didn't feel he was sincere about anything in which I was interested.

You know how it is. First impressions last a long time …
but finally, we became close and worked together as casual but
firm friends for three years.

Andy died one day when I was at work. Well … not
exactly. He actually died some time before that day, but
he was not dead for me until one day when I met another
acquaintance passing through Cairn's flight operations. I had
left the CAV around Christmas the previous year, and I had
seen Andy almost last of all those I knew so well there.

I was minding my own business when this man brought
up Andy. During our conversation, it occurred to me he was
absolutely unworthy to speak Andy's name, and I became
angry. As we were talking, he happened to casually mention
Andy had died. He elaborated a precious few details and
continued the conversation, oblivious to the steel band
wrapping itself around my throat. I went away and cried over
my loss.

It did not matter to the acquaintance a great man had
passed from this earth; perhaps the significance of it did not
register with him. He could not see my mind's eye racing over
a hundred, perhaps a thousand, quiet conversations I had shared
with my friend, or the jokes, or the common goals we had
shared as a privileged secret. He could never understand the

esteem I had felt for this cavalryman, or the sacrifice I would have made to prevent his untimely demise.

We were good friends, Andy and I, and we shared common values. He and I found precious little time to socialize, though we spoke of it often. At this moment, I would give anything to say we socialized some. But we loved our work; we did it well together, and I loved him as a brother.

Anyway, when I got home I called his wife, too late to do any real supporting, unable to help. She was great, but it occurred to me that I was not considered close enough to be notified. My heart sagged at the thought.

Andy was a soldier with me, and we were both glad for our relationship. He was an achiever, spoke his mind, looked better than John Wayne, and really liked the Army. He was a man of tradition … once I heard him recite the entire poem of Cavalrymen … *Garry Owen*. It is a rare talent and only indicated the spirit of his service. The greeting "Garry Owen" is a particular traditional CAV greeting that calls the greeted to pay attention for whatever else is spoken, like *Sempre Fi* to a Marine.

He adored his sweet wife and had a handful of good kids and dreams he hoped to pursue one day. He loved living and gave it his best shot in every effort. He was one of those pilots with the "right stuff," and his talent was envied in the unit.

Andy displayed honor, courage and integrity of an order seldom seen in the world today. His passing was a terrible loss to the Army. But he was my friend, and while my loss cannot be so clearly defined, I have learned a great lesson.

Sometimes in the pursuit of our careers, we get into the "zoom mode." We forget about the good things around us. Sometimes we need to be reminded of the priceless nature of the friendships we are all privileged to share.

As I have more thoughtfully considered this man, I can think of several other men I have known like him. Few of them have had such a tragedy, but I am grateful to have known and/ or worked with each one. This year I called a few of them just to give 'em a jolt of the ol' Christmas Spirit!

If you share this book and perhaps this lesson with your soldier, remind him that as he plods along in his career, he should remember his friends carefully. It is part of our career to share our comradeship as well as the responsibilities and dangers. Remind him/her that the whole soldier matters, and we should ask about his treasures ... the spouse, the kids, the dog. Ask him home to carve up a Sunday ham. You may be surprised how much you and that guy have in common.

This is a career lesson for the young soldier. There may come a day when you'll be glad you lent him this, another silken thread in the line that gives purpose to our life in the Army.

The Load We Bear

1989—We had to cooperate with Hanchey Army Airfield in all our training efforts. They handled our flight following, but we did not mix our training with their flight operations. We stayed clear as much as possible and were careful to comply with their direction. As the USPHT safety officer, I was responsible for a lot of stuff and went out there often. We also had practice areas in and around the airfield, and I was always around.

I was driving back from a coordination meeting there when I noticed a pilot walking along the side of the road, kicking a can, carrying a helicopter operator's manual.

I am no rocket scientist, but it was a mighty long way back to town. I am a quick study … I knew he was in trouble. And since I had a number of pilots out there, the chances were he was one of mine.

Now, Army pilots generally have a certain air about them, and they fit a certain profile of habit and thought process. I mean, generally speaking, they wear a fancy watch, speak with a "Chuck Yeager" drawl, and they *don't walk*. So I had a feeling this kid was in deep, whatever his problem was, and I stopped to offer him a lift.

He was a good-looking kid, a young warrant officer, and he was very polite in an Opie Taylor sort of way, but he didn't speak. He just smiled until I asked him if he wanted a ride, then got in. He wasn't one of mine, I was certain, and he smiled until I spoke.

What's your name? He told me.

"Why are you walking?"

"Tired of waiting for the bus."

"You know, it's a long way back to town." You can figure out the rest. Anyway, I finally got around to saying I had a mean wife, six kids and a three-legged dog. There was no reaction. Nothing. Usually I can break serious ice with some of my family goings-on, but nothing came of this. I said it again and asked if he were married.

"Well … yes … well no … well sort of. I'm a widower. That means my wife is dead." He had a big smile on his face, but it was a smile of stress and pain and real suffering.

It was a hundred and ten outside, but I felt cold down to my socks.

"How old are you, son?"

"Twenty-six."

"Where did you come from?"

"Korea … I was there when she died."

I was stunned. I got my heart pumping again and went on to ask what happened to her.

"Oh, yeah. She was killed. Hit by a train."

At first I could not fathom what he had said. Whatever I expected, I couldn't believe it and thought he might be kidding … or maybe just *wrong* might be a better word. How can you kid about something like this? He still had that big smile. Yep. I had to ask.

"How?" He didn't hear me.

"And my three sons," he went on.

I was numb now; I couldn't swallow, and I listened more carefully.

"With her sister. Yep, her sister was with her … and *her* two …" He wasn't smiling now. I could barely hear him. There were tears stuck in him like a backward fish hook, and they just couldn't come out. Hell, I am not sure, but the tears in me felt that way.

"Her two children?"

"Yeah," he answered. "And an old man from town, we all knew him, he came out with the rescue squad. Tried to revive my son. Had a heart attack. Died on the scene."

He took a deep breath and the smile was back. He was in control again. I fired a bunch of questions. He was one of us, a soldier in anguish, and we damn well better do this right.

"What are you here for?"

" An advanced helicopter course. Apache … AH-64."

"How are you doing?"

"Not good."

"What's the problem?"

"Can't concentrate. Not sleeping much."

"Why don't you come to dinner Sunday?"

"Yeah, I'd like that."

"We have a lot of kids, if they bug you, tell me."

"Oh, they'll be okay, but do you *really* have a three-legged dog?"

"Yep, and he's ugly, but we love him."

"Good. I want to play with your dog."

"We can arrange it."

He didn't have a prayer. My children ran him over. The dog liked him too.

I called someone in the command channels. It was Major "Doc" Martin, the USPHT flight surgeon and all-around good guy. He listened. He took notes. He promised action. He left me wondering just what he could do.

Now, it happened that I was due my annual flight physical, just by chance, two days later. I entered the clinic at the appointed time and took my seat. There were lots of folks there, and some VIPs came in behind me.

I saw a lady captain (flight surgeon) step out and call me by name, and I told a colonel to go ahead, since I was in no hurry. He was grateful. He was, after all, a colonel, and obviously more important than I. I got no reward for this little courtesy except maybe a more efficient Army.

The flight surgeon finished with him, stepped out and called me again. She seemed a little put out, but I ignored it. Another colonel had come in, and I waved him ahead. He was, after all, another colonel, and obviously more important than I. I got no reward for this little courtesy except *blah blah blah*. I hoped. But I was getting kind of antsy. I wanted to get done and get back. When she stepped out again, I ignored all others and stepped up to her. She grabbed my arm.

"Mr. Kingsley, didn't you hear me calling *you*?"

I was startled at my first meeting with **Captain Rhonda Cornum**, who would become a hero in the first Iraq War in 1991 by her courageous endurance of crash injuries and torture. She was a hell of a man.

She sat me down and started in. She did not know I was there for my physical. She wanted to talk about my young pilot, the one I had picked up on the side of the road. She wanted to know all the details. I could not tell her enough. She was certain she could get him help, bail him out of his advanced course and still save his career.

She did not even do my flight physical. She got on the phone and spoke to the young man's commander. She stayed on the phone after I left. She contacted personnel, then Department of the Army Warrant Officer Management, Washington DC. She went out and met the kid. And she did it all that day. I have seldom seen such worthy compassion in the Army.

They gave the kid a break. He was pulled out of school, and the Army took care of him.

He came by to see me one time before he left, and he thanked me for helping. He was already better. I don't mean the pain, but he wasn't pulling the train alone anymore, and he knew it.

I learned a lot from that experience. For whatever reason my family is here, and his isn't. I am eternally grateful to have them. And whatever I might have done for that kid, it is not near as much as he did for me.

Fort Rucker 1987-1988

A lot happened during the years between 1986 and 1988, and I have given them short shrift. I spent most of my tenure as the safety Subject Matter Expert for the Director of Gunnery and Flight Systems. I taught safety classes for all aviation students as assigned, maintained flight and instrument currency, ran up '58s being maintained in the crew chief training courses, and tried to negotiate a better end to my career, which I could see coming.

I was promoted to CW4. I was selected to attend the resident Warrant Officer Senior Course (WOSC), which was supposed to be a very highly regarded selection. I had already completed the reserve WOSC at Fort Lewis, expecting I might not be selected for the resident course.

It was nearly the last class of that sort. The Army decided to create the rank of CW5 and added a course (I think it was called the Warrant Officer Master Course), which eliminated the Senior Course. So all of us proud guys in the last few classes were mostly Fort Rucker residents, and it cost the Army very little to transport the personnel to flesh out the last few classes. But it was a good course, and I enjoyed it.

I bought that little place in Newton and moved my family out there. The home wasn't much, but I loved that 15 acres. My oldest son accidently shot himself in the eye with a BB gun, and we were very lucky the doctors were able to save the eye. My second son was thrown from a horse and suffered a severe injury to his right calf, but he recovered fully. My third child, the finest horsewoman I ever saw, was thrown off a horse that refused a jump and had her neck stepped on, but she was not badly injured, due to her helmet. My fourth child, the other finest horsewoman I ever saw, stumbled off a horse and broke her foot, and she still limps on it.

We raised our children in the country with pigs and farm animals, and it was a good life. It was hardest on my poor wife, who loved living in the country but not in that little house with six kids and a three-legged dog.

The Three-Legged Dog

In early November 1988, our dog, Andy, disappeared.

Remember here I loved country life, but I was still on active duty doing active duty stuff. The dog was as much baby-sitter as pal. His was a quiet presence; you know how it is around a country place. If there was fishing or camping, Andy was always there, but otherwise, all he ever did worthy of mention was chase away cows rummaging around our corn patch.

My kids had taken him for granted for a long time, but now he was missed. Every meal-time, as our faithful mutt failed to return, concern grew. He had never been gone overnight before, so this was rather unusual.

One Saturday morning I was getting ready to step into the shower when it happened.

"*Aarrrgghhhhhh!*" It was the kind of guttural groan that makes your heart stop, shrieked from the kitchen by a wretched soul. It was my sweet son, desperate to lend his help to some terrible situation he could not fully understand. It brought to mind the Biblical discussion of wailing and gnashing of teeth, and the "fight or run instinct" took over in me. I leaped away from the shower, nearly unclad.

"*He's lost his foot! Aarrrgghhhhhh!*" My blood froze. Kids, not all mine, were outside. And there were tools like axes, saws, plows. There were yearling bulls, cows, horses and things that could easily snuff a kid being silly or stupid. I ripped an Army webbed belt out of my uniform, the kind with the slip-lock buckle, which would allow me to cinch down a tourniquet ... should I need it ... for the kid I could see in my mind's eye, helpless outside.

I raced outside to see my daughter Nancy holding Andy by the collar, touching his head gently. The rest of the kids were standing around in one state of mourning or another. Nancy was crying, trying not to look at Andy's foot. She was prancing around as though her spirit wanted to fly away but her body just couldn't go along. I took the collar and sent her in the house.

Before she left, she asked, "Daddy, is Andy going to die?"

"Yes," I said firmly. We had animals ... animals die ... we even have to destroy them on occasion. She knew this. Tears streamed from her face as she went into the house.

"Dad, should we pray for Andy?" Donny asked.

"Yes," I told him. I knew we had to end this quickly, for the missing foot had been gone for at least two days, and the dog was suffering.

"Tell all the kids to pray for Andy. Call Jeff out here. Tell him to bring the gun."

Donny shrieked again. There was a look of horror, of terrible pain and disbelief that I will never forget. He bolted into the house, and screamed for his mama.

My sweet wife, having more kid-savvy than I, convinced me to take him to a vet and have him put to sleep. So my oldest son, Jeff, and I loaded Andy into the truck, and off we went to find a vet who would do this on a Saturday. The ride was eternal. There was no cell phone to bolster my fortitude. But the vet was very kind.

"The dog isn't too bad," he said. "I might save him," he went on, for a mere $ 250.00.

FORT RUCKER: 1986 - 1989

I'm kind of wimpy ... after all, I still wanted to be "the Dad," and it might be questionable after this. I borrowed his phone and called Mom. She gave me the okay, if the vet would take plastic money.

All seemed to go well, at first. Then came infection and *Doggie Intensive Care*. More than $400.00. That was a pretty healthy chunk of change, especially back then. But you couldn't just take the dog back and demand a refund ... and I was much more likely to be voted Dad of the Year should there ever be such a tally in my house.

Well, we had that wonderful dog for many more years, and I continued to be the wonderful dad. Andy with only three legs, could still chase those cows, but he was a bit more subdued than he used to be.

As I write these words, it is the holiday season, which wouldn't be complete without a footnote of the wonder it brought to our house.

Over Thanksgiving dinner, as Nancy blessed the food, she called to mind our beloved dog with wonderful words that only a child can whisper, and she gave heartfelt thanks. As she wrestled with the Lord over our many blessings, Nancy humbled all of us with her faithful plea...

"... and God, won't you please hurry up and grow his leg back?"

Fort Rucker 1988-1989

As much as I enjoyed the Fort Rucker area, I knew I had used up all the good will of the Warrant Officer Management Branch when I had sneaked into Fort Rucker by way of General Robinson. They did their very best to be civil to me about it, but I knew I was coming up for rotation in 1989, and I was looking for my career-ending to be something in my favor. I had actually wanted to do more than 20 years, but I also wanted to keep my family at home.

Warrant Officer Management figured I should just be happy to do whatever came up and they would provide their own motivation. I think they expected the hope of promotion to CW5 to be a powerful carrot, but actually I did not see anyone uphill willing to reward me for all I had done, whatever merit they felt that might be. I just wanted to be a good soldier and not do many more isolated tours. I struck a deal to go to Korea for a tour, and they promised to bring me back to Rucker for another tour. They did not pretend I had any expectation of promotion again, but I should get at least another three years at Rucker, and by the end of that time, I would have 23 years active, and I could see how it turned out, promotion or no.

I was blissfully living at Rucker having a great career in safety. I had been on the USPHT, I had settled in at Fort

FORT RUCKER: 1986 - 1989

Rucker, and I was happy there. I had been promised my isolated tour in Korea with a return to Rucker, as I wished. I felt I had finally made peace with Warrant Officer Branch. I had presumed, incorrectly, that my deal for a Korean tour had earned forgiveness for accepting my current Fort Rucker tour over their heads, and all their nasty little yellow stickies had been cleared. Apparently, I was wrong. But there is no sense trying to explain it without some sarcasm and humor.

"Little yellow stickies"—Each active-duty officer in those days had a career folder containing a record of all assignments and details, conversations and special information. When you called Warrant Officer Management, the manager who spoke to you reviewed that folder and reviewed your issues. Details that did not merit a specific correct entry got a little note on a yellow sticky paper that was stuck on the appropriate page in the file. I never spoke to the same manager twice, but each one knew everything that was current in my career. I am convinced that in addition to the requisite administrative notes, they highlighted my sins and all our discussions about my career. I once heard a rumor that in those stickies, I was listed as a dirty yellow polecat of dubious antecedents and conjectural progeny. It was only rumor, you understand … but it seems to fit their regard for my service.

One day after I had made my best effort to shape my illustrious career and satisfy the powers on high, I got a shocking call from LTC Harry. He was still my exec at DGFS, and he simply told me to run down to the Fort Rucker Aviation Museum and pick up the old 1986 precision team records, and bring them to his office. He casually mentioned that we had to get them sorted out for the next team, and he had already interviewed a few folks to flesh out the staff.

Now, this may seem normal to a civilian, but the USPHT was a once-in-a-lifetime event, and to take a second cut at it was beyond extraordinary. I was stunned. I was thrilled. But I was afraid what this might mean to my best effort to be a faithful, obedient warrant officer.

As we started going through the records, I thanked him for considering me again, but I had struck the deal with Warrant Officer Branch to go to Korea and return to Rucker. It was an agreement I did not dare break if I ever wanted more career than I could see from my chair.

He did not even blink. He just grunted and told me I did not need to worry about that. After all, this was the world competition again, and we were going to win it. General Parker would make that agreement good … that is, the promise to return to Rucker after a Korean tour … and there was nothing to worry about.

I knew there would be smoke on the horizon over *this* unconventional revision of Department of the Army orders, but I did not know how much. I had been very lucky the first time

FORT RUCKER: 1986 - 1989

I was sent to Rucker, and I loved my Fort Rucker assignment. But I was still not clearly aware of the shadowy world of warrant officer politics.

LTC Harry made good on his promise a few weeks later. I was given a copy of this letter, written about me to the Warrant Officer Management Branch.

LTC Harry was very proud of this letter and was taken aback by my suspicion of its veracity. It said, basically, that in my presence *the sun would pale, babies would not cry, women would swoon and men would step aside*. It was dutifully signed by General Parker. How could I doubt that??

In fairness, Warrant Officer Management Branch did what they had to do. They couldn't let just any old hillbilly warrant officer run over them, however important his plans might seem to be. And knowing how much fluff there was in this letter, I was an idiot. Even I knew it just could not play out that way.

UNITED STATES
PRECISION

HELICOPTER
TEAM
JOURNAL

Cover for the 1989 USPHT JOURNAL

LTC Harry was called up again to lead the team, and he assigned me as his Safety Officer. A lot of interesting things occurred in this train-up. The entire competition series conducted up to the selection of the team was a sort of fraud.

It became clear to us that all the pilots who had been in the previous competition, trained as they were for the intensity of the effort, were more skilled than any of the new pilots who tried to win a spot on the team. LTC Harry chose and approved every person on the team, staff and competitors. As much audacity as that shows, his training eye made few errors, and in the actual event, *any of the seven crews who went would have been World Champion (by virtue of their score in the competition) if all the others had been absent.*

In fact, the degree of the victory in 1989 was so astonishing there was consideration by the international judges of eliminating the USPHT from the competition for cheating. Cheating because we flew too much, cheating because we bribed our judges or their judges, or cheating just because you *had* to cheat to win by such a margin. Just ask a Russian.

Jimmy Greene, the former navigator for World Champion Jon Iseminger could not return for this team, so Jon chose his own navigator for this trip. Rudy Hobbs was a very bright and energetic instructor pilot. He was simply snatched up became one of the Team. Jon did all the instruction and training needed… and Rudy became an invaluable part of the crew and team

The USPHT judging staff was refined somewhat and approved by LTC Harry. They were trained on this trip; they were taught to be assertive in their decisions, no matter who the pilot was, and they were required to be on time and under budget during every event.

In this trip, LTC Harry refined the competition rules and training constantly, so that the entire team was constantly in turmoil perfecting their techniques. There was a degree of hatred for the way he tormented the crews. Still is. But LTC Harry had these crews so refined in their skills that the Russians were very suspicious about the Americans who talked so openly about their methods and were so willing to help.

Let me cite one example. During the training, the rules would be changed almost weekly, so at every event, rules were constantly being changed. The legs of navigation might be lengthened or shortened … they might have different identification panels on the ground … they might even have one panel available to one crew's navigation and then changed for another crew coming along behind. They might remove one of the slalom gates, or change the length of the hover event lanes or shorten the hovering (height ropes and weights). Thus the constant resentment about every change and every new judgment still exists today.

During a competition briefing in the 1989 competition, as though delivered by an angel, the Russians stood up in a meeting and suggested two changes to an event. They were big changes, and they required a vote from the judges and from the crew commanders (i.e., Bob Harry and others). Bob Harry jumped up and objected to the change as unfair, unpracticed and unauthorized. The Russians seized this opportunity to embarrass the Americans, to impose their will on the judges, and to change the competition rules.

The American judges, knowing full well the team had practiced these changes dozens of times, stood up and supported their Russian judge colleagues, bonding their friendship by supporting that change, and setting up the Russians for their own folly. Harry stomped off and pretended to be offended.

We found him later laughing and still reminding the team to keep their heads up, that the competition, the judges, the international jury and all the powers of heaven could still combine to defeat them. But the Americans kicked so much butt in that event that the international jury met to discussed the propriety of this change … and letting the Americans win so convincingly; the jury even discussing penalizing the team for some unknown and underhanded trick they could not explain.

Well, we won. Though only allowed to have five competitors and an extra two crews as backups, all seven crews were honored by the WHC. Every score was higher than all competitors, and the offense felt by the international judges was so brutal, that even after we flew out of country we did not know for sure whether the last penalty against Jon Iseminger would be tossed out or applied to his score.

After we returned home, we were all flown to Washington DC to see the president. But only the real men got to meet him. George W. Bush had no time for all of us. The crews visited him, and the rest of us toured Washington DC until their meeting was over. I do not recall even leaving the bus. You can read all the details in my book ***We Came to Dominate***.

Then we, the faithful support staff, did what every father of the bride should do:

Show up, put up, pay up and shut up.

We came. We saw. We conquered.

FORT RUCKER: 1986 - 1989

1989 USPHT Support Staff   Left to Right...

Back Row... CW3 Mike Gann Asst Tng; SPC Darlene Graber, Admin Asst; CW3 Chris Van Cuyk, Asst Tng; LTC Robert E. Harry, Commander; Cpt Kevin McGrath, Training Officer; CPT David Dippold, S-1, DAC William Hayes, PAO;

2nd Row... CPT Keith Martin, Flight Surgeon; DAC Wanda Bellamy, Secretary; CPT Herb Burgess, S-3; SPC Otto Fernandez Admin Specialist; CPT Robin Lynch, S-4; CW4 Dan Kingsley, Safety

Kneeling... MSG Jim Sutton; Team NCOIC; SSG Richardo Manuel, Supply NCO; CPT John Delaney, Executive Officer; SSG Connie Sell, Operations NCO;

Insert... CPT John Allen, Maintenance Officer

1989 World Champion Helicopter Crew
SSG John Degand   CW3 Jon Iseminger
Inspecting Rotor Head... CW3 Rudy Hobbs

1989 Team Aircraft and

1986 President Regan presented USPHT T-Shirt By LTC Bob Harry

1989 USPHT meeting President Bush & Representative Dickensen. Tallest left: Cpt Kevin McGrath. By Flag : MSG Jim Sutton
L-R: CW2 Ken Wright; Commander LTC Robert E. Harry; Sgt Lonnie Rash; Sgt Scott Harbarger; Hon Rep Dickenson; General Carl E. Vuono
CW3 Paul Hendricks; CW3 George Egbert; CW3 Rudy Hobbs; 3rd Place WHC Pilot CW3 Rick Church; Twice World Champion Pilot Jon Iseminger;
2nd Place WHC Pilot CW4 John Loftice . Seated: President of the United States - George Bush

WHEN FAT MEN FLEW

We returned to Fort Rucker, and Jon Iseminger was
paraded around the Army and placed in the Warrant Officer
Hall of Fame, as he richly deserved. I am not sure he ever felt
the stress was worthwhile, but he was the face of the team
without any question.

We all filed reports and boxed them up for the USPHT
display, which was going to be set up in the Fort Rucker
museum ... and for the future defense of the World Helicopter
Championship, which we were certain would be happening one
day soon.

It never happened.

The only exciting part of our return to the aviator ranks
there was a big rebellion amongst the command staff at Fort
Rucker, specifically against the team. The team was specifically
allowed to keep their USPHT patch on their flight uniforms.
It was apostasy to the rules of the Army to have such a patch.
Anyone with command authority and a pair of 'nads insisted on
hollering to all who would listen (except General Parker) that
this arrogance was unauthorized and illegal and just another
perk without a purpose.

Too bad. I was able to wear it without problems after that.

Thus the end of this most exciting adventure, even if it
was the most challenging in my career. It disappeared like
the vapor of a warm cow patty on a bright, brisk morning.

FORT RUCKER: 1986 - 1989

We all went back to our business. It was kind of like running a marathon but not quite catching your breath after it was over.

Some Confusing Personal Facts

Just before our train-up ended (prior to the competition), I was having some heart palpitations. I sort of tucked those away as uneventful loafer stuff. I just did not have time for them.

In the meantime, the warrant officer manager (a full colonel) spoke pleasantly over the phone ... and met me at Rucker to discuss my career. He promised (again) that if I went to Korea (inferring ... without wailing, complaining or hollering too much), I would still return to Rucker for my next tour. He looked honest. He seemed sincere. I was sure I had pulled it off, finally.

So I later I spoke to his assistant, the CW5 with him, the *real* executioner of the orders ... and his growling, snarling response was no comfort to me. He insisted that if the manager said it, it would be so. He did not mention the colonel was going to depart his job very soon ... *and he would not be the manager much longer.*

I suspected that, and I hated it, but I needed no translation. I was an old warrant myself, and in warrant officer speak, I was gonna get my tallywhacker bent in the door, as all disobedient children do. And we *all* knew that couldn't be good. I had broken their sacred code—not once but *twice*—by getting orders changed against their prescribed course of action. Yep. That old "bent in the door" thing was beginning to hurt already.

My First Heart Issues

Heck, I never had a heart attack. It only seemed that way, and it caused a lot of problems for me, for my self-esteem, my ego and my flight pay. I ended up writing a funny little poem on the issues involved the moment a pilot loses his wings … but that is later in the chapter.

I mean, there I was on the USPHT. I was busier than that proverbial one-legged man in a butt-kicking contest, and I was under stress each day. You may not truly realize the pain-in-the-neck label that goes with the office of Safety Officer, but it makes him the centerpiece of every controversial issue. In other words, if it did not deal with flight time, training or money, it was my problem. That means either I was failing or it was not a problem. With additional duties such as the part-time Public Affairs Officer and the general do-it boy for the commander, I was out of my mind. I started having trouble sleeping ... then I was getting extra heart beats.

When I try to describe this … it is not easy. You know how your heart goes *ka-thump, ka-thump … ka-thump*, as though it is keeping time with "Mary Had A Little Lamb"? Well, mine decided to start going ka-thump *bang* ... ka-thump *bang,* as though it were off to the "Camp Town Races."

Not often, but once in a while, I would get these little mouse-running-the-creaky-wheel-in-your-chest feelings. Not while I was under a heavy physical load, but when I was making serious decisions and enduring stressful moments. I did not like it one bit, and *there was only one thing to do* ... and I did it.

Shut up! Tell no one!

Last thing I needed was to lose my flight status, my flight pay, and my position on the team. Being a line-unit safety officer was low enough on the pecking order, but I assure you that being grounded ... well, that's like being a stallion without a ... well, you figure it out.

So I said nothing until training was nearly complete, and the worst they could do was let the team go to France without me.

You may notice here that it did not occur to me that I could be *dead,* or even worse, injure someone else. Not for a minute.

"What did you say?"

During the competition training, I trapped my friend and team flight surgeon, Captain "Doc" Martin, in his office one day and told him my problem. He nearly jumped out of his chair and made me sit down for a listen. Then he ordered up a Holter monitor (a chest mounted recorder to take a 24-hour read), and long story short, there were a few extra heartbeats, but nothing terrible. He got me a waiver to fly. I went to France with the team. We won the World Helicopter Championship again. So, for me, it was all worth it.

I was really patting myself on the back for 'fessing up to my sins, but I did not bother the doc with my continued extra heartbeats. They got rather worse ... that is, after a few minutes of these irregular heartbeats, I was ready to lie down and take a break. Then they would stop. But I felt that once the team completion was over, I could relax some and do my year in Korea with no problems. So I sucked it up. I told no one.

But I learned a great lesson. Self-medication, like self-diagnosis (by such an esteemed and knowledgeable person such as myself), is not as useful as I had hoped.

16

Korea, 1989

I returned home with the team and immediately shipped out to Korea. In no time I was embroiled in the unit issues. I ended up in Korea for only three months, and the chronology of these moments may seem a bit confusing, but they were critical to my remaining career.

One of my major issues there was a problem warrant officer. To respect the privacy we all deserve, I am gonna spare you his name.

This was, I believe, the most difficult moment I ever had in my career. He was an aviator in my unit who was impervious to guidance. Rules (the things we had to comply with all the time) or orders (assignments for duty) were abused or ignored on a broad scale, and it is amazing he was tolerated by the unit. He had what I consider a high-risk profile that now, in hindsight, is clear and precise. At that time, it was not so much.

He could not obey rules. He was dangerous. He hid all this behind a façade of courage and initiative. He was an instructor pilot and had no use for anyone interfering with his decisions, and he would use what power he pretended to have to abuse and intimidate his fellows.

I was not part of the command channel, and as such forbidden to provide evidence for court, but I provided eyes for the commander. The commander is responsible for enforcement of rules, for obedience to orders, for successful mission completion, for all training, and for every facet of the unit. So a safety officer provides input; the commander acts in the interest of his command.

Now, on the second day in-country, I wandered into our flight operations center at Camp Page, Korea. I saw a CW2 looking exactly like Rambo. I mean, he didn't have the build, but the swagger was perfect.

I had to take a second look at him. I had been in the Army all day long, and generally, aviation warrant officers are superb experts in aviation, pretty much slovenly in their appearance and laid back in their bearing. Not always ... but generally.

KOREA, 1989

This kid was wearing a turtle-neck sweater under his Nomex flight suit. It was Air Force issue underwear, I was told later by this kid, just so I understood it was *authorized*. He had a Gerber (a very popular soldier-of-fortune sort of combat knife) strapped onto one boot. His boots were spit shined and not standard issue. They were some very expensive German mountain boots with the very wide and very high sole. I think it made him look taller.

He came right over and shook hands. He seemed certain that my particular attention was *envy* … and he seemed to preen for me. He asked me what aircraft I flew. I told him I wanted to fly the OH-58 (the Kiowa Scout helicopter … more flexibility for the safety mission than the AH-1). He promptly informed me that *he* was the only '58 instructor in the battalion. In fact, if I recall correctly, he told me he was the only SIP in the unit, and he would get to me when he had time. The truth was that he was the only '58 IP (Instructor Pilot) in the unit and not qualified as an SIP. In "pilot talk," an SIP is no arbitrary designation. It means as a Standardization Instructor Pilot, his training and appointment are the yardstick of unit compliance to regulations, flight procedures and training.

Well, no big deal. I was the new guy. I could hardly imagine the load of the *only* '58 instructor in the entire battalion. Anyway, there were other CW4s there to watch over this kid, and surely not all of them were asleep. I was still confused over this kid's real place, and one of the senior warrants would square it with me. And after all, this was my first look at him. In fact, it was my first look at the unit.

I did not know it then, but the kid was being mentored by a hard-drinking, hard-fighting, divorced old warrant officer who made a lot of bogus excuses for the kid. The mentor was a primary enabler to dysfunctional behavior. As you will see, it would take five years to get all of the story out.

I immediately began to hear unsolicited rumblings. That very day. And I did as I always do, I kept a sort of journal of unit issues.

For starters, the kid often and regularly intimidated his fellows. Specifically, if he were not getting cooperation from someone, he would threaten them with an *unannounced check ride*. An unannounced check ride is the standard way for an Army aviation unit to ensure that training is current and skills are good across the board. Everybody gets an unannounced check ride from time to time, but it can be abused, and abuse is forbidden. So I thought the first guy who told me this might be falling short in his personal skills, or jealous, or gossiping … but all *three* of them could not be.

Then came whispers of flight violations. Some were petty, open to interpretation. No sweat. Rumor had it that he had flown some single pilot missions on NVGs (Night Vision Goggles) with a crew chief and landed his aircraft on a bridge that was under construction.

Regulations in those days required two qualified NVG pilots in a flight. Landing on an unmarked, uncharted bridge was beyond comprehension. Who could believe the unit (not just the unit, but the battalion) instructor pilot would deliberately break such a rule. But after this, a young lieutenant (non-aviation, and certainly non-NVG qualified officer) came to me and said the kid had scared him to death doing this, too.

The kid had his own nickel-plated 9mm semi-automatic pistol he carried to the field, with his own ammunition. He kept the gun in his hooch, as opposed to having an official license and keeping it as required in the armory. And rumor had it he carried it to town.

He was recently divorced.

He had recently submitted a request for an extension to remain in Korea.

He had recently been passed over for CW3.

He was a very heavy drinker.

And somehow, no one else in the entire battalion saw any red lights except me? I may be proud, but I knew I was not clairvoyant. There was more, but you get the idea.

I called the kid and asked him in to see me. I was already grounded by this time with a heart problem but was cleared DNIF (duty not to include flight). I was still accountable for the flight safety of the battalion. Knowing all this, he was inclined to dismiss my counsel. He demanded to know why I wanted to see him.

I told him I had prepared a Memorandum For Record for the battalion commander about him, and I wanted him to see it first. He asked me who the heck I thought I was, and I explained it so he would understand.

"I am CW4 Kingsley, your safety officer, and I think you might want an opportunity to see this first. And you might want your commander to come along."

Before I get too far, as the new ASO, I had an office with a computer in it. It was unusual, but I kept detailed notes on all things, and especially this series of events, including my Memorandum for Record on this activity. These notes would become critical to this kid five years later.

So the kid brought his company commander, a fine West Point, just-made-the-major-list captain to our meeting. He was a good man, there to ensure that truth, justice and the American Way prevailed in this hanging, as he suspected it would be. He knew how hard this kid worked (I give it to him … he *did* work hard) and how much responsibility was on his shoulders (ditto the last … I give it to him). The kid was suave and cocky, and the two of them read the list separately. I think there were 12 items on the list. The kid got madder and madder but said nothing.

The captain became flustered as he read on. He finally spoke. "And who says it is illegal to land on a bridge?" he sputtered.

"Sir, just tell me this was on his mission-brief, and I will make one of these up for *you* too."

The captain looked over at his warrant officer. They said nothing. The aviator denied only one item, a minor flight violation.

I did not realize how much of an outcast I would become over this memorandum. Even the men who had confided in me over these issues asked not to be revealed. The kid's mentor, the salty old CW4, would later come to me drunk one night and threaten me. I was hoping he would be just as drunk if he ever tried to make it good. But I am sure this old warrant was trying to protect the kid, sure he could straighten him out. The warrant certainly would not allow a wimpy safety officer to railroad his protege.

The commander, it turned out, was in a pickle over this kid. He was unquestionably one of the finest commanders I ever worked for (in very measurable ways) and made it policy to reward aggressiveness. This habit, rewarding aggressiveness, is the one common denominator I have found in great commanders. After all, they must fight alongside the aggressive soldiers they have *mentored.*

This commander had given this young aviator a "1" block. That means he had rated him higher than all other warrant officer aviators in his command, a very bold thing for a CW2. The commander had also groomed the CW2 for a very prestigious award, the Army Aviation Association of America Aviator of the Year for Korea from that unit. I believe the commander did these things to reward the kid's work in the unit and to get him promoted. Getting promoted after being passed over was a real tough nut to crack.

I went up to see the commander the same evening I saw the kid. I waited an hour because the kid was already in there with his battalion and company commanders. When I was finally called in to see the battalion commander with the memorandum, he was furious. He swore he knew nothing of the pistol (the kid was the commander's pilot in the field) or of any of the other charges. No one else had brought any of these charges to his attention.

He wanted the names of those gossip mongers *now.* I refused. I explained the rules on safety officer information … rules he knew well … and I told him how these men had asked not to be revealed. I told him that none of them had come as a group, but singly. It was a unit-wide awareness that brought this to me, not a gossip circle. He raged about my audacity. He did not quite say it, but he indicated he believed this was all just a lot of gossip. But he said he would look into the charges.

I did not know it at the time, but the old CW4 mentor to this struggling aviator had already been to see the commander. I am sure the kid spread this memo far and wide, but the commander complained bitterly of my "dirty tricks" and my "unfairness" to this kid.

I believe the commander was poorly advised by his trusted senior warrant officer, and I think he simply could not decide who was being truthful ... or perhaps he had decided before I got there.

When I made this memo, I had also included recommendations to settle this issue for the safety of both the command and the kid. The recommendations were detailed, brutal and without any wiggle room. I fully understood I had no right to punish or enforce. But a recommendation without teeth is a pacifier. Among these were:

- relief of his position as unit OH-58 Instructor Pilot

- mandatory in-country flight evaluation.

- psychological evaluation

- termination of his effort to extend in Korea.

I had to leave country two months later due to what I thought was a heart problem, so I did not hear the end of it for several years. But not much happened in that two months.

The commander never used me in a safety function after that, except to keep up the paperwork and inspect a few things. I did not participate in training or in any long-term planning. The men I had started so well with were obviously not willing to be associated with me, and they still feared being associated with my "abuse" of the little tyrant IP. The local flight surgeon, having received a request from the commander to review these recommendations, asked me what the heck I was trying to do. I told him same thing I told the commander … the kid had to be stopped.

On the last day I was there, as I was having breakfast, the commander saw me and wished me luck. As well as I remember, that was that.

Arrival in Camp Page, Korea

Okay, back to my initial arrival at Camp Page. I was not feeling rested at all, and I was immediately wrestling with unit problems. I felt as though I had not slept in a year, and if I could just catch up on my rest, all would be well.

KOREA, 1989

I knew it was going to be a long year away from my family, so I had to stay busy with a plan, however overly optimistic it might be. I discovered that the unit seemed divided between two camps of men ... those who practiced the "whatever happens in Korea stays in Korea" life, and those who spent their spare time doing their duty and devoted to family in some fashion. Remember that the accepted vices of alcohol, tobacco and daring activities were in full effect here. Coupled with the emotional drain of being away from family, these often led to problems on the professional level.

As a member of the Church of Jesus Christ of Latter-Day Saints (a Mormon), I had a few tangible goals that fit my lifestyle.

1. I wanted to be the successful safety guru of the Attack Helicopter Battalion. I wanted to make a difference in both morale and safety in some substantive, measurable way.

2. I wanted to fulfill my commitment in Korea and return to Fort Rucker to retire ... put in 24 years and maybe a few more. The Warrant Officer Branch was mad at me, but even if they did not promote me, they had promised me those orders, and I wanted to get them in my hand.

3. I wanted to actively practice my faith and find whatever peace there was to find in Korea.

4. I still had visions of becoming a CW5, the god of warrant officers. Maybe even be allowed to serve in the hallowed halls of the USASC, the US Army Safety Center.

5. I wanted to stay out of trouble and stay close enough to my family so that I did not lose my emotional balance. That was a major problem in Korea.

As soon as I arrived in Korea, I discovered that all my Warrant Officer Branch promises had been broken; I was headed for Fort Campbell no matter what, and if I did not like it, I could just eat rocks and bark at the moon. I actually had a printed copy of orders handed to me with the old dates of my planned first trip to Korea. Nothing to do about it now.

Well, I was a big boy. I didn't even call them. Orders is orders, and I sucked it up. At least, *until by a strange twist of fate, I found a way to make 'em even madder.* It was just the way it worked out.

Having just come from a very stressful assignment, I was determined to kick back some but still do a professional job. I was expecting the quarters to be primitive … but when I signed in, I learned that the "field grade" quarters were not complete. They thought it would make me unhappy, but I did not care. They promised me if I could accept it, they would give me an entire Quonset hut and partition it into rooms with wall lockers, provide me furniture as requested and stock it with all the appliances I wanted. In addition, there was some sort of remedial housing allowance they would pay me; and I agreed. Happily.

I went to my first church meeting in town and met the local LDS soldiers there. I asked those men home, and from then on, I made my hooch the local Latter Day Saint gathering place twice a week.

A sergeant had 400 movies and one of those old 14-inch DVD players weighing at least a hundred pounds. He chose one movie each week. He and a gorilla would haul the player over to my place and set it up, play it and take it down each day they were there. We often had 15 or more on our movie night, always consisting of those soldiers who were family oriented and usually did not drink heavily.

Before I left home, I had cut out two dozen pictures of wife and kids. When I got to my housing, I hung them up on the wall as a trio of collages. You know the stuff ... Mom giving haircuts, the boys eating watermelon, the girls doing girly stuff ... the boys doing boy stuff ... and Mom looking like all the woman she was. She even got a portrait for me that absolutely captured the girl I loved. And these pictures were not simply of family. They were of me, of my world, of my goals and all I held dear. Even the crusty guys loved those pictures.

One day a soldier came in and passed these three frames on the wall. He stopped to stare at them. One at a time, he examined each frame and every picture in it. I watched him as he deliberately went from one to another, and back again. He started to cry. It was not the wimpy cry of a child, or whining, or complaining. It was the cry of a brave man whose crust was suddenly cracked by what a soldier gives for his career. He became a good friend. And he wrote home about our movie nights.

Finally ... No More Denial

Back in the unit, I was really busy trying to get the feel for things, and I hit the ground running. I was keeping a safety log in my office and often spent my late nights working.

One day around lunch, when everybody was at chow, I got that funny mouse-in-my-chest sort of feeling and decided to walk it off. No good. It was not very painful, just uncomfortable and heck ... annoying.

I simply could not think. I felt sort of confused, and I started out for a serious walk. I ended up down at our medical section and stopped in. A couple of guys were sitting around the waiting room, and a female warrant officer PA (Physician's Assistant) was in an exam room, taking care of a patient. The clerk asked what I wanted—I think he wanted to help me find who I was looking for and let me leave—and I said I was having some chest and breathing problems. The warrant officer came out immediately. She casually told PFC *So-and-so* to hook me up, so I stripped to the waist. He fumbled around and got a pattern.

Next thing I heard was, "*Shit! Get out!*"

I sat up and saw that she was waving all her patients out.

"*Not* you. " She pointed at me. She turned away and yelled again, "Unless you have something important, come back in the morning!"

She and I were alone behind the curtain except for PFC S*o-and-so*, who darted in and out. She ripped off the leads and rearranged them.

"*Shit …*" she whispered again.

She hooked up an IV and opened it wide. It made my arm cold. She took my blood pressure and pulse as she fired questions at me. No smoking. No drinking. No drugs. Blood pressure was okay. She asked me what I had done that day. All pretty bland stuff.

"Calm down," she said. "Just don't worry."

Just what did that mean, anyway?

I explained that I had experienced this once before, but not so bad, on the USPHT. I had also obtained a waiver after some testing and a Holter. I had been in country for about a month.

"Okay. Just calm down," she said again. It was beginning to peeve me the way she kept telling me that.

I told her I *was* calm. I also told her that usually this cleared after a few deep breaths.

"After a few deep breaths?" She was incredulous. I did not know if she did not believe me or if I was just lucky to be alive or *what.*

I was getting frustrated now. I did not know how to respond, so I decided to let her start asking, and I would answer questions. Finally I just told her to make this stop so I could go back to work. That's when she got silent.

She let the IV run, and after another 20 minutes, she called the hospital in Seoul. She was obviously talking to a doctor. I could not quite catch her entire conversation, but I remember that she got off the phone and then got back on, talking to someone higher in the pecking order.

She said something like, "I know it can't happen, but it *is.* It has been that way an *hour*, and medevac is enroute to pick him up!" With that, the conversation was over, and she told me (again) to be calm.

About this time the IV's input started backing up in my bladder, and I announced I had to pee. She was gracious enough to let me stand up and do it in a bottle, and then I lay back down.

A few minutes later, two of the medevac crew (a crew chief and a medic) showed up and put me on a stretcher, and I had to pee again.

"Just give us 15 minutes, and you will be in Seoul," one of them said.

By the time I was in the aircraft, the November cold hit me. They had left me a single blanket, no shirt, and were hurrying when the crew chief's mike-boom hooked the IV line and ripped open the bag.

Now, in addition to a bursting bladder, I was soaked and cold. I was half-naked, and my only source of warmth was also soaked and cold. I heard those damn words again.

"Calm down. In 15 minutes you will be in Seoul!"

"You said that five minutes ago!" I croaked. The safety margin of my bladder was now in for a terrific test.

Fortunately for me, the UH-60 landed directly on the hospital pad, and they wheeled me right in. To my horror, every training nurse, new doctor, PA and nurse assistant in South Korea huddled around me to lend their wisdom.

"I have to pee! Gotta do it! Now!"

Someone handed me a bottle and I got real mad. *"Get out! Get out!!"*

The doctor nodded at them to leave. I started to jump off the table and the doctor started to get hold of me to prevent it. I shot her a look that would have injured a bigger man, and she stopped in her tracks. Between a liter of saline ... the soaked blanket ... my missing shirt and my swollen belly, I could hardly find the darn thing, much less aim it. I hopped off, got hold of my diminutive manhood and got a stream going, generally in the direction of that dang jug.

When I finished I collapsed on the gurney, and they hooked me up again. For an hour. By then, I was exhausted. My regular urination aside, the continued odd heartbeats were driving me nuts. And they seemed to baffle the doctor as well.

Finally, the doctor leaned over and whispered, "Mr. Kingsley, if I give you this shot, you will never fly again."

"Lady, I got kids ... a wife ... I was looking for a job when I got this one ... just make me better. If I die here, she will kill me."

The doctor said I had a mature attitude. I told her my wife was a mean woman, and if I checked out, she would chase me into the next life just to get even. The doctor laughed and gave me the medicine.

KOREA, 1989

The PVCs stopped immediately.

Suddenly I felt like a million bucks. That little mouse in my chest went away, and I was ready to do a 10K run. Or so I thought till I tried to stand up … after which I lay back down quietly and slept for twelve hours.

The burden of that day hit me next morning. My career was in tatters. For some strange reason, the Army says a pilot who can't fly isn't much of a pilot, you see. And my unit would be losing me early, so I was suddenly one of those wimps who couldn't finish a full tour in Korea. No wonder the warrant officer manager was always so grouchy.

Anyway, as I became conscious, I began feeling sort of "snaky," as I described it to the nurse. She checked, and my blood pressure was down to 70/40, which was low enough for them to be concerned. I asked what medicine I was on and asked to read about it.

"Okay, here's the book."

It was a physician's desk reference of drugs, with such items as their effects, side-effects and dosages. I looked up my medicine. There, under the section titled "Side-Effects" was the dreaded "I" word.

"Pt [patient] may experience nausea, drowsiness, im—" There was that word. I couldn't read anything else.

"Im—" Oh, darn it all anyway, it was a very bad word. My world, which had become more depressing by the moment for the past two days, became very dark indeed.

I had been feeling … well … distracted. I mean, three other patients in the room, nurses night and day to visit me with medicine and blood pressure readings, and medicine that sort of numbed my senses. I had not been feeling very amorous. But now my worst fears were awakened.

The dreaded "I" word, which had never occurred to me, became the focus of my entire thought process. I did not call my wife. I stopped eating. I needed to get my bearings. I was, for a day, severely depressed.

Next morning, my doctor came in, and I asked her about the medicine. Why, she wanted to know.

"Doc … that stuff can make you … You may not feel like … well, you know …" I tried to stammer around the dreaded "I" word. She knew very well what I was saying.

She laughed. She had no idea how black my world looked. I understand she was not equipped to appreciate my issues, so she might not be able to empathize with me … but I got so mad I nearly jumped out of my bed to choke her.

Suddenly, whatever depressed feelings I might have felt were washed away in the indignity. I felt angry but better, instantly.

I went back to my unit, grounded but still working.

I called my wife and broke the news that I might not be the same man she had known. She was unbelievable. She didn't care.

"Just get home. We'll worry about it then … together."

It made all the difference. And trust me, we had problems. But she made sure impotence was never one of them.

Dear Dady

My very short tour in Korea was a source of family bonding for us. I quickly learned there was a lot of difference between being *alone* and being *away*. Many soldiers, even the married ones, were alone. We all knew it was part of the game if you wanted to be in the Army. But though you never heard from anyone having problems at home, it was a hard time.

In my spare time, I wrote and recorded stuff for my family. I just had no other way to connect with them.

I suffered without my family, so my sweet wife mailed old and new family pictures regularly for me to rotate through the three picture frames I kept on the wall of my room. Men would often comment on my display of family, and as I related earlier, one even wept.

When I arrived in Korea, I was very fortunate to be sent to a little unit that had a small library and other facilities on the compound. I began to read children's books on mini-cassette tapes, and I sent them to my children. I soon went through all the books the library had, and I drove the librarians nuts by asking them to go through the lending system around Korea to get more.

My youngest three children were thrilled.

I did some pretty clever things. For example, as I was speaking to the kids, I would say, "Now, don't tell your mom these things, but … *gab, gab, gab* …" They would leap out of bed, holler for their mom as loud as they could and make her sit down and listen to all the dirt. It was cute the first dozen times, but after that, she got pretty tired of it, especially since *it was always the same tape.*

Of course, the kids had favorite tapes, ones Mom got tired of hearing. Then there were Mom's tapes, during which they would sneak in and listen them closely. But the fact they received so *many* really bugged my poor wife, who in a bad moment would ponder the lot of a woman alone with six kids and feel cheated of my time and maybe even of my affection.

KOREA, 1989

One day, after having blasted me with the only real problem she would admit to during my whole tour (she did wonderfully well), she yelled that this week she had received only one letter, while the kids had received two tapes. *Two.* And it had better stop, or words to that effect.

Well, the moment went by as bad ones do; she was sorry and I was sorry, and soon it was forgotten. Until just before Thanksgiving Day 1989. I opened my mail from home and found a little letter all folded and taped up so no one could read it before it reached its intended addressee. In it, I got this heart full of my daughter, Elizabeth:

Dear Dady,

I heard mom talking to you on the telephone. She said that you should not send the little kids any more tapes with storys. Dad the little kids love those storys. You just can't stop sending us little kids tapes with storys on them. She said you don't half to read storys you only need to read one page of a story. Dad please understand. Please write back.

Love,

Beth

I broke down and cried over this sweet letter, and I immediately wrote back.

My Dear Daughter;

I received your wonderful letter today. I am so very happy to have the love of such a good daughter. You only heard part of Mama's talk, however. She told me how good you have been, and how she could not make it without all your wonderful help. She made me very proud of you.

Tell the kids I will always love them, and I will send you more tapes. I will just have to send more to Mom. OK? I love you!

Daddy

At Thanksgiving, I still read this letter. I am the luckiest man alive.

So I went back to my unit, and I was put on meds. I still felt snaky a lot, but I limped along awhile until I had another episode.

They changed my meds. I asked my doctor what was wrong. He was incredulous. "We are not sure, but we are adjusting the meds to fix it." They had lost my records, and the doc was sure they were still at the hospital in Seoul.

438

KOREA, 1989

After my third episode, I got real ugly and insisted they do something else besides give me pills. I got a ride to Seoul and an appointment with the hospital commander. It seems they had no cardiologist. They were not going to get one. They could not answer my questions and did not seem particularly interested. They had lost my records (from my medivac and the treatment at that time), and they were treating me as well as they knew how. The colonel told me I had nothing to worry about. There was no urgency. No concern. I was gonna get better because they said so.

I was … ugly about it. I told the colonel that if I died here, I would make sure he was terribly embarrassed. Then I went back to Camp Page.

WHEN FAT MEN FLEW

17

Back to Fort Rucker, December 1989

Two weeks later I had orders to Eisenhower Hospital for evaluation. But I contacted Doc Martin, who signed me into Fort Rucker. He sent me for a complete workup in Texas. After four months, if I recall correctly, it turned out to be stress, not heart. Then it was a lot of psychological evaluation until they figured out what would come next. They call that a Medical Evaluation Board, and I felt completely left out of that process.

I was not entirely happy at this time, with this diagnosis or my situation. My entire known world was collapsing around me, and I was still not quite tuned into reality.

Flight pay represented a quarter of my pay, and after six months, that was history.

I still did not believe these doctors, as this all seemed like just another lame excuse for the sick, lame and lazy. I was just another guy who could not hack Korea.

I saw shrinks and counselors, attended every 12-step program in the books, took breathing exercises and stopped taking meds. I believe my only successful treatment was in 12-step Codependents Anonymous, with its basic philosophy being that you got to make your own decisions, and the consequences are yours to bear.

One day while I was feeling bad and sorry for myself, I wrote this lame poetry. Remember that humor is where pain goes to die…

Ode to the Grounded Aviator

Listen, my young friend, impatient to play
with your toy so sleek and so trim.
That airplane can wait! You can learn of your fate
in times that may one day be grim!

It will happen to you, as has happened to me,
so be kind; don't forget such things.
'Tis sad when a man gives his life, it is true,
but far sadder when he loses his wings.

BACK TO FORT RUCKER, DECEMBER 1989

Give ear to my story; it's more than profound;
 you'll be caught unaware and dumbfounded.
It is dreaded and feared, so vile and so bleak—
the moment they say, "You are grounded."

"How can it be so?" ask in whispers so low,
 friends who so far have dodged such a blow.
But deep in a part of each aviator's heart
 comes this: "Happens to wimps *like him*, you know."

Now, no malice bear I to that noteworthy guy,
and we'll still see him over the years;
Maybe re-classed, maybe retired,
and perhaps selling blenders at Sears.

Back to that day when the truth was revealed,
and the pilot discovered mortality,
"But doc I can fly, I'm a heck of a guy!
Come on and get back to reality!"

Alone in a chair, his body near bare,
 being poked by the doc, oh so gingerly,
he knows the odds and allows the doc's prods,
 while desperately clinging to dignity.

Stripped there in a gown, he sits dazed, with a frown,
awaiting the worst of the news.
The doc comes back in, reading the pale grin, saying,
"Brace yourself, man, for my views."

The news was a rag, and his heart, how it sagged,
as he mentally tried to recover.

WHEN FAT MEN FLEW

"Can't let him see what he's doing to me.
When I'm home, I can always call Mother."

"My heart isn't bad, it's just wasting no time.
My knee can still go 15 miles!
My Adidas, you'll see, make a new man of me,
 and we'll get through these hard times with smiles!"

The doctor replies with words to disguise
his faith in his patient's resolve,
Giving guidance galore of what is in store
 and the new things his diet must solve.

"Give up salt, give up sugar ..." and now give up meat?
Good grief, I'll probably flip!
"Give up food, lose some weight ..."*Eat all that I hate?*
"I'll do it! Just sign the old *up slip!*"

The doctor does know, as he feigns to let go,
the chances this jerk will repent.
"Lose the weight, get in shape. Work out every day.
And, oh yes, give up chocolate for Lent."

The first time he wins, and the second,
you see, and a third he'll give heck to the fray.
But in the end comes the same, the end of the game,
 and thus that terrible day.

Well, life doesn't end when it makes that sad bend,
though the aviator sees things much slower.
"I'll just lean out the mix, slow back the speed,
 and set the collective a little bit lower."

444

BACK TO FORT RUCKER, DECEMBER 1989

Even so when some cocky young buck lifts his face
To the sky to brag about aviator itch,
The old guy nods with a smile, but thinks all the while,
"Let me at 'em! I can out-fly that Son of a ...
Gun!"

But the Army was good to me. All told, they kept me on medical hold for about a year and kept me at Fort Rucker until I retired. Except for things I wanted to do and couldn't, I had it pretty easy after that, especially considering they could have pitched me into the street.

I was grounded and kept wearing my Nomex (the Nomex flight suit), like all good pretend pilots. I kept up my SFTS (Synthetic Flight Training System) instrument minimums. I tried to get into the Safety Center regarding anything that might matter. But no one wanted to hear it. I was willing to teach again at DGFS, but there was no interest in a grounded aviator.

I don't remember how it happened, but after helping out some, I ended up being the OIC (Officer In Charge) of Fort Rucker Aviation Learning Center. I enjoyed that job very much. I felt I was making a difference to young soldiers, both flight school and maintenance crew.

It is funny now, but I kept having dreams, nightmares actually, about missing deadlines for ATM (Aircrew Training Manual) requirements, failing of a check-ride, failure to show up for a test, missing a simulator appointment. I had spent a career keeping up with them. Now I actually dreamed of being in a line unit, flying a mission, and suddenly realizing I was not current in some way. Old stuff came back to me. Once, flying lead for a night mission, I nearly hit wires on a night flight in Germany. I dreamed about that event repeatedly many times.

A lot of things went on during my medical hold. LTC Harry was put on alert to lead another team. He sent me down to the Fort Rucker Aviation Museum and gather the old records from the USPHT to use for the 1992 Team. I had no idea who Harry was going to impress, but when I went down there, I discovered that the display for the team had never been put up. It was old hat now, and all my precious pictures, which I had taken and given to them, were buried under dust and trash. The museum seemed glad someone would take them (i.e., put them elsewhere), and under the pretense of gathering records, I pilfered every picture and picture frame I had made. I scanned, copied and set up my own little token of history. I delivered all the records to LTC Harry and returned all the stuff he did not want to the museum, where it may still be gathering dust.

One of the clever things I got away with was a 1992 USPHT patch. The 1989 patch was the last one worn for the 1989 Team. But the 1992 patch was made in an optimistic moment, and I even dared to hope I might be asked back again rather than retire. It never happened.

1992 USPHT Patch - never issued

Well, the first desert war came along, and there I was at Fort Rucker, doing not much for the Army. I loved my job, but I wanted to go do something, anything, that mattered. It just felt as though a Cobra guy only matters if he is out killing tanks, and even then, the elite were already transitioned to Apache. For all my medical hold, I was found fit to serve but not to fly. I could still be in safety, even in a ground unit.

I called the Department of the Army Warrant Officer Manager who took one look at my file and announced he had no place for me. He offered, generously (?) and with great gusto, to allow me to go to missile tech school and go back and forth to Korea as a missile tech each year. He told me I would have to withdraw my retirement papers and leave immediately for school. I whined about leaving home, family and six kids (i.e., every year, not on a combat mission but on regular, extended isolated tours), and his best offer was that he would "try" to get me returned to Rucker each year. I knew my change of primary MOS was a problem for him, but I knew how popular this MOS was, and I thought it was a favor to him.

So I had heard this line before. The short story is that I refused. I was locked into retirement, so he really could not move me unless they declared an emergency extension. He thought he was punishing me for my past missteps, and said I would have to keep my current job until the war was over. He wished me well and hung up.

The darn war lasted only a hundred hours, and I loved my job at Rucker, so I was only disappointed it ended so soon.

That was the end. I got out in 1991.

Now remember here that I was feeling pretty sorry for myself, since my world of experience had come to a screeching halt. Like all old soldiers, I can remember taking offense at this and that, but the reality was that the Army was as good to me as I could have hoped. And I am still very grateful.

Anyway, I started getting pretty huffy. I refused the little parade they give for those second stringers who bail out into a 20 years or disability retirement. I was going to refuse to take the last physical fitness (PT) test, but my pride took over. I had never failed one. The S-1 (admin weenie) told me if I did not do it, I would not get my MSM (Meritorious Service Medal) for my 23 years of service. I did not matter to him, and he was inconvenienced by another administrative task which would not bear some sort of fruit for him. He just wanted to clean up his administrative reports.

Hell, they did not care, and I like to say I did not care, but I was just mad. It was no one's fault, but I was tired, and the lack of dignity seemed to be piling up. The glory of getting such a distinguished medal is really diminished when it is just for passing a PT test. But I passed the PT test, and it must have caused him a big pain in the neck. Several weeks after, a small box in a plain brown wrapper with no labels or other suspicious marks, arrived at my home. I got my MSM and the official paper that declared (summarizing here) that, *of all the warrant officers in the Army, I certainly was one.*

I reviewed it carefully. I have it stored with my trinkets, but I never mounted it on my chest ribbons. I had many letters of commendation, Army Achievement Medals, Army Commendation Medals, and certificates of achievement I felt had more merit than that medal. I was a CW4; I had a Broken Wing; and I was still good looking. The Army owed me nothing.

I signed out of the unit and wandered the post my last day, being sure I did not fail to return equipment or clear hand receipts. I left nothing undone.

WHEN FAT MEN FLEW

18

Retirement

This is not the end of this story.

When I got out, 200,000 other soldiers got out with me.
All the local jobs were taken, and I suppose I had failed to have
enough connections to land good work. Cobro Corporation
took me on as a contract safety instructor. I worked as a
contract writer for a short time for a man who could not be
happy, and I quit that job. I did not get any of the other contract
work I expected. I did a lot of menial stuff, too. I want back
to college for a year, but I had too many kids to keep that
up. I painted houses, threw papers, worked a dozen clerk
jobs, stabbed at some safety jobs, and was secretary for an

organization bidding on the Fort Rucker Maintenance contract, which we lost.

I finally ended up as the Director of Safety, Workers Comp and Environmental Protection in a … wait for it … *condom plant*. Sparing you a lot of detail, I still know all the secret specs of those free military condoms available to every soldier who needs …well … protection. In fact, if you mounted one on a 155 mm howitzer, it would reduce the max effective range to less than 500 meters. We really prided ourselves on a quality product, I can tell you.

Yep. I was protecting my soldiers. C'mon, isn't that worth something? Actually, my specialty there was hazardous materials, ammonia and confined space safety. But eventually, my job went to China … and most of us were laid off.

A friend handed my resume to Northrop Grumman, and they brought me on as a computer operator in a combat simulations system. Basically I was teaching battle rhythm skills to field grade and command officers by manning the OPFOR side of the simulation. It was only part time, but I had that job for more than 15 years, and it kept the wolf from my door. I ended up working in the Special Forces cell. The people I knew there were mostly vets, and they were of such high quality that I loved going there, and I loved working with them.

RETIREMENT

We Wear the Chains We Weave in Life

Three years after I left the military, I was still living near Fort Rucker when I got a call from the local JAG office. The officer, Captain S*o and so*, told me he wanted to discuss an Army aviator accused of dangerous conduct. I thought there must be a mistake, since I was retired. No, he said. I had been recommended as an prosecution character witness by someone. Who, I wondered. It was a former battalion commander who had said I knew the history of a man being given a Flight Evaluation Board (FEB).

Now, to be given an FEB, you may recall from an earlier story here, the crewman may be unhealthy, unqualified, or have done something less than honorable in the Army. An FEB is considered an administrative action. It is *not* punitive.

The JAG captain went on to mention the officer's name, and the knot returned to my stomach. I told him *No.* "Go and talk to Colonel S*uch and such*, my former battalion commander, who, I am sure, can answer every question. *He* is the expert, and *he* knows all about this guy."

"Mr. Kingsley, that colonel will not testify. He said *you* would be able to tell the board all they needed to know."

I could not prevail on him to tell me why the former battalion commander would not testify. I am sure his misplaced support of the kid was a big mistake, and that it had caused him problems after I left Korea. That battalion commander was a great leader. This was simply a mistake created by successful manipulation of an idiot. I bit my tongue and relented. Yes, I knew him, and yes, I would testify.

The day came, and I felt all the same stress I had experienced in the unit. I waited in a room of witnesses and discovered that after my departure from Korea, this kid had been made the AAAA Aviator of the Year from Korea as the commander had intended. It was a very high honor. And he had been promoted to CW3, as the commander had hoped. In fact, the commander had rebuilt the kid's career, as he had planned.

He was transferred to Fort Rucker and was teaching new young aviators, and one of their proud critiques of his flight skills had caught the commanding general's eye. Something about how CW3 Knucklehead had been the only man with courage enough to teach the new aviators the edge of the envelope.

The "envelope" of the aircraft refers to the limits of airspeed, angle of bank, engine temperature and torque limits, center of gravity limits and other flight limits created by design or regulation requirements. This critique had been intended as highly complementary by two young aviators in reference to his teaching dangerous and illegal maneuvers and proudly proclaiming them to be acceptable, more or less a measure of his personal skill and courage. In fact, many of the specific charges in the FEB were similar to the ones in my memorandum. This FEB was held for recent violations that had brought this to the attention of the commanding general. But the investigation showed these activities had been going on his entire career.

During the proceeding, the young military defense lawyer had called me scornfully to the stand. He tried to paint me as an old, jealous has-been, bearing down on this poor young flight instructor out of envy and spite. I am not sure how successful he was in making an impression on the board to discredit my effort, but the other ten or so witness simply overwhelmed the board.

The kid was relieved of his wings.

It did not end there. In 1994, I published an article about this aviator in the Army Aviation Digest. I felt it was important to share this picture of high-risk performance by an Army aviator. It's entire purpose was to awaken line unit safety officers to aid in active management of such behavior. But I went out of my way to paint the picture without listing names, dates, or unit. Army Aviation Digest was very glad to get the story, and it was well received.

A year later, I was called by the JAG again. Yes, same captain, and yes, they wanted to have me as a witness for the same kid. This time they were conducting a Retention Board hearing, evaluating his right to remain on active duty as an enlisted man.

I was very angry about this, and I told Captain *Such and Such* that this man was dangerous, that he did not respond to things with rational thought. If I saw him on my little street in my little town, I would feel threatened. I may have been more assertive than that.

The captain began to lecture me on how important this was and how foolish I might be in my unwarranted concern. I told him to spit it out. What did he want? I explained about the kid's actions in Korea, including the pistol he carried, and he assured me I would not have to worry about it. I did not believe him, but he said they needed my testimony to make this happen. I agreed to come in.

I went into another hearing with some of the same witnesses, but it was a different board. A funny thing happened.

First, I saw the board president (a colonel who had once been a captain in my stairwell in Germany years before) and we greeted each other warmly. The proceedings were going smoothly when the president called for a break.

It turned out that the board secretary (a member of the board without voting privileges), a CW4, had realized *he* had been my replacement in the 501st at Camp Page, Korea. We had never met, but he had found my records buried in the safety computer, with all the details and all the issues I had found, including my memo.

He had advised the board president that this might cause a conflict of interest and might compromise the proceeding. But the board president decided to continue.

When I was called to testify, the kid had himself a slick lawyer specializing in military courts martials, and in his hand was a copy of the magazine that had the article I had written.

He began to play the same tune of bitter, old, fat retired wanna-be warrant officer trying to cast dirt on his poor client. He asked if I had written this about his client. I told him I had never mentioned his name. He asked me again. I told him I had never mentioned the unit, the time frame, or any of the players. He became more insistent, and I said yes, it was clearly about him.

He opened up and demanded to know why I would slander such a fine man. I did not hesitate. I told him the kid was a danger to himself and his unit. The lawyer sort of smirked and asked me if that was all I was trying to do, implying again that my intentions were less than honorable or professional. I was steamed. I had already endured all this turkey could heap on my integrity, and now a slick lawyer was going to out-talk all the witnesses?

I looked directly at the board and blurted out that if the kid were retained on active duty, no matter what rank, he would retire as a CW4, and I felt it was a travesty to everyone in the Warrant Officer Corps.

The attorney was stunned at this sudden flip of the discussion. He tried to shut me up, and get me off the stand. But the board president interrupted him. The board president stood and faced me.

Mr. Kingsley, just what does that mean?

I explained there was no question of his guilt. But if he remained on active duty, his reserve rank of warrant officer would remain active. He would remain a reserve warrant on active duty as an NCO. During the rest of his enlisted career, he would continue to be promoted with each reserve promotion board for which he was eligible. He would become a reserve CW4. He would be allowed to pin on his CW4 the day he hit 20 years, and he would retire as a CW4. The only cost, the only effort required by him was a new uniform.

The colonel was incredulous. He demanded to know if that were right, and his CW4 secretary confirmed it. He then turned to the attorney and demanded to know if it were true.

The attorney stammered something about not knowing military retirement law ... and dismissed me as quickly as possible.

The kid lost. Last time I knew, he was preparing for appeal and discharge.

I may have tried to find vindication in this outcome for all my personal offense, but it was a shallow victory. We could have saved this officer and provided the Army another fine pilot. But instead of responding to guidance and proper mentoring, fixing the attitude, improving his performance and becoming a better officer, he played all the rules like a fine violin, and he did it without integrity or honor. His effort was not for the good of the Army or to teach right principles or proper aviation skills, but to brag and pretend to greatness he did not possess. In addition, his deliberate actions in those five years cast doubt on my own motive and integrity. In the end, 12 witnesses were brought for each of these counts, but he was finally found out by the testimony of his own students. He denied every issue.

I am sorry to say that all such judgments can be negotiated, changed, reduced and vaporized. I never saw him again or heard of any other outcomes. I do not care. It matters that he was prevented from further bad aviation decisions.

"Old Bones," 1991

Hard as it might be to believe, I was quite the stud when I started out to make a military career in ... well, many years ago. My first weeks in boot camp, which were so tough for some kids at the Marine Corps Recruit Depot in San Diego, were, for me, spent getting great exercise and loving the challenge.

I was Superman, then, but time has a way of tugging on Superman's cape.

I went to a doctor once for a separated shoulder. I had been hurt in a game of "combat football." Combat football was created to be a "physical fitness sport" and was made famous in the Army of the mid-to-late 1970s. I loved it.

"How did it happen?" the doctor asked. Football, I answered. "A real killer game too, you know. I really creamed the guy."

The doctor looked me in disbelief. "How old are you?" I could feel the lecture coming on. Anyway, I was thirty-two. Still a kid. A tough guy. A macho, tough guy, if you asked me.

"Twenty-eight," I answered firmly. I was determined not to have another "over thirty" lecture. It didn't work.

"No thirty-year-old man should play football," he said, "especially if he expects to pass a flight physical after age forty." I nodded solemnly. But I knew better.

RETIREMENT

As time went on, I started going to the doctors more often for such complaints as bad legs, bad knees, bad back .I went once and complained that I was getting serious lower back pain after I did sit-ups. The doctor brightly stated he had a cure for that.

I was thrilled. Maybe, after all these years and military doctors, I had at last found the man who could start getting me back into fighting trim.

He paused for effect. I looked at him. He looked at me. He must have felt I suffered a deplorable lack of curiosity. He said it again.

"Okay, Doc, what is it?" I tried to appear more excited than I was, just in case this guy was holding out.

"Just don't do any more sit-ups." He was serious.

"Say what? No more sit-ups?"

He seemed disappointed that I should be so incredulous. Obviously this guy couldn't appreciate the wimps who fall by the wayside, claiming old age and bad backs to keep out of the serious exercise business.

"Only do partial sit-ups," he said. "If it hurts, don't sit all the way up. It will relieve the strain on those old bones of yours and still give you plenty of needed abdominal muscle activity."

More Wimpsville. Just great.

Well, I tried it. It didn't help my image, but when the choice is walking upright with the rest of mankind or keeping the image … well … what can I say?

So, now I am retired, and I practice that stuff a lot … especially the part about "if it hurts, don't." My back and knees don't bother me nearly as much. Why, heck, if they called me back to active duty today, I am sure I could still cut the mustard.

But now each day when I go home, I drive past the post gym where all the young soldiers are out there jogging around the track, running for their very lives, ageless in their thought and their stride.

I pause to think, *There is an ice-cold pop and a soft chair waiting just down the road.*

I wave at anyone I know, especially at the young guys I used to know, who are now the **old** guys.

Sometimes I even watch them in my rearview mirror.

And I drive on.

The End

About the Author

The author is retired and living in Buffalo, NY.

You can contact him at... scoutdriver74@gmail.com

CPSIA information can be obtained
at www.ICGtesting.com
Printed in the USA
LVHW051406210723
752765LV00014B/534